SUPERMAN: RED SON

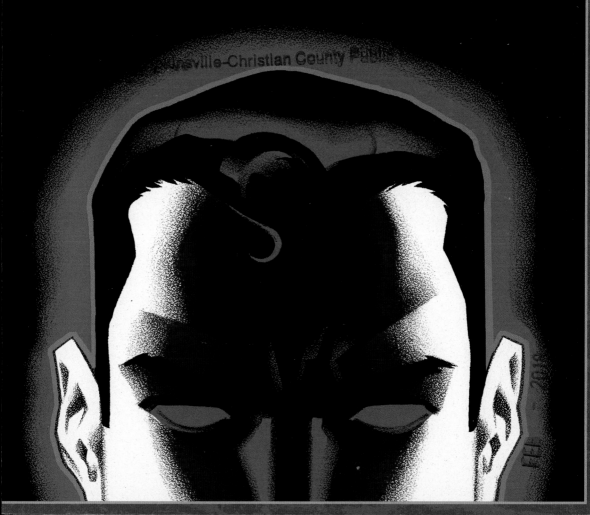

SUPERMAN:

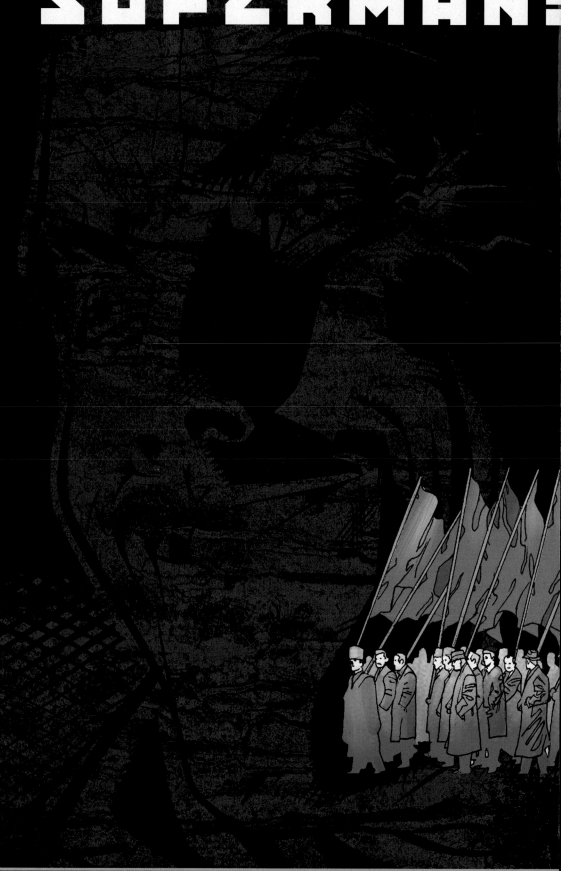

RED SON

MARK **MILLAR**
writer

DAVE **JOHNSON** with
ANDREW **ROBINSON**
("Red Son Rising" & "Red Son Ascendant")

KILIAN **PLUNKETT** with
WALDEN **WONG**
("Red Son Ascendant" & "Red Son Setting")
artists

PAUL **MOUNTS**
colorist

KEN **LOPEZ**
letterer

DAVE **JOHNSON**
original covers painter

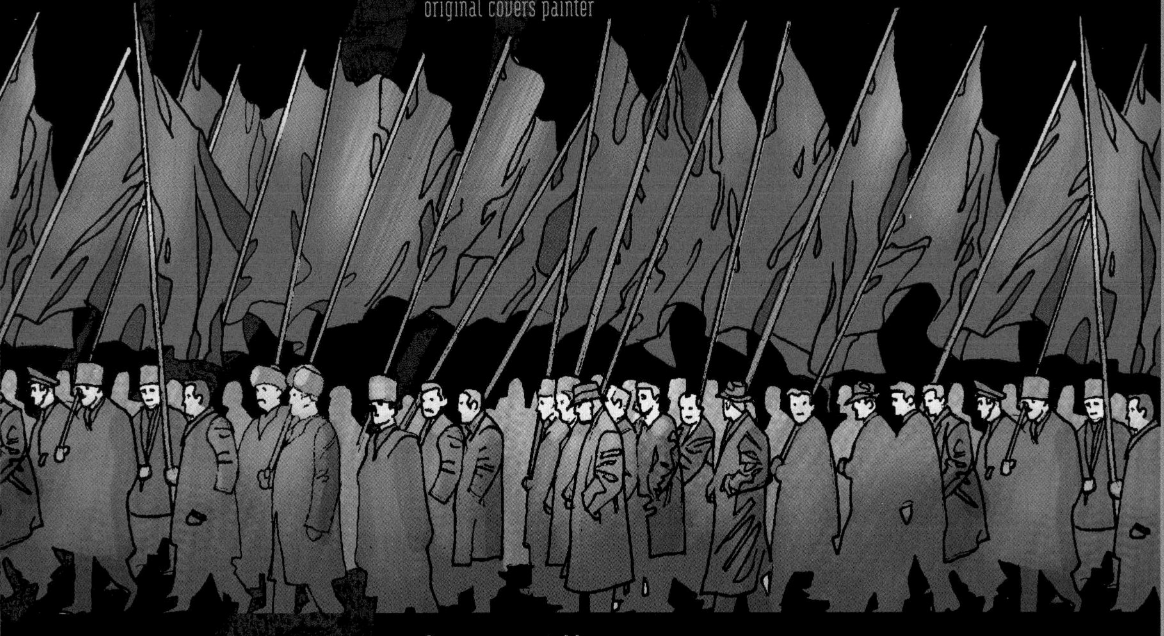

Superman created by
JERRY SIEGEL & JOE SHUSTER
By special arrangement with the
JERRY SIEGEL FAMILY

LET OUR ENEMIES BEWARE:

THERE IS ONLY **ONE** SUPERPOWER NOW.

MIKE McAVENNIE TOM PALMER, JR. Editors – Original Series MAUREEN McTIGUE Assistant Editor – Original Series
JEB WOODARD Group Editor – Collected Editions ANTON KAWASAKI Editor – Collected Edition STEVE COOK Design Director – Books
ROBBIE BIEDERMAN Publication Design
BOB HARRAS Senior VP – Editor-in-Chief, DC Comics
DIANE NELSON President DAN DiDIO and JIM LEE Co-Publishers GEOFF JOHNS Chief Creative Officer
AMIT DESAI Senior VP – Marketing & Global Franchise Management NAIRI GARDINER Senior VP – Finance SAM ADES VP – Digital Marketing
BOBBIE CHASE VP – Talent Development MARK CHIARELLO Senior VP – Art, Design & Collected Editions JOHN CUNNINGHAM VP – Content Strategy
ANNE DePIES VP – Strategy Planning & Reporting DON FALLETTI VP – Manufacturing Operations
LAWRENCE GANEM VP – Editorial Administration & Talent Relations ALISON GILL Senior VP – Manufacturing & Operations
HANK KANALZ Senior VP – Editorial Strategy & Administration JAY KOGAN VP – Legal Affairs DEREK MADDALENA Senior VP – Sales & Business Development
JACK MAHAN VP – Business Affairs NICK NAPOLITANO VP – Manufacturing Administration CAROL ROEDER VP – Marketing
Eddie Scannell VP – Mass Account & Digital Sales COURTNEY SIMMONS Senior VP – Publicity & Communications
JIM (SKI) SOKOLOWSKI VP – Comic Book Specialty & Newsstand Sales SANDY YI Senior VP – Global Franchise Management

SUPERMAN: RED SON

Published by DC Comics. Copyright © 2014 DC Comics. All Rights Reserved.

Originally published in single magazine form in SUPERMAN: RED SON 1-3. Copyright © 2003 DC Comics. All Rights Reserved. All characters, their distinctive
likenesses and related indicia featured in this publication are trademarks of DC Comics. The stories, characters and incidents featured in this publication are
entirely fictional. DC Comics does not read or accept unsolicited submissions of ideas, stories or artwork.

DC Comics, 2900 W. Alameda Avenue, Burbank, CA 91505
Printed by Solisco Printers, Scott, QC, Canada. 5/20/16. Third Printing.
ISBN 978-1-4012-4711-9

Library of Congress Cataloging-in-Publication Data

Millar, Mark.
  Superman. Red Son / Mark Millar, Dave Johnson, Kilian Plunkett, Andrew Robinson, Walden Wong.
    pages cm
  Summary: "The critically acclaimed Superman: Red Son now collected in a brand new edition! In this vivid tale of Cold War paranoia, the ship carrying the
infant who would grow up to become Superman lands in the midst of the 1950s Soviet Union, where he is raised on a collective. As he becomes a symbol to the
Soviet people, the world changes drastically from what we know — bringing Superman into conflict with Batman, Lex Luthor and others. This volume collect
Superman: Red Son #1-3"— Provided by publisher.
  ISBN 978-1-4012-4711-9 (paperback)
  1. Graphic novels. I. Johnson, Dave, 1966- II. Plunkett, Kilian. III. Robinson, Andrew (Andrew C.) IV. Wong, Walden. V. Title. VI. Title: Red Son.
  PN6728.S9M567 2014
  741.5'973—dc23
                          2013049659

Cover painting by DAVE JOHNSON
Logo design by STEVE COOK

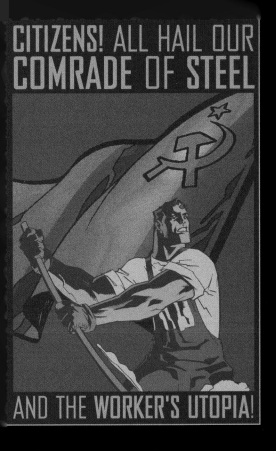

CITIZENS! ALL HAIL OUR COMRADE OF STEEL AND THE WORKER'S UTOPIA!

CRIME DOESN'T EXIST. ACCIDENTS NEVER HAPPEN. ALL DUE TO PRESIDENT SUPERMAN!

INTRODUCTION

BY TOM DESANTO

Mom, apple pie, Chevrolet, and Superman. With all due respect to Mickey Mouse, there is perhaps no greater American icon than the Man of Steel. When Mark Millar first told me the premise of RED SON — of taking the American icon of Superman and putting him in the ultimate what-if scenario — I was shocked. Imagine Superman wasn't red, white, and blue... imagine Superman was red...Communist red? Instead of baby Kal-El landing in the loving arms of Ma and Pa Kent in the good ol' U.S. of A., he lands in the loving arms of Josef Stalin back in the U.S.S.R. No longer Superman American icon, but Superman Soviet comrade — needless to say, the premise is more than intriguing. In the hands of a lesser writer the story would have fallen into cookie cutter, black-and-white, America good, Soviets bad, feel-good propaganda. Thank God Mark Millar is not a lesser writer. And thank God his favorite color seems to be gray.

Superman mythology. Having read the book three times, I find such an attention to detail that I am still discovering something new in the words or art that I somehow had missed before. All the elements that make Superman great are there: Lex Luthor, Lois Lane (oops, I mean Lois Luthor), Jimmy Olsen, even Batman, Wonder Woman, and the greatest Green Lantern of them all, Hal Jordan. All of them the same, yet different — all reinvented. Even though the traditional "S" on his chest has been replaced by the hammer and sickle, one thing is still the same — Superman believes he is doing the right thing. He has the best of intentions, but we all know what the road to hell is paved with. Yet Superman still wants to make the world safe, except this time he is willing to force us to see that his way is the best way.

Ben Franklin once wrote, "Those who would sacrifice their freedom for safety will find they inherit neither." That line, written over two hundred years ago, may have more meaning now than ever before. Good writing challenges the way you think. Great writing changes the way you think. RED SON is great writing. Mark actually started writing RED SON around 1995, and we all know it is a much different world than those days. Millar was able to gaze into his Orwellian crystal ball and see Superman as the poster child for Big Brother. The all X-ray vision seeing, all super-hearing listening, all-knowing,

All that morally questionable gray is captured in what seems to be 1950s Technicolor glory. Fortunately the artistic palette of Dave Johnson's and Kilian Plunkett's pencils, Andrew Robinson's and Walden Wong's inks, and Paul Mounts' colors combine to create a Kafkaesque, Max Fleischer cartoon that collides with the best of propaganda art. It is not like you are reading a graphic novel but watching a movie. This book is everything I love about comics — a great morality tale with art that leaps off the page and into your mind's eye.

Even if you have never read a comic before, you can pick up RED SON and follow the story and enjoy a great ride. But don't be fooled; it is much more than that. RED SON is a sharp social commentary on capitalism vs. communism and current American foreign policy. Not bad for a funny book. If you are a comic fan, then you will notice the detail to the

all-powerful Big Brother. All-encompassing security, like a baby in a super blanket — just one thing...don't think for yourself and don't challenge the system. Free will or freedom in exchange for absolute security — I don't think Ben Franklin would have liked that idea. Just remember Superman is watching you. But who's watching the watchmen? Mark Millar is, that's who.

Be good,

TOM DESANTO

October 9, 2003

A self-described pop culture junkie and longtime comic book fan, Tom DeSanto is a writer/ producer who has worked on such films as the Transformers *franchise,* X-Men, X2, *and other projects.*

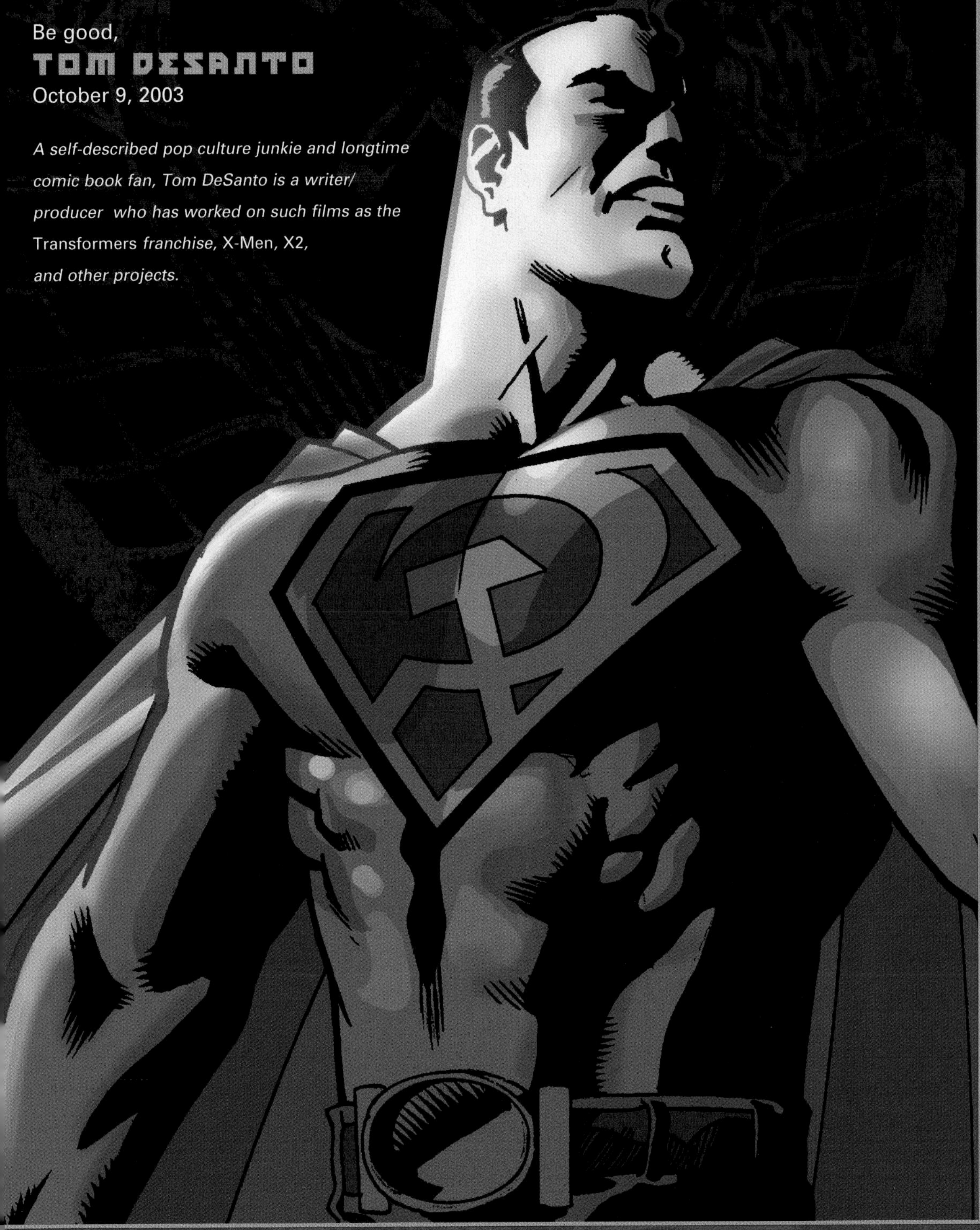

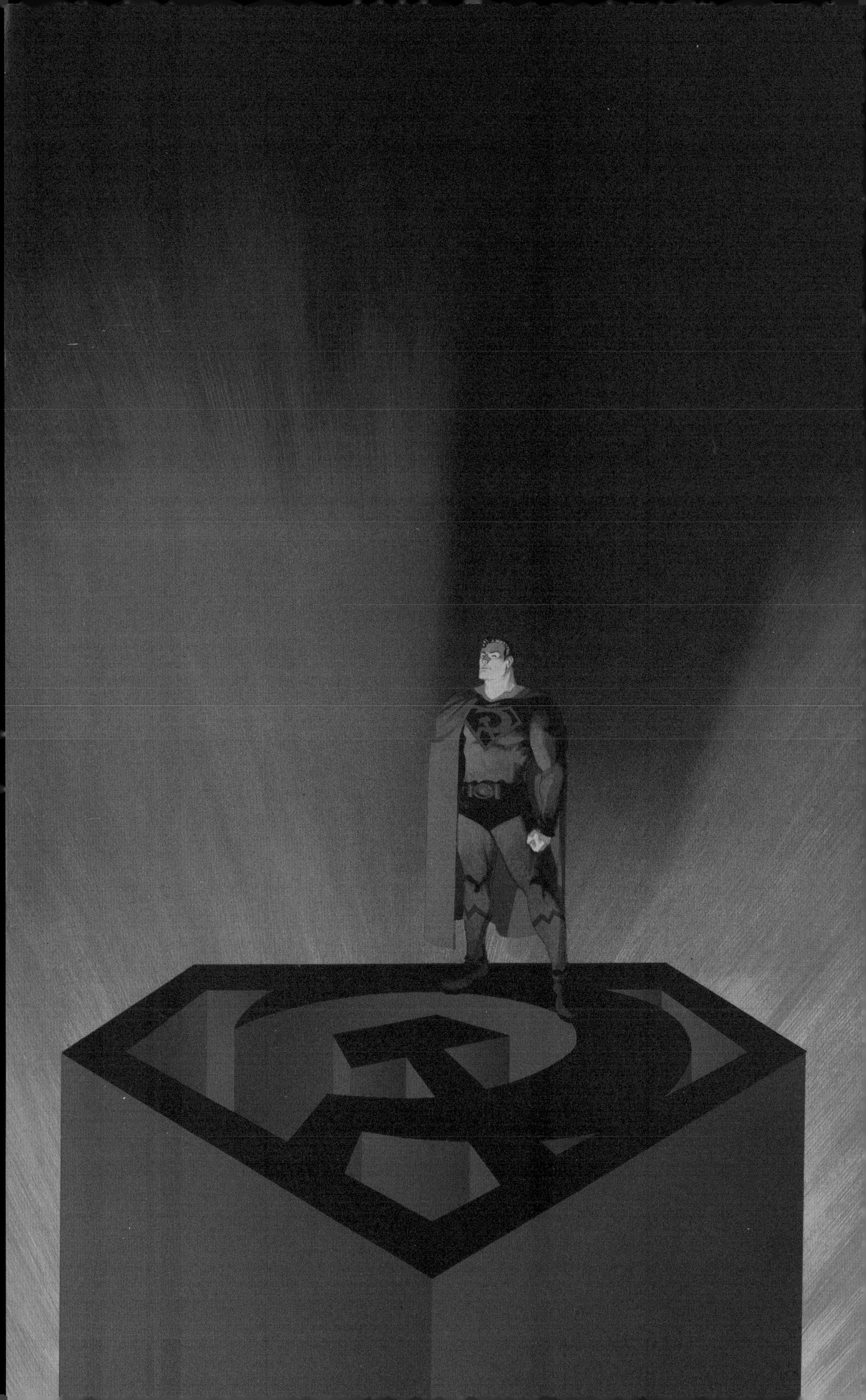

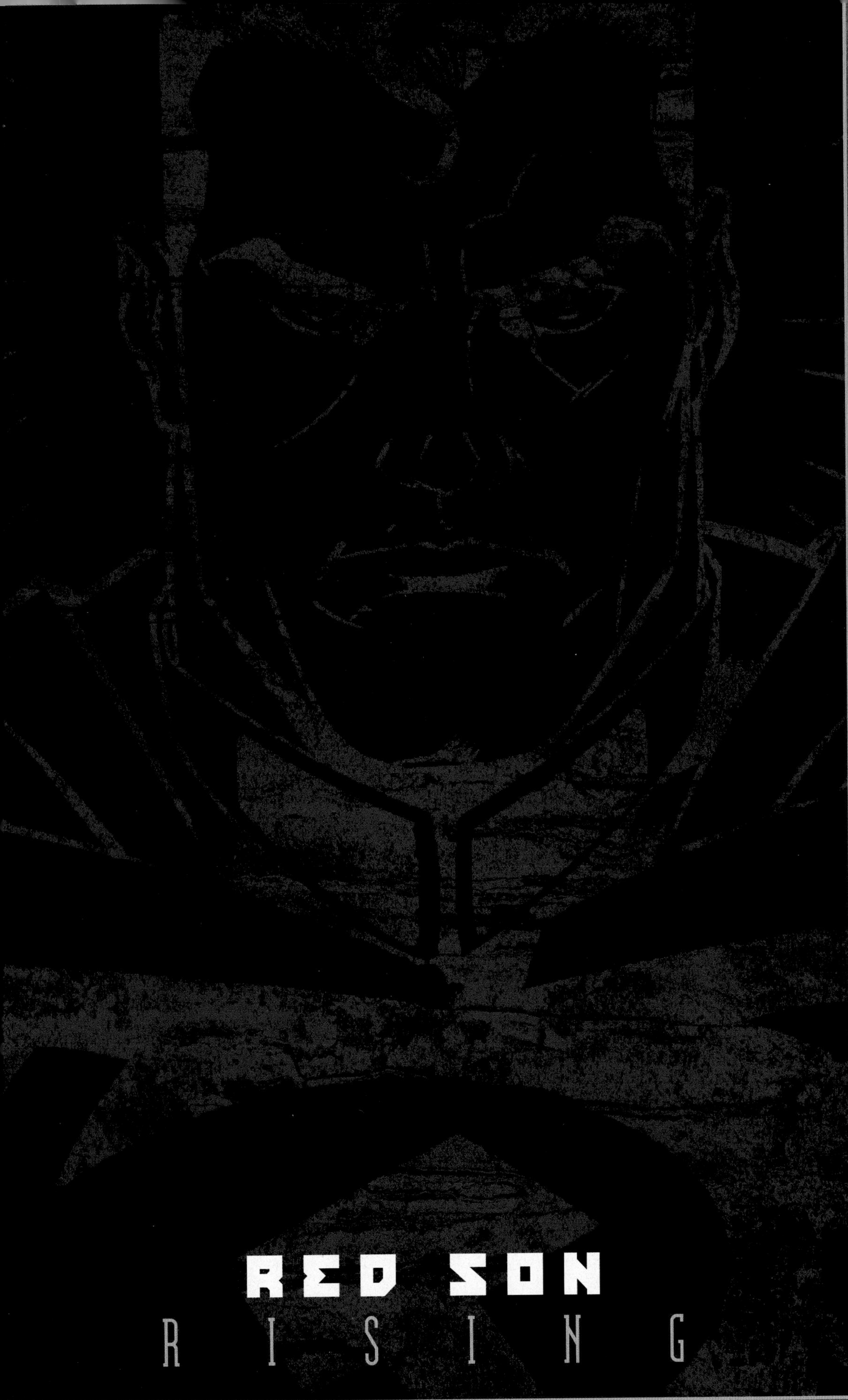

RED SON
R I S I N G

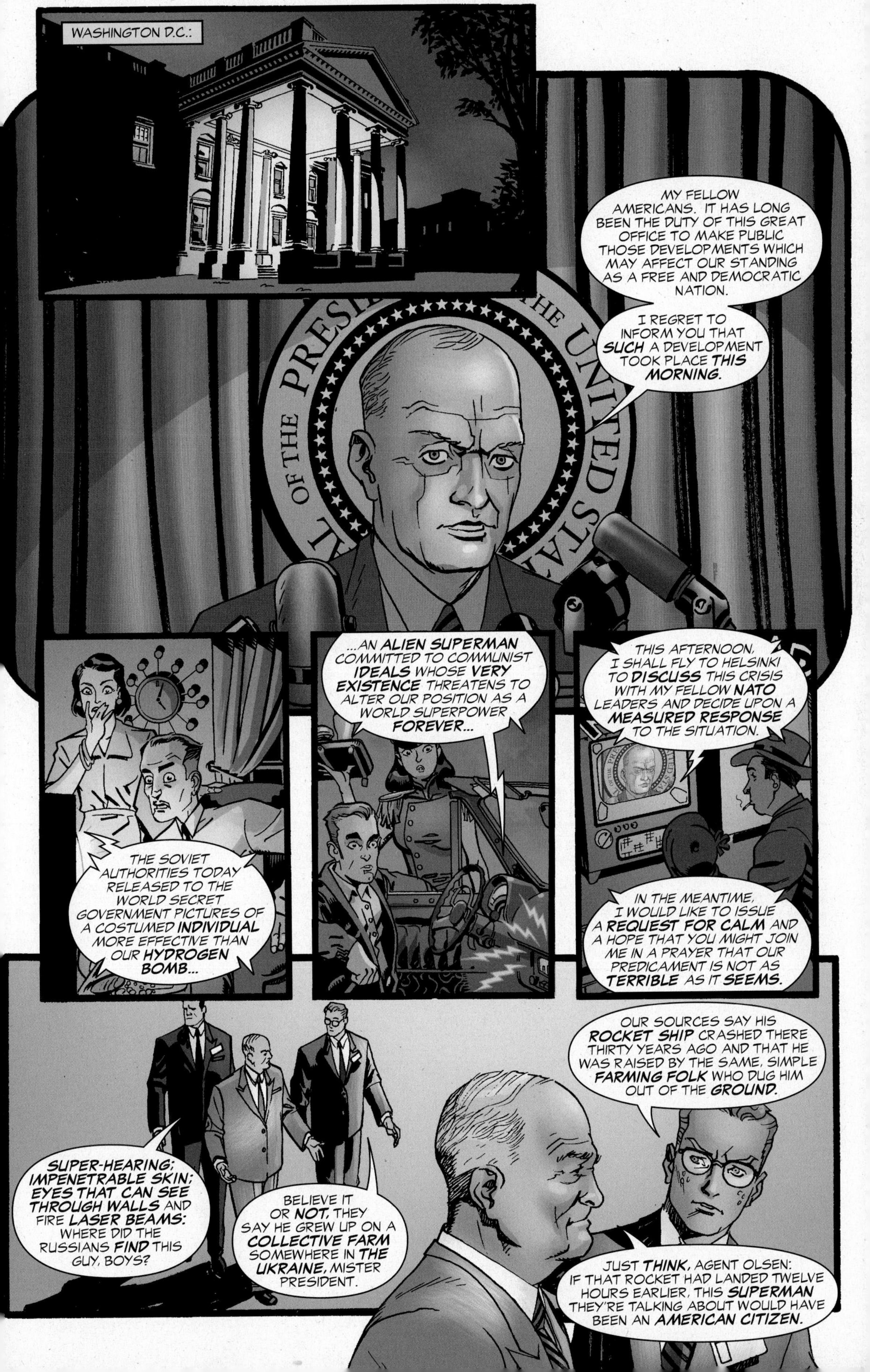

WASHINGTON D.C.:
MY FELLOW AMERICANS. IT HAS LONG BEEN THE DUTY OF THIS GREAT OFFICE TO MAKE PUBLIC THOSE DEVELOPMENTS WHICH MAY AFFECT OUR STANDING AS A FREE AND DEMOCRATIC NATION.
I REGRET TO INFORM YOU THAT SUCH A DEVELOPMENT TOOK PLACE THIS MORNING.
THE SOVIET AUTHORITIES TODAY RELEASED TO THE WORLD SECRET GOVERNMENT PICTURES OF A COSTUMED INDIVIDUAL MORE EFFECTIVE THAN OUR HYDROGEN BOMB...
...AN ALIEN SUPERMAN COMMITTED TO COMMUNIST IDEALS WHOSE VERY EXISTENCE THREATENS TO ALTER OUR POSITION AS A WORLD SUPERPOWER FOREVER...
THIS AFTERNOON, I SHALL FLY TO HELSINKI TO DISCUSS THIS CRISIS WITH MY FELLOW NATO LEADERS AND DECIDE UPON A MEASURED RESPONSE TO THE SITUATION.
IN THE MEANTIME, I WOULD LIKE TO ISSUE A REQUEST FOR CALM AND A HOPE THAT YOU MIGHT JOIN ME IN A PRAYER THAT OUR PREDICAMENT IS NOT AS TERRIBLE AS IT SEEMS.
SUPER-HEARING; IMPENETRABLE SKIN; EYES THAT CAN SEE THROUGH WALLS AND FIRE LASER BEAMS: WHERE DID THE RUSSIANS FIND THIS GUY, BOYS?
BELIEVE IT OR NOT, THEY SAY HE GREW UP ON A COLLECTIVE FARM SOMEWHERE IN THE UKRAINE, MISTER PRESIDENT.
OUR SOURCES SAY HIS ROCKET SHIP CRASHED THERE THIRTY YEARS AGO AND THAT HE WAS RAISED BY THE SAME, SIMPLE FARMING FOLK WHO DUG HIM OUT OF THE GROUND.
JUST THINK, AGENT OLSEN: IF THAT ROCKET HAD LANDED TWELVE HOURS EARLIER, THIS SUPERMAN THEY'RE TALKING ABOUT WOULD HAVE BEEN AN AMERICAN CITIZEN.

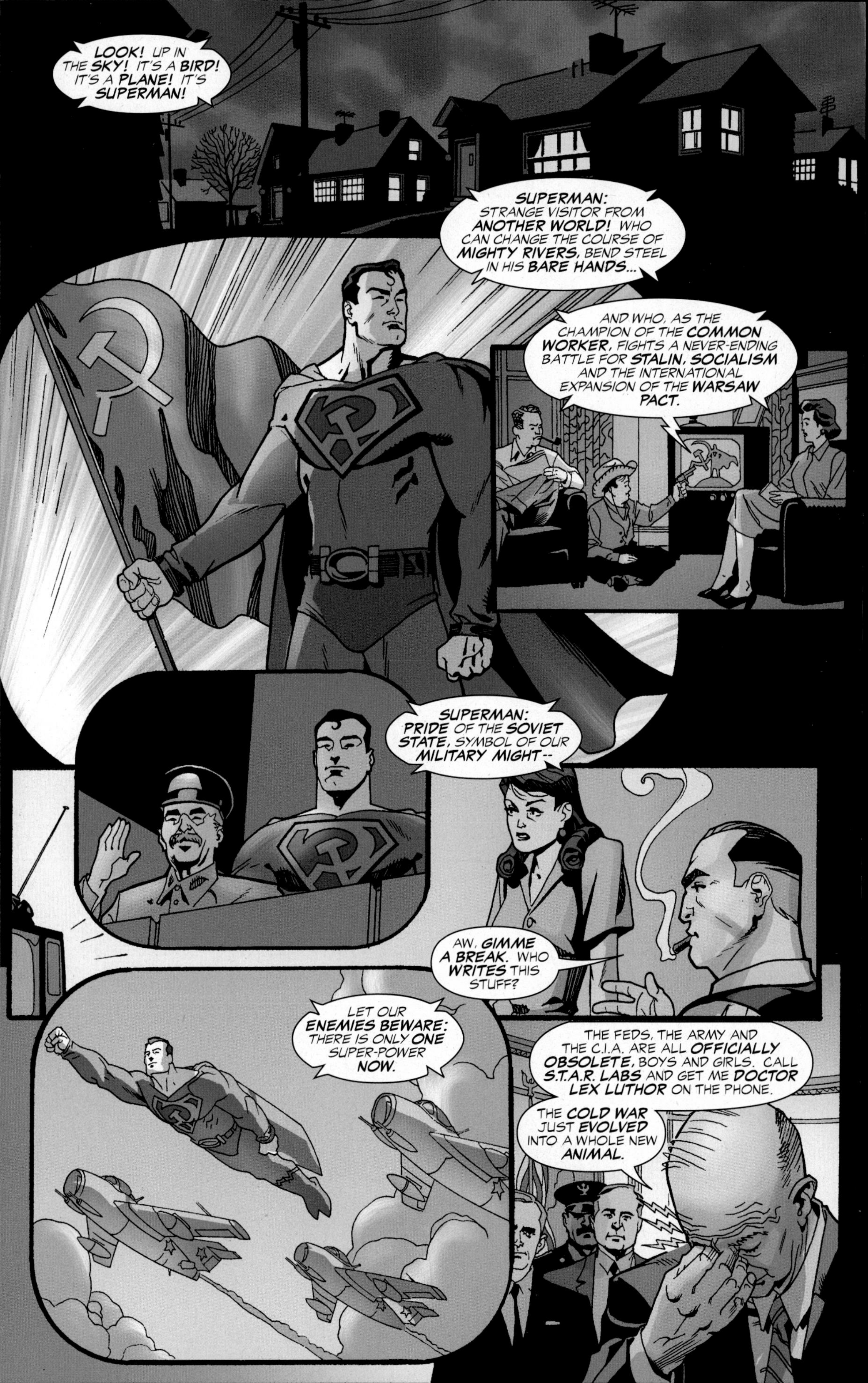
LOOK! UP IN THE SKY! IT'S A BIRD! IT'S A PLANE! IT'S SUPERMAN!
SUPERMAN: STRANGE VISITOR FROM ANOTHER WORLD! WHO CAN CHANGE THE COURSE OF MIGHTY RIVERS, BEND STEEL IN HIS BARE HANDS...
AND WHO, AS THE CHAMPION OF THE COMMON WORKER, FIGHTS A NEVER-ENDING BATTLE FOR STALIN, SOCIALISM AND THE INTERNATIONAL EXPANSION OF THE WARSAW PACT.
SUPERMAN: PRIDE OF THE SOVIET STATE, SYMBOL OF OUR MILITARY MIGHT--
AW, GIMME A BREAK. WHO WRITES THIS STUFF?
LET OUR ENEMIES BEWARE: THERE IS ONLY ONE SUPER-POWER NOW.
THE FEDS, THE ARMY AND THE C.I.A. ARE ALL OFFICIALLY OBSOLETE, BOYS AND GIRLS. CALL S.T.A.R. LABS AND GET ME DOCTOR LEX LUTHOR ON THE PHONE.
THE COLD WAR JUST EVOLVED INTO A WHOLE NEW ANIMAL.

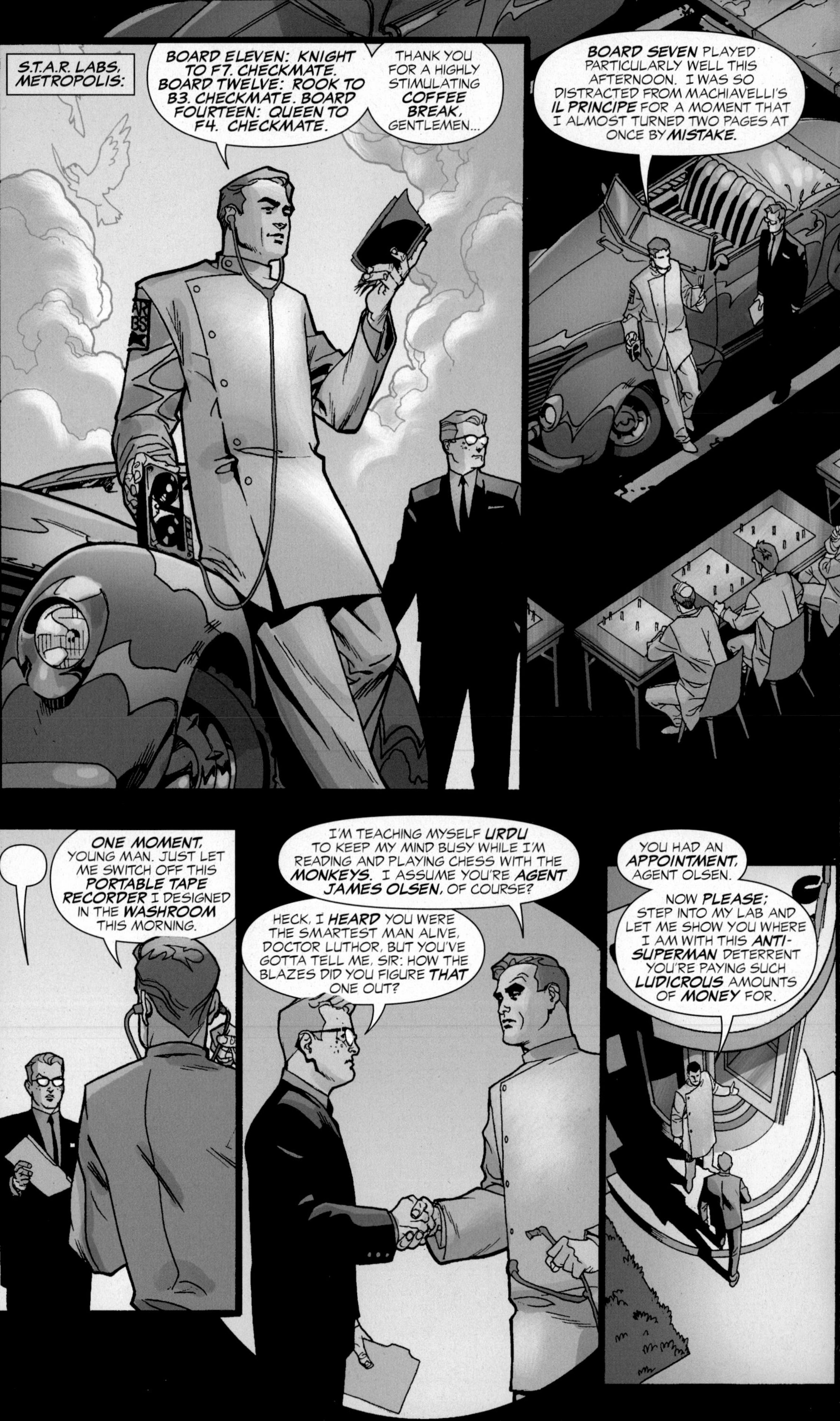
S.T.A.R. LABS, METROPOLIS:
BOARD ELEVEN: KNIGHT TO F7. CHECKMATE. BOARD TWELVE: ROOK TO B3. CHECKMATE. BOARD FOURTEEN: QUEEN TO F4. CHECKMATE.
THANK YOU FOR A HIGHLY STIMULATING COFFEE BREAK, GENTLEMEN...
BOARD SEVEN PLAYED PARTICULARLY WELL THIS AFTERNOON. I WAS SO DISTRACTED FROM MACHIAVELLI'S IL PRINCIPE FOR A MOMENT THAT I ALMOST TURNED TWO PAGES AT ONCE BY MISTAKE.
ONE MOMENT, YOUNG MAN. JUST LET ME SWITCH OFF THIS PORTABLE TAPE RECORDER I DESIGNED IN THE WASHROOM THIS MORNING.
I'M TEACHING MYSELF URDU TO KEEP MY MIND BUSY WHILE I'M READING AND PLAYING CHESS WITH THE MONKEYS. I ASSUME YOU'RE AGENT JAMES OLSEN, OF COURSE?
HECK, I HEARD YOU WERE THE SMARTEST MAN ALIVE, DOCTOR LUTHOR, BUT YOU'VE GOTTA TELL ME, SIR: HOW THE BLAZES DID YOU FIGURE THAT ONE OUT?
YOU HAD AN APPOINTMENT, AGENT OLSEN.
NOW PLEASE; STEP INTO MY LAB AND LET ME SHOW YOU WHERE I AM WITH THIS ANTI-SUPERMAN DETERRENT YOU'RE PAYING SUCH LUDICROUS AMOUNTS OF MONEY FOR.

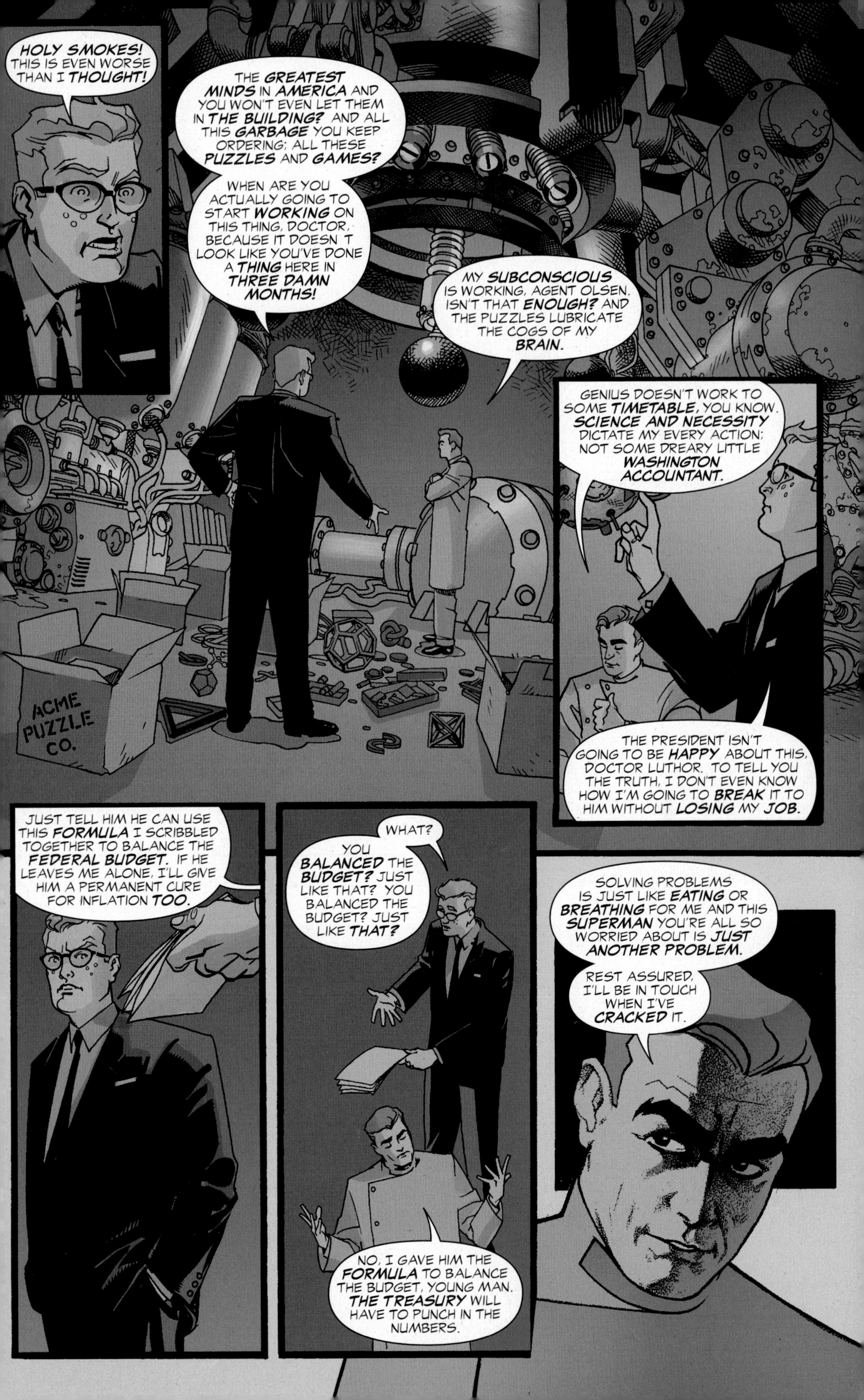
HOLY SMOKES! THIS IS EVEN WORSE THAN I THOUGHT!
THE GREATEST MINDS IN AMERICA AND YOU WON'T EVEN LET THEM IN THE BUILDING? AND ALL THIS GARBAGE YOU KEEP ORDERING; ALL THESE PUZZLES AND GAMES?
WHEN ARE YOU ACTUALLY GOING TO START WORKING ON THIS THING, DOCTOR, BECAUSE IT DOESN T LOOK LIKE YOU'VE DONE A THING HERE IN THREE DAMN MONTHS!
MY SUBCONSCIOUS IS WORKING, AGENT OLSEN. ISN'T THAT ENOUGH? AND THE PUZZLES LUBRICATE THE COGS OF MY BRAIN.
ACME PUZZLE CO.
GENIUS DOESN'T WORK TO SOME TIMETABLE, YOU KNOW. SCIENCE AND NECESSITY DICTATE MY EVERY ACTION; NOT SOME DREARY LITTLE WASHINGTON ACCOUNTANT.
THE PRESIDENT ISN'T GOING TO BE HAPPY ABOUT THIS, DOCTOR LUTHOR. TO TELL YOU THE TRUTH, I DON'T EVEN KNOW HOW I'M GOING TO BREAK IT TO HIM WITHOUT LOSING MY JOB.
JUST TELL HIM HE CAN USE THIS FORMULA I SCRIBBLED TOGETHER TO BALANCE THE FEDERAL BUDGET. IF HE LEAVES ME ALONE, I'LL GIVE HIM A PERMANENT CURE FOR INFLATION TOO.
WHAT?
YOU BALANCED THE BUDGET? JUST LIKE THAT? YOU BALANCED THE BUDGET? JUST LIKE THAT?
NO, I GAVE HIM THE FORMULA TO BALANCE THE BUDGET, YOUNG MAN. THE TREASURY WILL HAVE TO PUNCH IN THE NUMBERS.
SOLVING PROBLEMS IS JUST LIKE EATING OR BREATHING FOR ME AND THIS SUPERMAN YOU'RE ALL SO WORRIED ABOUT IS JUST ANOTHER PROBLEM.
REST ASSURED, I'LL BE IN TOUCH WHEN I'VE CRACKED IT.

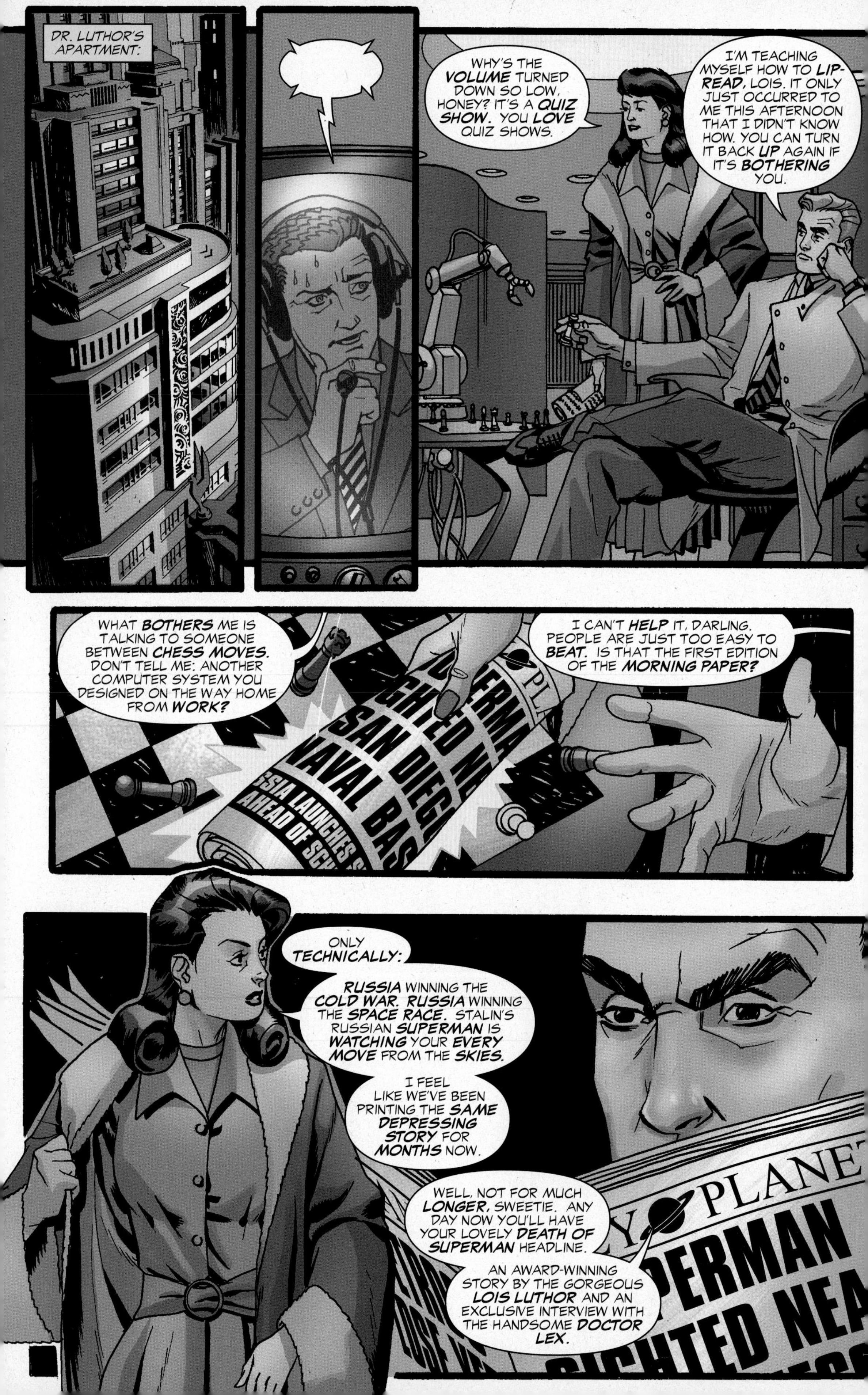
DR. LUTHOR'S APARTMENT:
WHY'S THE VOLUME TURNED DOWN SO LOW, HONEY? IT'S A QUIZ SHOW. YOU LOVE QUIZ SHOWS.
I'M TEACHING MYSELF HOW TO LIP-READ, LOIS. IT ONLY JUST OCCURRED TO ME THIS AFTERNOON THAT I DIDN'T KNOW HOW. YOU CAN TURN IT BACK UP AGAIN IF IT'S BOTHERING YOU.
WHAT BOTHERS ME IS TALKING TO SOMEONE BETWEEN CHESS MOVES. DON'T TELL ME: ANOTHER COMPUTER SYSTEM YOU DESIGNED ON THE WAY HOME FROM WORK?
I CAN'T HELP IT, DARLING. PEOPLE ARE JUST TOO EASY TO BEAT. IS THAT THE FIRST EDITION OF THE MORNING PAPER?
ONLY TECHNICALLY:
RUSSIA WINNING THE COLD WAR. RUSSIA WINNING THE SPACE RACE. STALIN'S RUSSIAN SUPERMAN IS WATCHING YOUR EVERY MOVE FROM THE SKIES.
I FEEL LIKE WE'VE BEEN PRINTING THE SAME DEPRESSING STORY FOR MONTHS NOW.
WELL, NOT FOR MUCH LONGER, SWEETIE. ANY DAY NOW YOU'LL HAVE YOUR LOVELY DEATH OF SUPERMAN HEADLINE.
AN AWARD-WINNING STORY BY THE GORGEOUS LOIS LUTHOR AND AN EXCLUSIVE INTERVIEW WITH THE HANDSOME DOCTOR LEX.

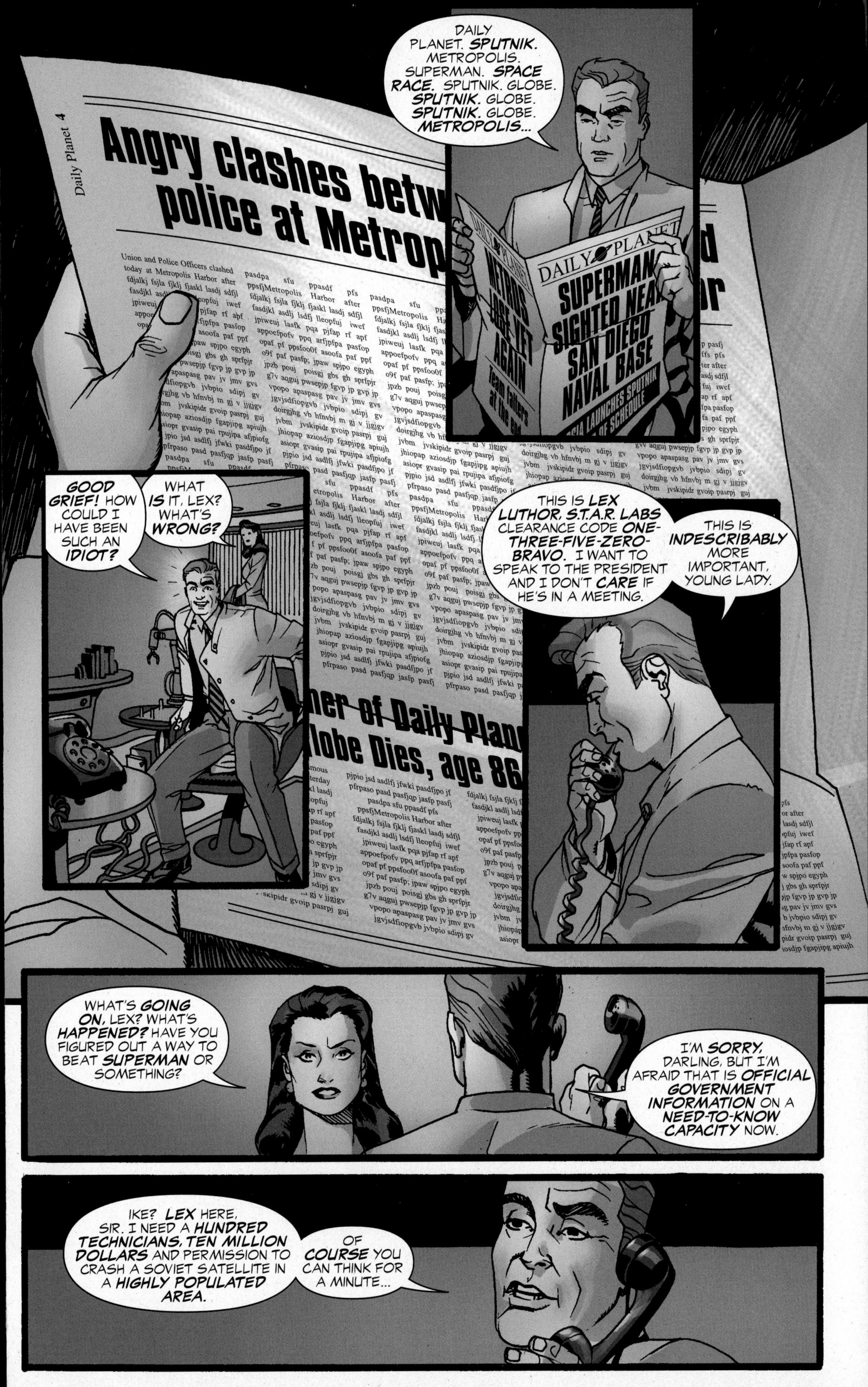

DAILY PLANET. SPUTNIK. METROPOLIS. SUPERMAN. SPACE RACE. SPUTNIK. GLOBE. SPUTNIK. GLOBE. SPUTNIK. GLOBE. METROPOLIS...
GOOD GRIEF! HOW COULD I HAVE BEEN SUCH AN IDIOT?
WHAT IS IT, LEX? WHAT'S WRONG?
THIS IS LEX LUTHOR, S.T.A.R. LABS CLEARANCE CODE ONE-THREE-FIVE-ZERO-BRAVO. I WANT TO SPEAK TO THE PRESIDENT AND I DON'T CARE IF HE'S IN A MEETING.
THIS IS INDESCRIBABLY MORE IMPORTANT, YOUNG LADY.
WHAT'S GOING ON, LEX? WHAT'S HAPPENED? HAVE YOU FIGURED OUT A WAY TO BEAT SUPERMAN OR SOMETHING?
I'M SORRY, DARLING, BUT I'M AFRAID THAT IS OFFICIAL GOVERNMENT INFORMATION ON A NEED-TO-KNOW CAPACITY NOW.
IKE? LEX HERE, SIR. I NEED A HUNDRED TECHNICIANS, TEN MILLION DOLLARS AND PERMISSION TO CRASH A SOVIET SATELLITE IN A HIGHLY POPULATED AREA.
OF COURSE YOU CAN THINK FOR A MINUTE...

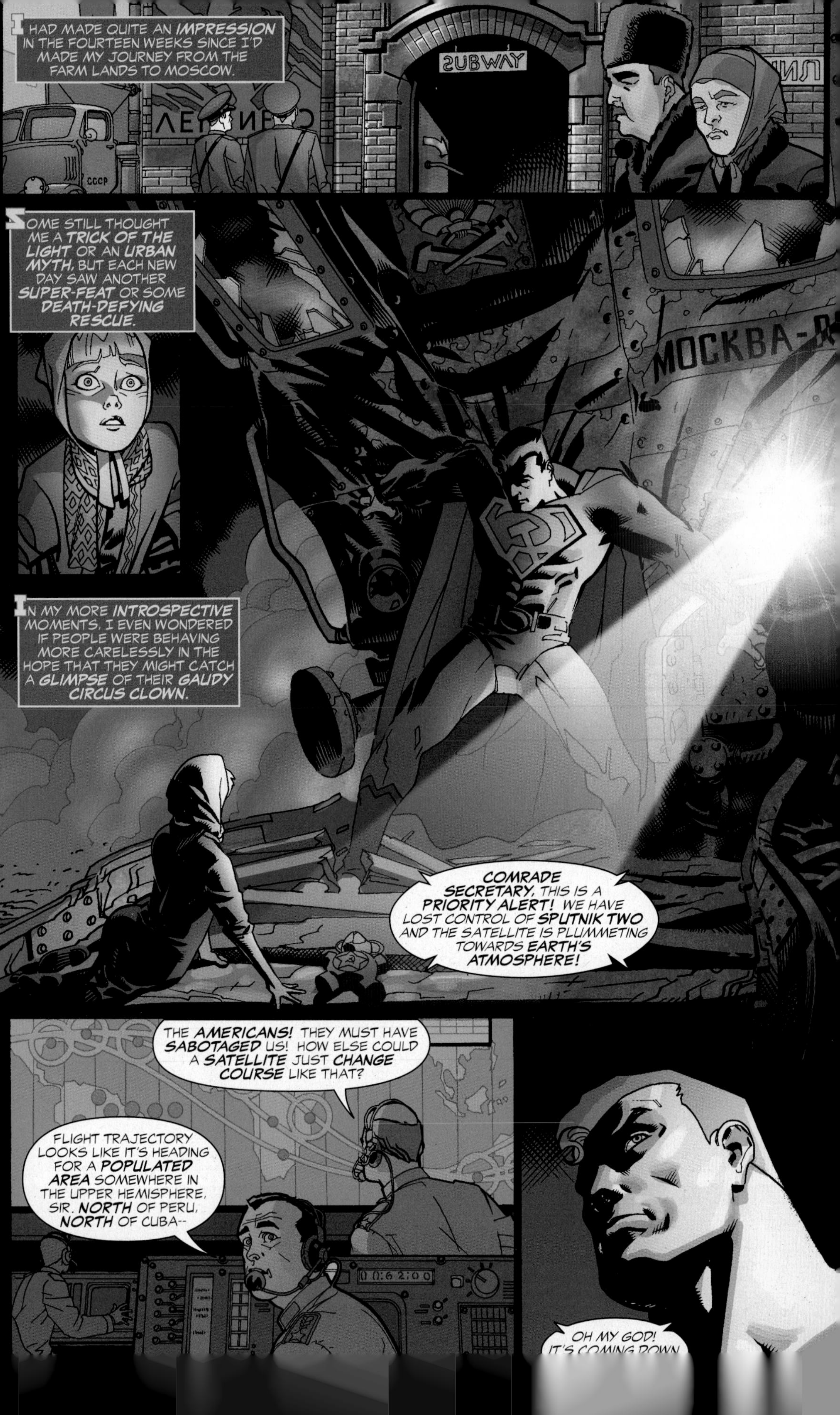
I HAD MADE QUITE AN IMPRESSION IN THE FOURTEEN WEEKS SINCE I'D MADE MY JOURNEY FROM THE FARM LANDS TO MOSCOW.
SUBWAY
SOME STILL THOUGHT ME A TRICK OF THE LIGHT OR AN URBAN MYTH, BUT EACH NEW DAY SAW ANOTHER SUPER-FEAT OR SOME DEATH-DEFYING RESCUE.
IN MY MORE INTROSPECTIVE MOMENTS, I EVEN WONDERED IF PEOPLE WERE BEHAVING MORE CARELESSLY IN THE HOPE THAT THEY MIGHT CATCH A GLIMPSE OF THEIR GAUDY CIRCUS CLOWN.
COMRADE SECRETARY, THIS IS A PRIORITY ALERT! WE HAVE LOST CONTROL OF SPUTNIK TWO AND THE SATELLITE IS PLUMMETING TOWARDS EARTH'S ATMOSPHERE!
THE AMERICANS! THEY MUST HAVE SABOTAGED US! HOW ELSE COULD A SATELLITE JUST CHANGE COURSE LIKE THAT?
FLIGHT TRAJECTORY LOOKS LIKE IT'S HEADING FOR A POPULATED AREA SOMEWHERE IN THE UPPER HEMISPHERE, SIR. NORTH OF PERU, NORTH OF CUBA--
OH MY GOD!

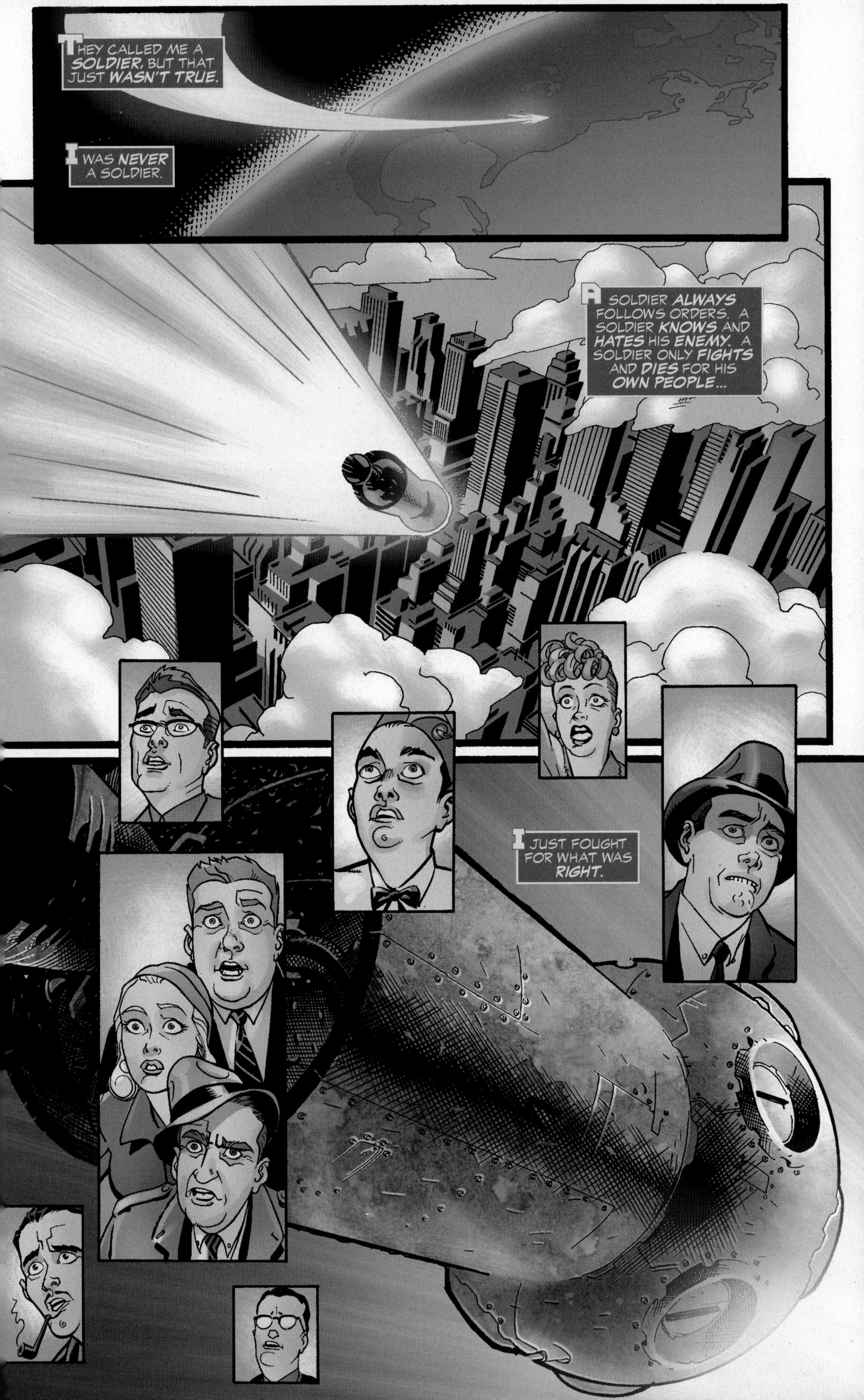
THEY CALLED ME A SOLDIER, BUT THAT JUST WASN'T TRUE.
I WAS NEVER A SOLDIER.
A SOLDIER ALWAYS FOLLOWS ORDERS. A SOLDIER KNOWS AND HATES HIS ENEMY. A SOLDIER ONLY FIGHTS AND DIES FOR HIS OWN PEOPLE...
I JUST FOUGHT FOR WHAT WAS RIGHT.

SPUTNIK TWO WEIGHED FIVE THOUSAND POUNDS.

THIS MASS MULTIPLIED BY AN ACCELERATION FACTOR OF A *HUNDRED METERS PER SECOND* WOULD HAVE DELIVERED A FORCE POWERFUL ENOUGH TO LEVEL THE *ENTIRE CITY.*

IN HINDSIGHT, THERE ARE *SO MANY WAYS* THIS PREDICAMENT MIGHT HAVE BEEN *SOLVED.*

BAKK!

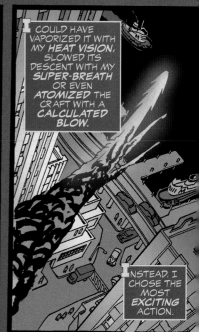

I COULD HAVE VAPORIZED IT WITH MY *HEAT VISION,* SLOWED ITS DESCENT WITH MY *SUPER-BREATH* OR EVEN *ATOMIZED* THE CRAFT WITH A *CALCULATED BLOW.*

INSTEAD, I CHOSE THE MOST *EXCITING* ACTION.

THOOOM!

THE POWERS WERE STILL *NEW* TO ME THEN, YOU UNDERSTAND.

EXACTLY THREE SECONDS AFTER HITTING THE ROOF OF THE **NEWSPAPER OFFICE**, I REALIZED THE DAMAGE DONE TO THE **BUILDING'S SUSPENSION**.

METROPOLIS WAS ALIVE WITH **NOISE** AGAIN, BUT I COULD STILL HEAR LOOSE BRICKS START TO FALL **TWO MILES WEST**.

A CLUSTER OF SUPPORT CABLES **GROANED** AND **SNAPPED**. PEOPLE BELOW SCREAMED FOR **SOMEONE** TO **SAVE** THEM.

SKRRR!

NOT MY PEOPLE...

BUT I **NEVER** REFUSE A CRY FOR HELP.

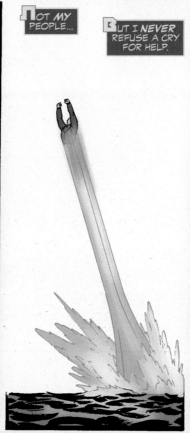

ALL THE **LIES** THEY SPREAD ABOUT ME. THE **PROPAGANDA** THEY ENGINEERED AT THE HEIGHT OF THE **COLD WAR**. NONE OF IT **MATTERED** FOR A WHILE ON THAT **BRIGHT AFTERNOON**.

JUST FOR A **SINGLE MOMENT**.

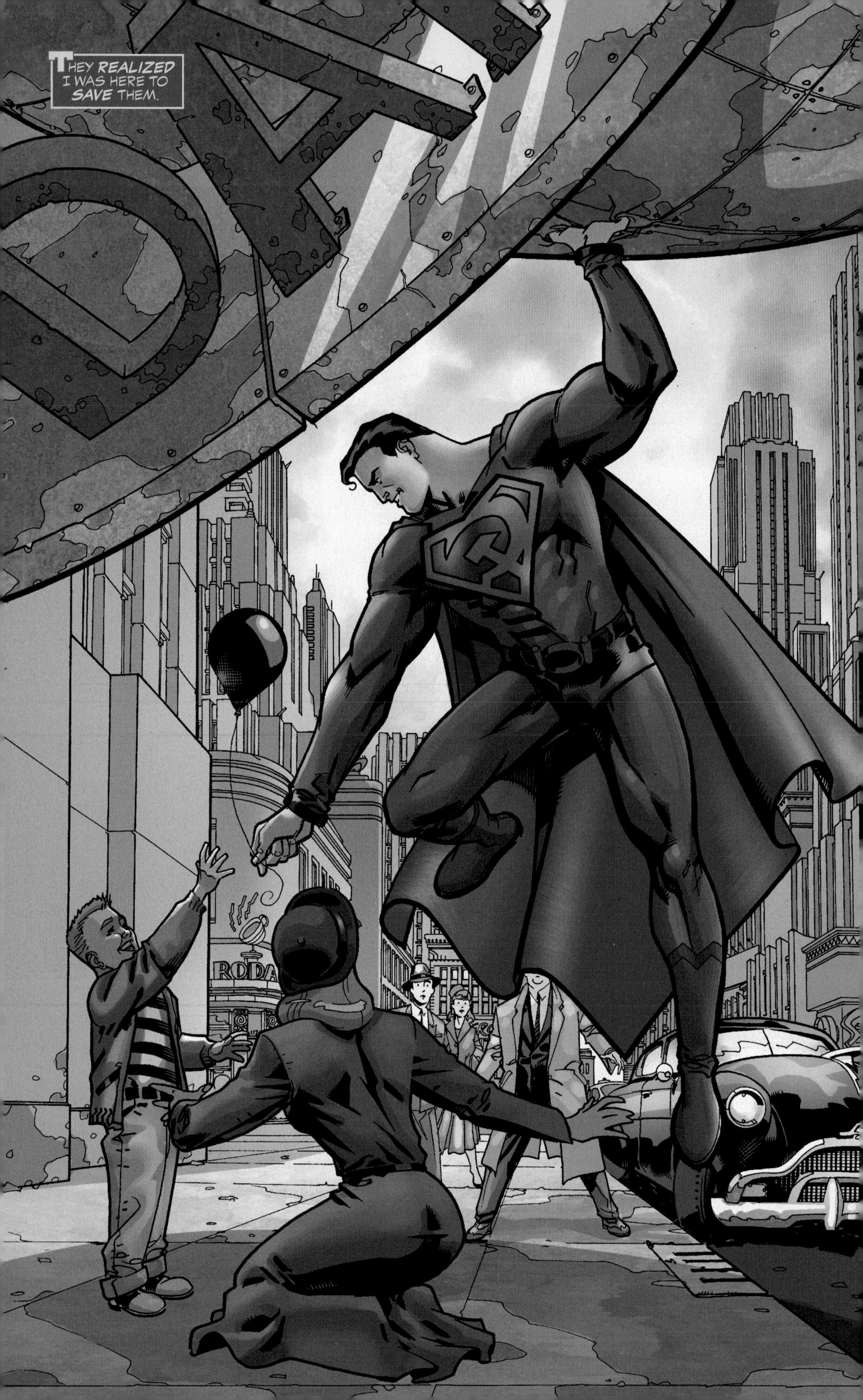
THEY REALIZED I WAS HERE TO SAVE THEM.
RODA

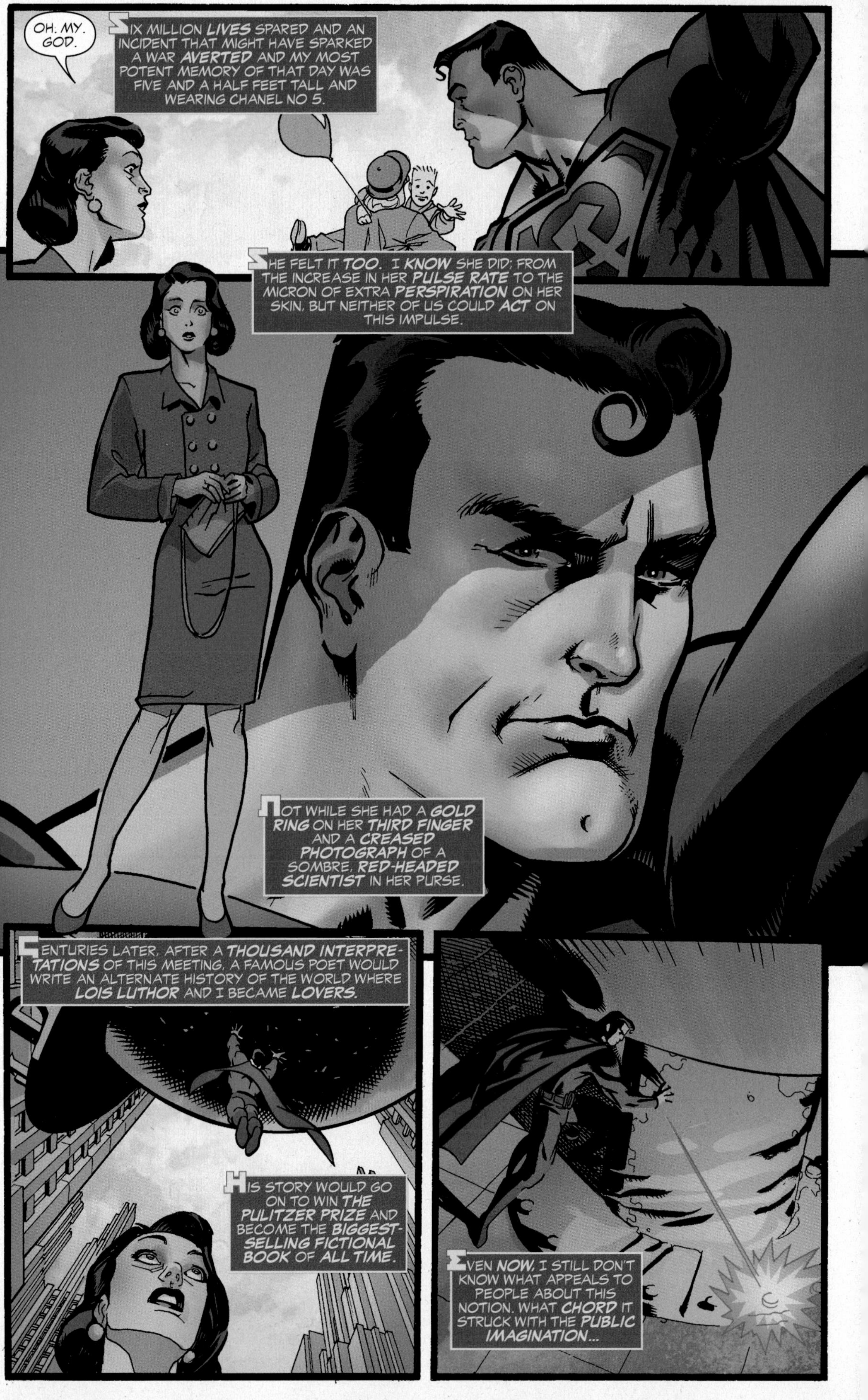

OH. MY. GOD.
SIX MILLION LIVES SPARED AND AN INCIDENT THAT MIGHT HAVE SPARKED A WAR AVERTED AND MY MOST POTENT MEMORY OF THAT DAY WAS FIVE AND A HALF FEET TALL AND WEARING CHANEL NO 5.
SHE FELT IT TOO. I KNOW SHE DID; FROM THE INCREASE IN HER PULSE RATE TO THE MICRON OF EXTRA PERSPIRATION ON HER SKIN, BUT NEITHER OF US COULD ACT ON THIS IMPULSE.
NOT WHILE SHE HAD A GOLD RING ON HER THIRD FINGER AND A CREASED PHOTOGRAPH OF A SOMBRE, RED-HEADED SCIENTIST IN HER PURSE.
CENTURIES LATER, AFTER A THOUSAND INTERPRETATIONS OF THIS MEETING, A FAMOUS POET WOULD WRITE AN ALTERNATE HISTORY OF THE WORLD WHERE LOIS LUTHOR AND I BECAME LOVERS.
HIS STORY WOULD GO ON TO WIN THE PULITZER PRIZE AND BECOME THE BIGGEST-SELLING FICTIONAL BOOK OF ALL TIME.
EVEN NOW, I STILL DON'T KNOW WHAT APPEALS TO PEOPLE ABOUT THIS NOTION. WHAT CHORD IT STRUCK WITH THE PUBLIC IMAGINATION...

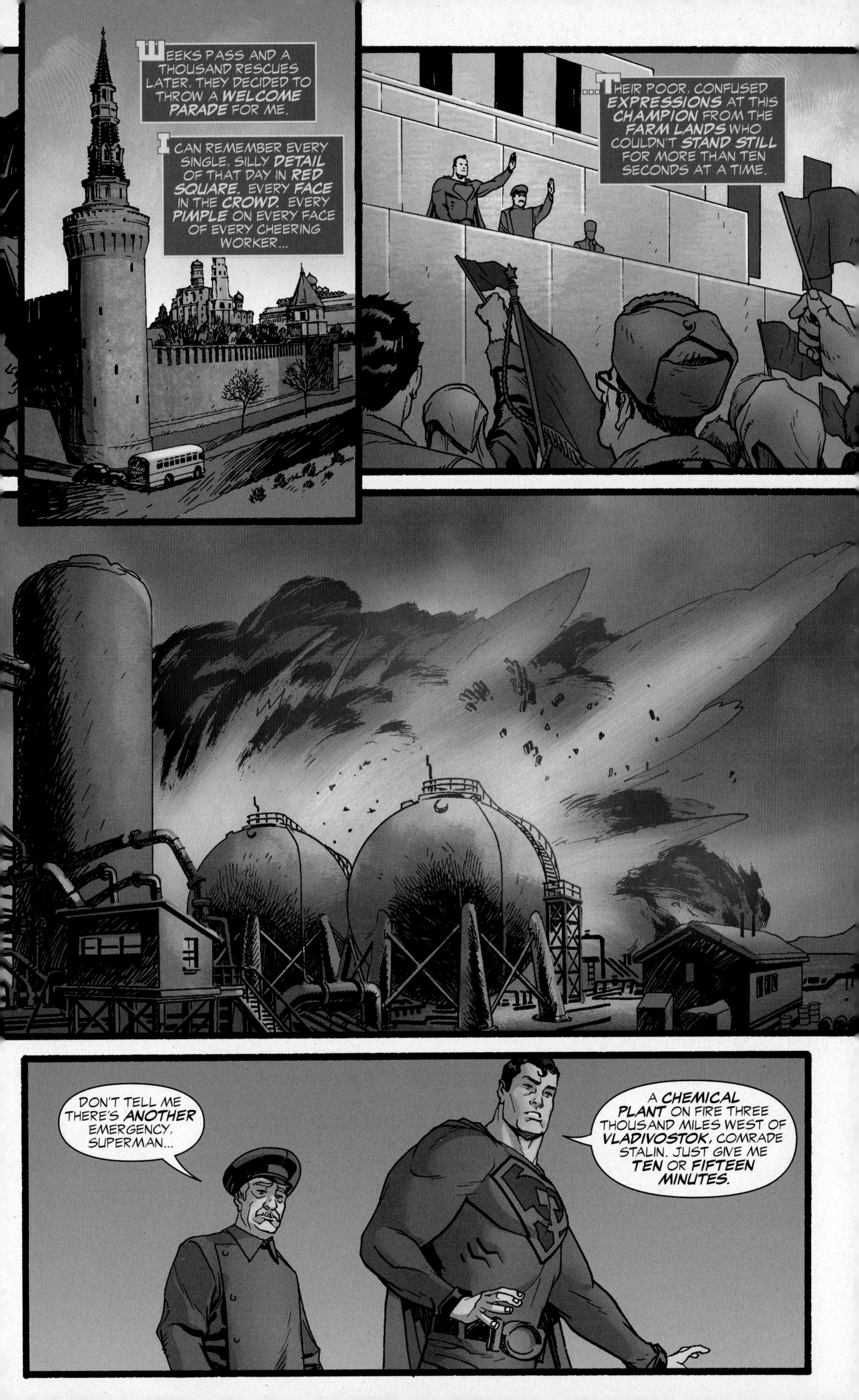
WEEKS PASS AND A THOUSAND RESCUES LATER, THEY DECIDED TO THROW A WELCOME PARADE FOR ME.
I CAN REMEMBER EVERY SINGLE, SILLY DETAIL OF THAT DAY IN RED SQUARE. EVERY FACE IN THE CROWD. EVERY PIMPLE ON EVERY FACE OF EVERY CHEERING WORKER...
...THEIR POOR, CONFUSED EXPRESSIONS AT THIS CHAMPION FROM THE FARM LANDS WHO COULDN'T STAND STILL FOR MORE THAN TEN SECONDS AT A TIME.
DON'T TELL ME THERE'S ANOTHER EMERGENCY, SUPERMAN...
A CHEMICAL PLANT ON FIRE THREE THOUSAND MILES WEST OF VLADIVOSTOK, COMRADE STALIN. JUST GIVE ME TEN OR FIFTEEN MINUTES.

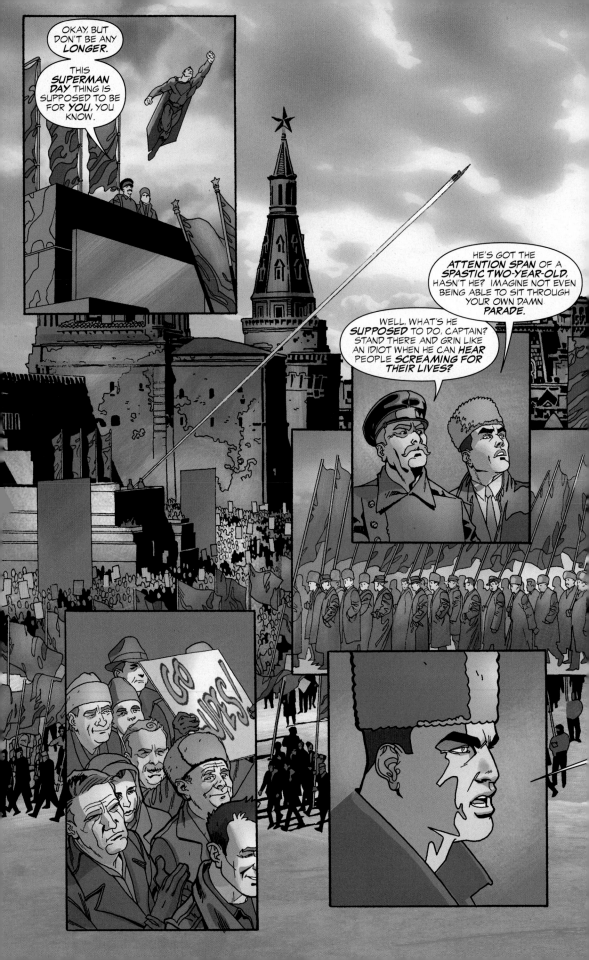

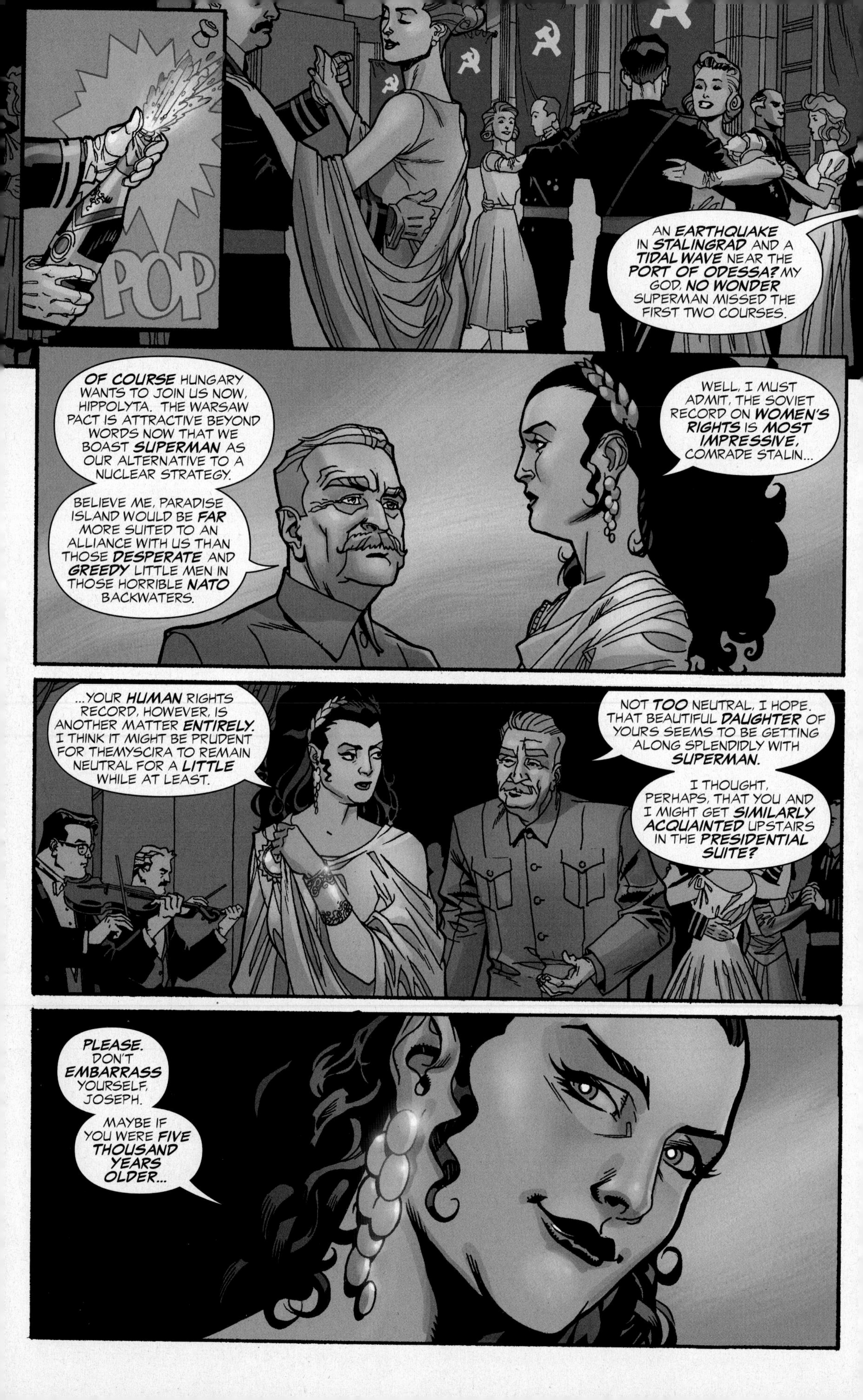

POP
AN EARTHQUAKE IN STALINGRAD AND A TIDAL WAVE NEAR THE PORT OF ODESSA? MY GOD, NO WONDER SUPERMAN MISSED THE FIRST TWO COURSES.
OF COURSE HUNGARY WANTS TO JOIN US NOW, HIPPOLYTA. THE WARSAW PACT IS ATTRACTIVE BEYOND WORDS NOW THAT WE BOAST SUPERMAN AS OUR ALTERNATIVE TO A NUCLEAR STRATEGY.
BELIEVE ME, PARADISE ISLAND WOULD BE FAR MORE SUITED TO AN ALLIANCE WITH US THAN THOSE DESPERATE AND GREEDY LITTLE MEN IN THOSE HORRIBLE NATO BACKWATERS.
WELL, I MUST ADMIT, THE SOVIET RECORD ON WOMEN'S RIGHTS IS MOST IMPRESSIVE, COMRADE STALIN...
...YOUR HUMAN RIGHTS RECORD, HOWEVER, IS ANOTHER MATTER ENTIRELY. I THINK IT MIGHT BE PRUDENT FOR THEMYSCIRA TO REMAIN NEUTRAL FOR A LITTLE WHILE AT LEAST.
NOT TOO NEUTRAL, I HOPE. THAT BEAUTIFUL DAUGHTER OF YOURS SEEMS TO BE GETTING ALONG SPLENDIDLY WITH SUPERMAN.
I THOUGHT, PERHAPS, THAT YOU AND I MIGHT GET SIMILARLY ACQUAINTED UPSTAIRS IN THE PRESIDENTIAL SUITE?
PLEASE. DON'T EMBARRASS YOURSELF, JOSEPH.
MAYBE IF YOU WERE FIVE THOUSAND YEARS OLDER...

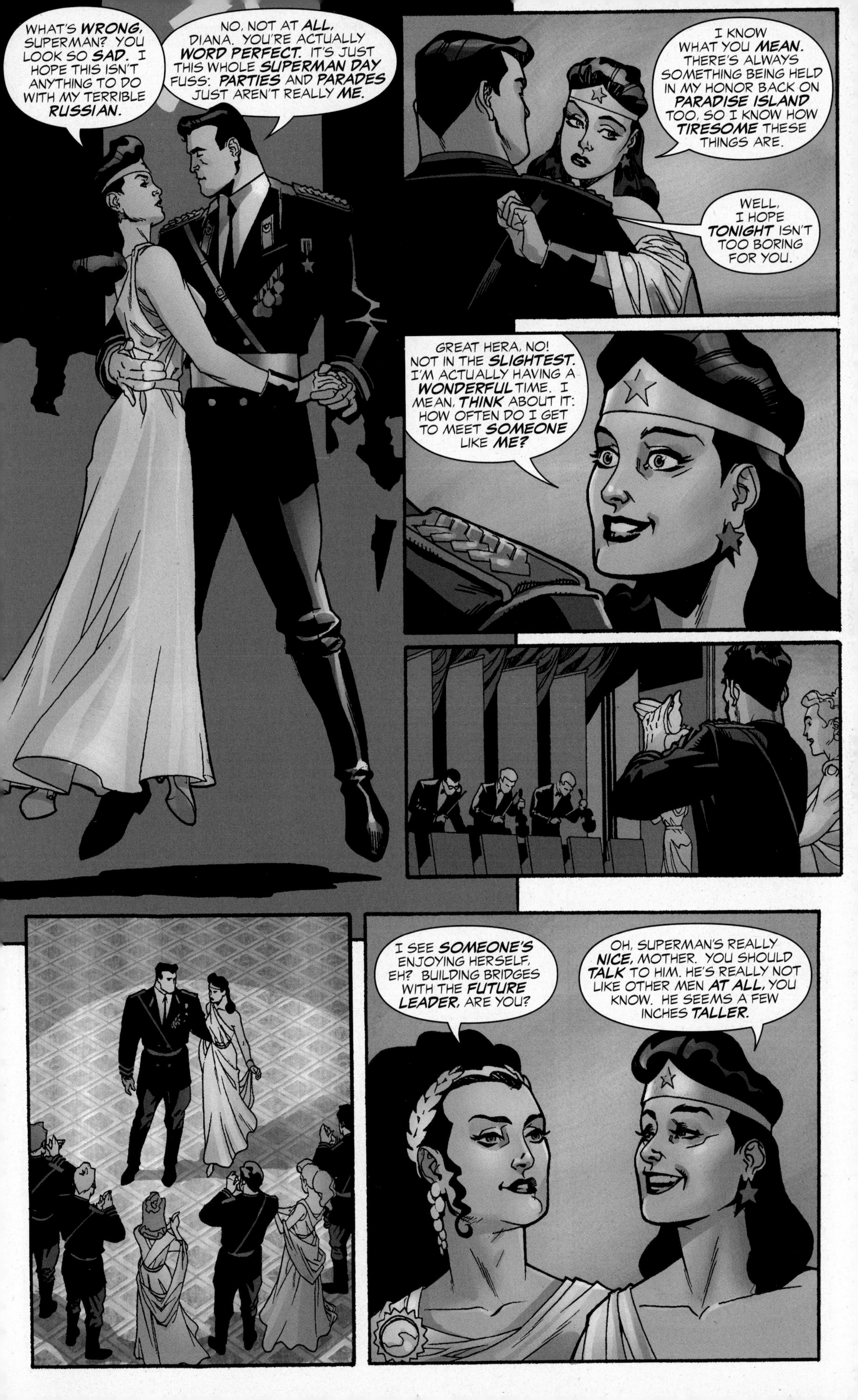
WHAT'S WRONG, SUPERMAN? YOU LOOK SO SAD. I HOPE THIS ISN'T ANYTHING TO DO WITH MY TERRIBLE RUSSIAN.
NO, NOT AT ALL, DIANA. YOU'RE ACTUALLY WORD PERFECT. IT'S JUST THIS WHOLE SUPERMAN DAY FUSS: PARTIES AND PARADES JUST AREN'T REALLY ME.
I KNOW WHAT YOU MEAN. THERE'S ALWAYS SOMETHING BEING HELD IN MY HONOR BACK ON PARADISE ISLAND TOO, SO I KNOW HOW TIRESOME THESE THINGS ARE.
WELL, I HOPE TONIGHT ISN'T TOO BORING FOR YOU.
GREAT HERA, NO! NOT IN THE SLIGHTEST. I'M ACTUALLY HAVING A WONDERFUL TIME. I MEAN, THINK ABOUT IT: HOW OFTEN DO I GET TO MEET SOMEONE LIKE ME?
I SEE SOMEONE'S ENJOYING HERSELF, EH? BUILDING BRIDGES WITH THE FUTURE LEADER, ARE YOU?
OH, SUPERMAN'S REALLY NICE, MOTHER. YOU SHOULD TALK TO HIM. HE'S REALLY NOT LIKE OTHER MEN AT ALL, YOU KNOW. HE SEEMS A FEW INCHES TALLER.

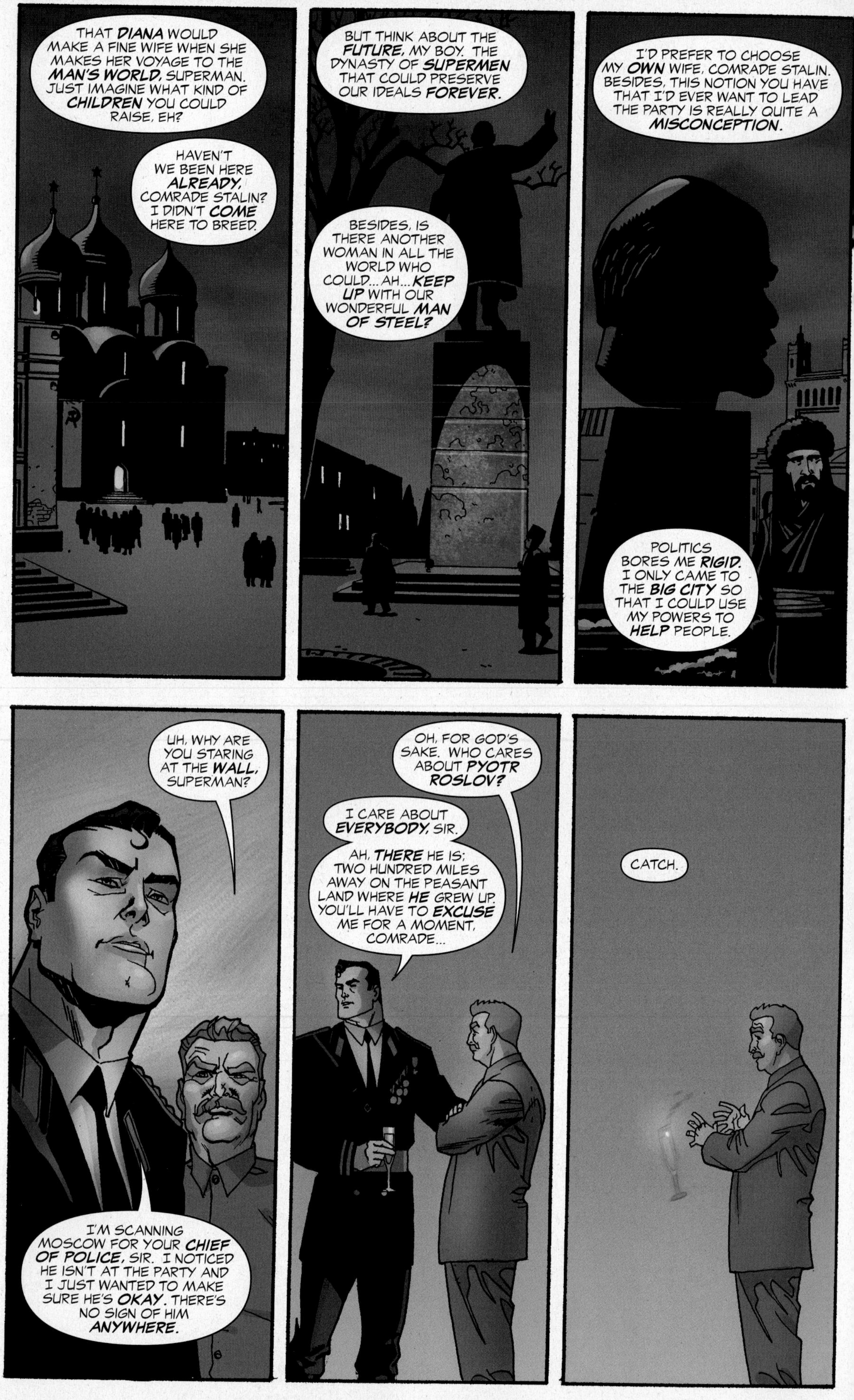
THAT DIANA WOULD MAKE A FINE WIFE WHEN SHE MAKES HER VOYAGE TO THE MAN'S WORLD, SUPERMAN. JUST IMAGINE WHAT KIND OF CHILDREN YOU COULD RAISE, EH?
HAVEN'T WE BEEN HERE ALREADY, COMRADE STALIN? I DIDN'T COME HERE TO BREED.
BUT THINK ABOUT THE FUTURE, MY BOY. THE DYNASTY OF SUPERMEN THAT COULD PRESERVE OUR IDEALS FOREVER.
BESIDES, IS THERE ANOTHER WOMAN IN ALL THE WORLD WHO COULD...AH...KEEP UP WITH OUR WONDERFUL MAN OF STEEL?
I'D PREFER TO CHOOSE MY OWN WIFE, COMRADE STALIN. BESIDES, THIS NOTION YOU HAVE THAT I'D EVER WANT TO LEAD THE PARTY IS REALLY QUITE A MISCONCEPTION.
POLITICS BORES ME RIGID. I ONLY CAME TO THE BIG CITY SO THAT I COULD USE MY POWERS TO HELP PEOPLE.
UH, WHY ARE YOU STARING AT THE WALL, SUPERMAN?
I'M SCANNING MOSCOW FOR YOUR CHIEF OF POLICE, SIR. I NOTICED HE ISN'T AT THE PARTY AND I JUST WANTED TO MAKE SURE HE'S OKAY. THERE'S NO SIGN OF HIM ANYWHERE.
OH, FOR GOD'S SAKE. WHO CARES ABOUT PYOTR ROSLOV?
I CARE ABOUT EVERYBODY, SIR.
AH, THERE HE IS; TWO HUNDRED MILES AWAY ON THE PEASANT LAND WHERE HE GREW UP. YOU'LL HAVE TO EXCUSE ME FOR A MOMENT, COMRADE...
CATCH.

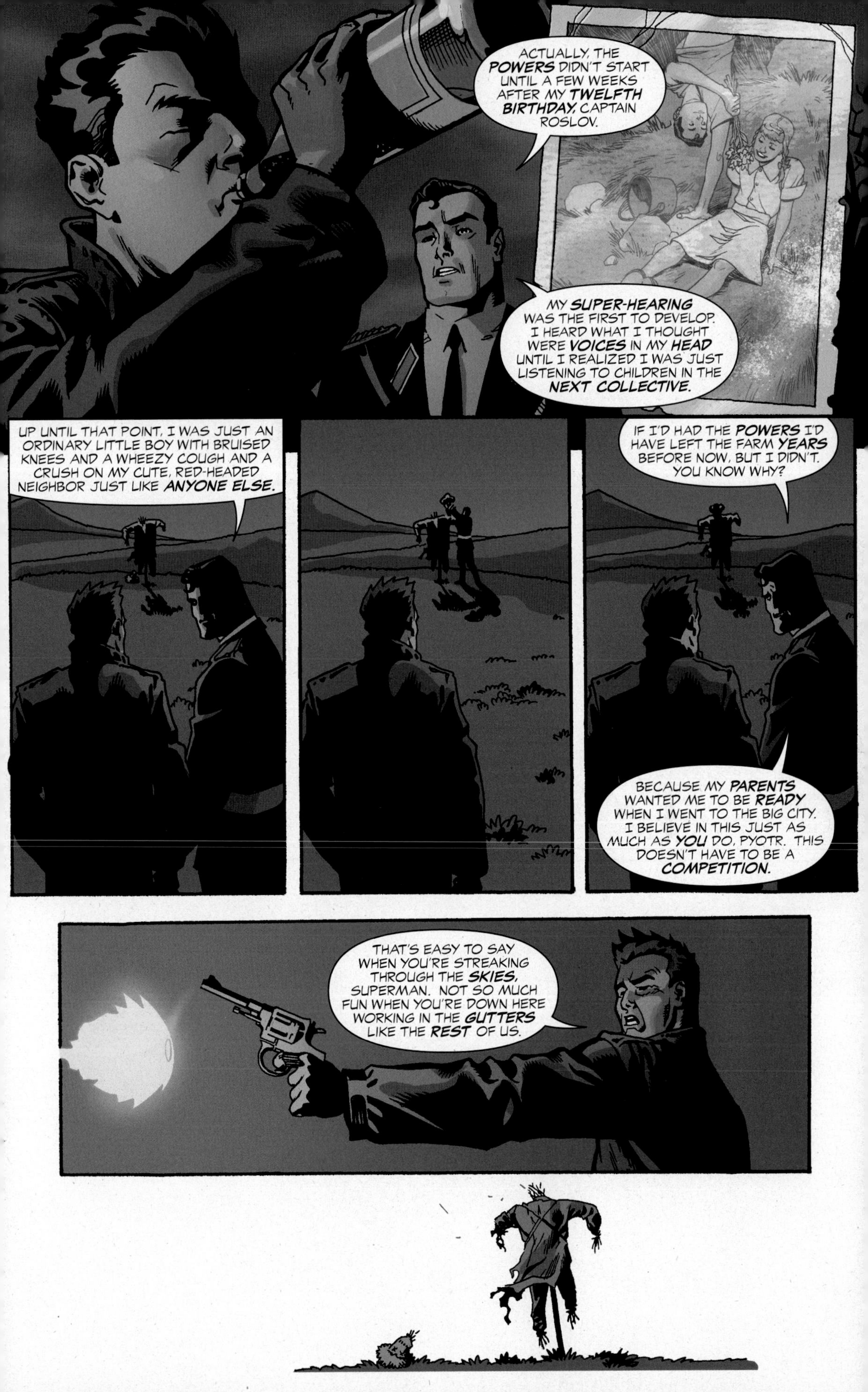
ACTUALLY, THE POWERS DIDN'T START UNTIL A FEW WEEKS AFTER MY TWELFTH BIRTHDAY, CAPTAIN ROSLOV.
MY SUPER-HEARING WAS THE FIRST TO DEVELOP. I HEARD WHAT I THOUGHT WERE VOICES IN MY HEAD UNTIL I REALIZED I WAS JUST LISTENING TO CHILDREN IN THE NEXT COLLECTIVE.
UP UNTIL THAT POINT, I WAS JUST AN ORDINARY LITTLE BOY WITH BRUISED KNEES AND A WHEEZY COUGH AND A CRUSH ON MY CUTE, RED-HEADED NEIGHBOR JUST LIKE ANYONE ELSE.
IF I'D HAD THE POWERS I'D HAVE LEFT THE FARM YEARS BEFORE NOW, BUT I DIDN'T. YOU KNOW WHY?
BECAUSE MY PARENTS WANTED ME TO BE READY WHEN I WENT TO THE BIG CITY. I BELIEVE IN THIS JUST AS MUCH AS YOU DO, PYOTR. THIS DOESN'T HAVE TO BE A COMPETITION.
THAT'S EASY TO SAY WHEN YOU'RE STREAKING THROUGH THE SKIES, SUPERMAN. NOT SO MUCH FUN WHEN YOU'RE DOWN HERE WORKING IN THE GUTTERS LIKE THE REST OF US.

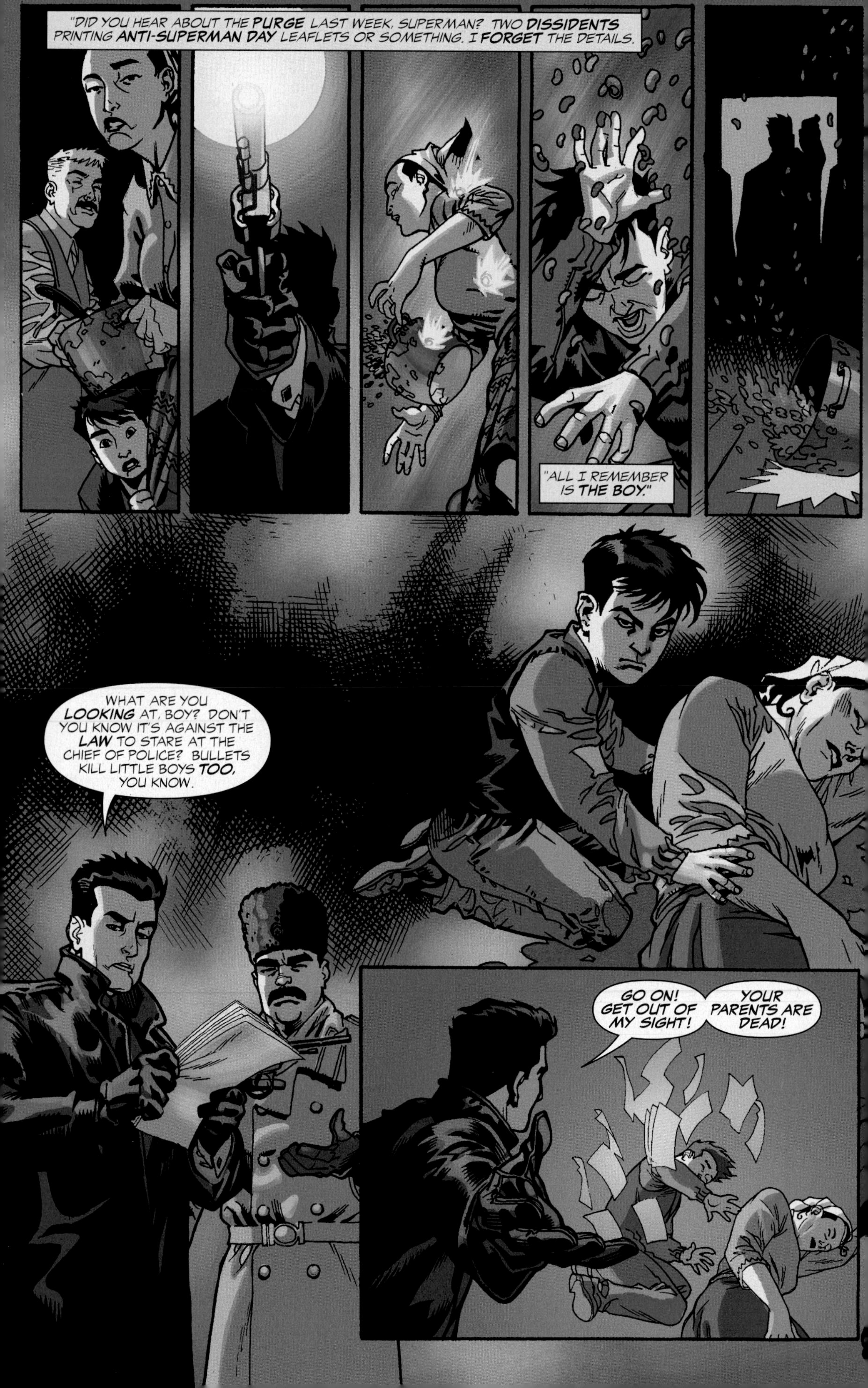
"DID YOU HEAR ABOUT THE PURGE LAST WEEK, SUPERMAN? TWO DISSIDENTS PRINTING ANTI-SUPERMAN DAY LEAFLETS OR SOMETHING. I FORGET THE DETAILS.
"ALL I REMEMBER IS THE BOY."
WHAT ARE YOU LOOKING AT, BOY? DON'T YOU KNOW IT'S AGAINST THE LAW TO STARE AT THE CHIEF OF POLICE? BULLETS KILL LITTLE BOYS TOO, YOU KNOW.
GO ON! GET OUT OF MY SIGHT!
YOUR PARENTS ARE DEAD!

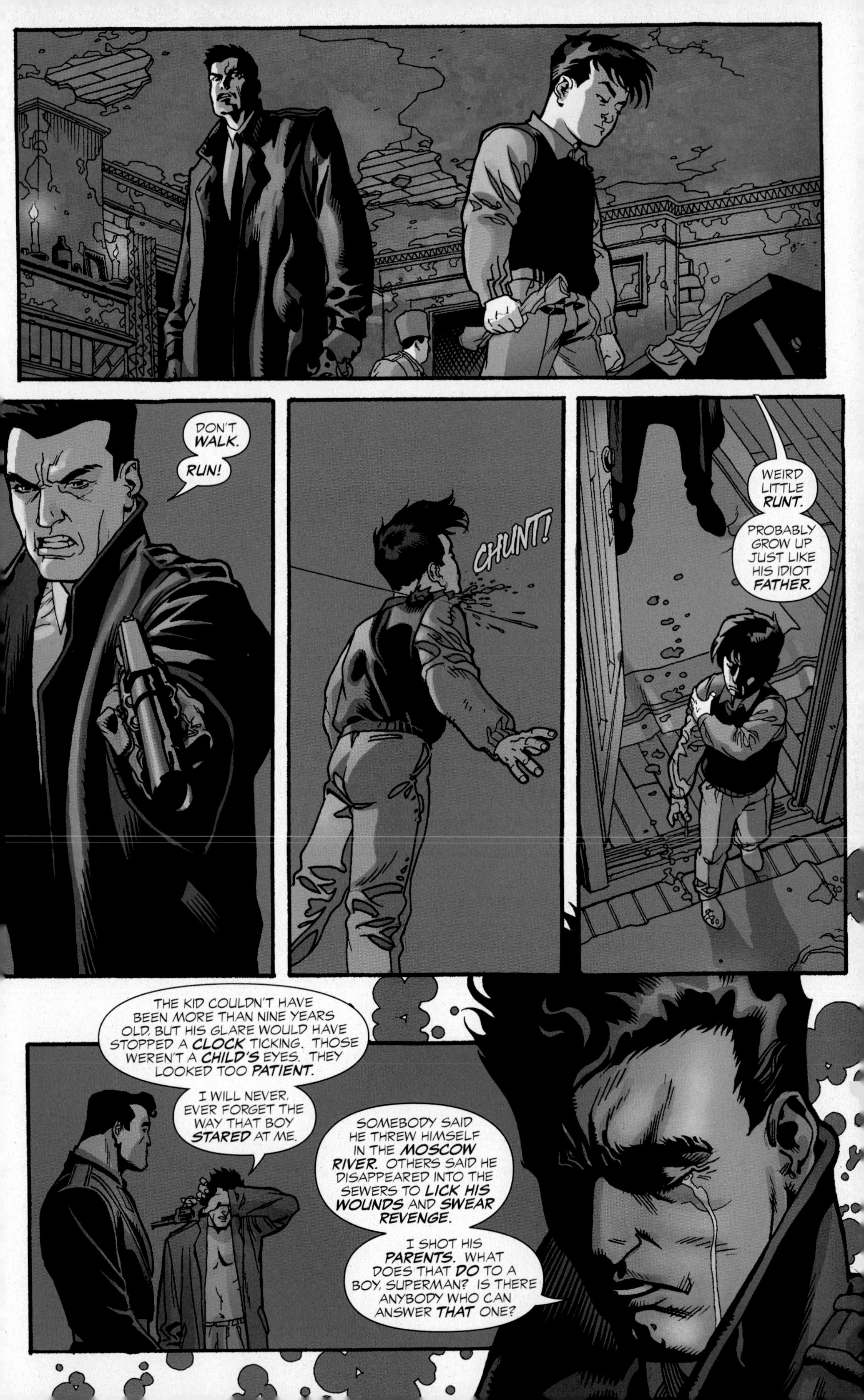
DON'T WALK.
RUN!
CHUNT!
WEIRD LITTLE RUNT.
PROBABLY GROW UP JUST LIKE HIS IDIOT FATHER.
THE KID COULDN'T HAVE BEEN MORE THAN NINE YEARS OLD, BUT HIS GLARE WOULD HAVE STOPPED A CLOCK TICKING. THOSE WEREN'T A CHILD'S EYES. THEY LOOKED TOO PATIENT.
I WILL NEVER, EVER FORGET THE WAY THAT BOY STARED AT ME.
SOMEBODY SAID HE THREW HIMSELF IN THE MOSCOW RIVER. OTHERS SAID HE DISAPPEARED INTO THE SEWERS TO LICK HIS WOUNDS AND SWEAR REVENGE.
I SHOT HIS PARENTS. WHAT DOES THAT DO TO A BOY, SUPERMAN? IS THERE ANYBODY WHO CAN ANSWER THAT ONE?

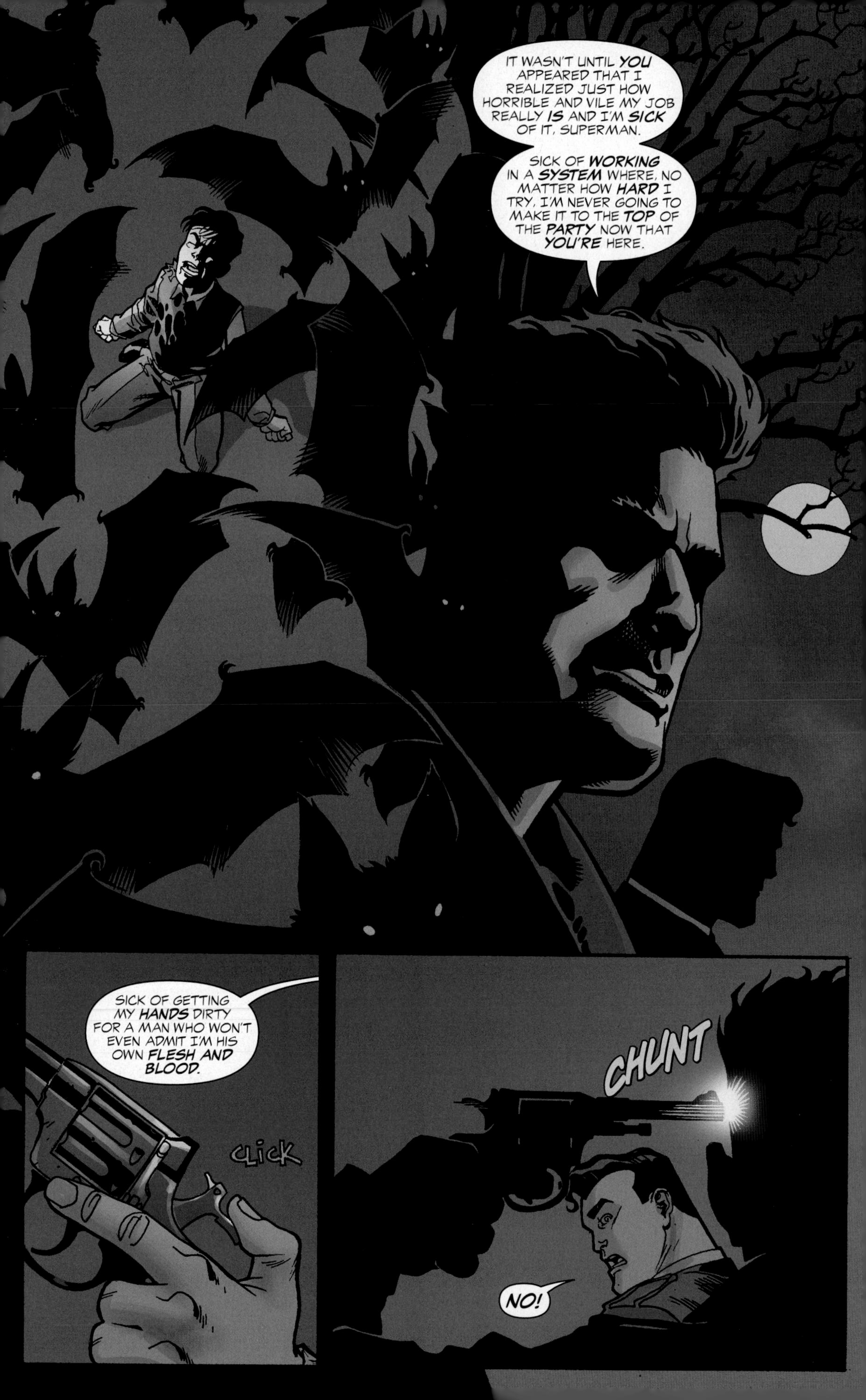
IT WASN'T UNTIL YOU APPEARED THAT I REALIZED JUST HOW HORRIBLE AND VILE MY JOB REALLY IS AND I'M SICK OF IT, SUPERMAN.
SICK OF WORKING IN A SYSTEM WHERE, NO MATTER HOW HARD I TRY, I'M NEVER GOING TO MAKE IT TO THE TOP OF THE PARTY NOW THAT YOU'RE HERE.
SICK OF GETTING MY HANDS DIRTY FOR A MAN WHO WON'T EVEN ADMIT I'M HIS OWN FLESH AND BLOOD.
CLICK
CHUNT
NO!

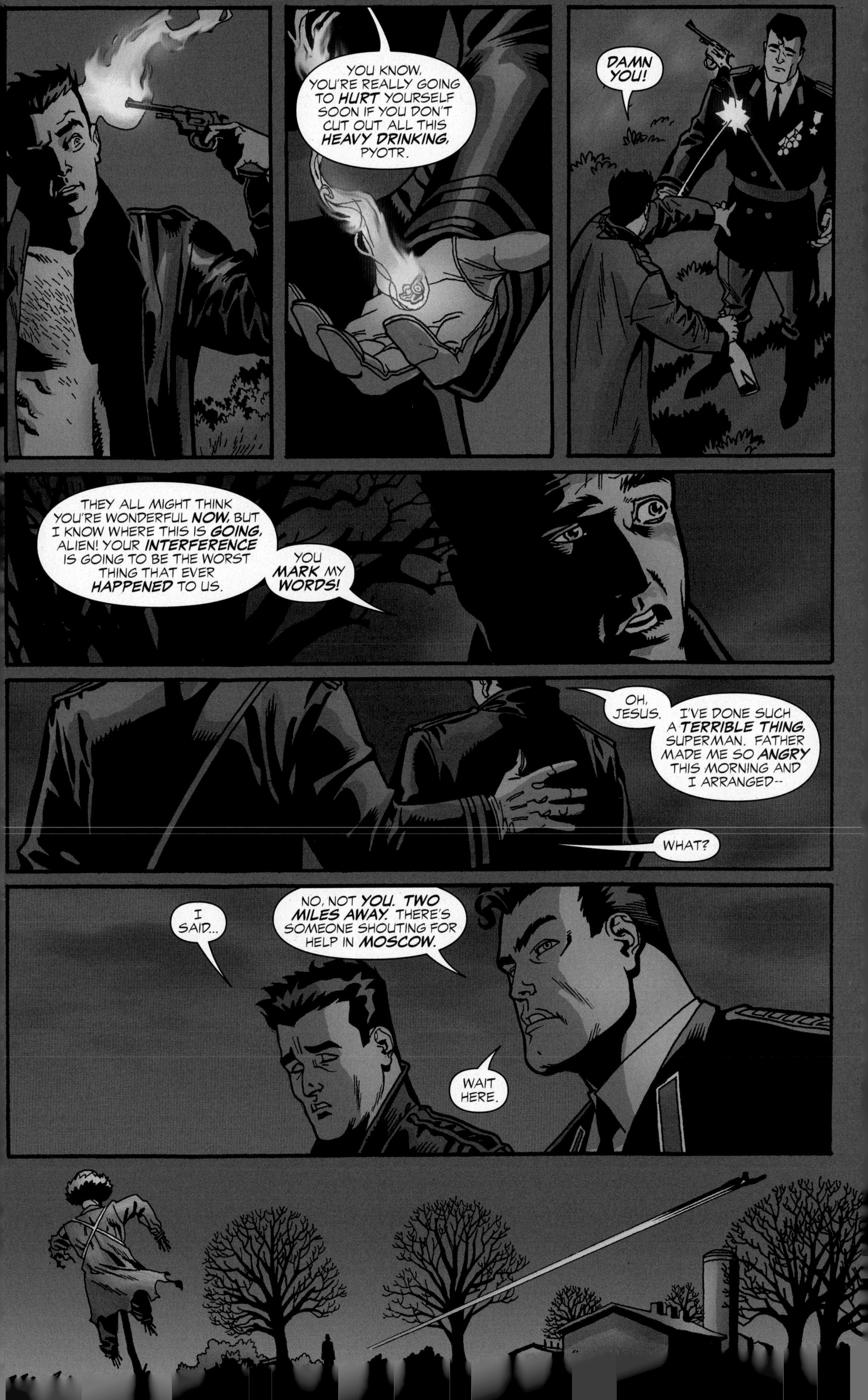
YOU KNOW, YOU'RE REALLY GOING TO HURT YOURSELF SOON IF YOU DON'T CUT OUT ALL THIS HEAVY DRINKING, PYOTR.
DAMN YOU!
THEY ALL MIGHT THINK YOU'RE WONDERFUL NOW, BUT I KNOW WHERE THIS IS GOING, ALIEN! YOUR INTERFERENCE IS GOING TO BE THE WORST THING THAT EVER HAPPENED TO US.
YOU MARK MY WORDS!
OH, JESUS.
I'VE DONE SUCH A TERRIBLE THING, SUPERMAN. FATHER MADE ME SO ANGRY THIS MORNING AND I ARRANGED--
WHAT?
I SAID...
NO, NOT YOU. TWO MILES AWAY. THERE'S SOMEONE SHOUTING FOR HELP IN MOSCOW.
WAIT HERE.

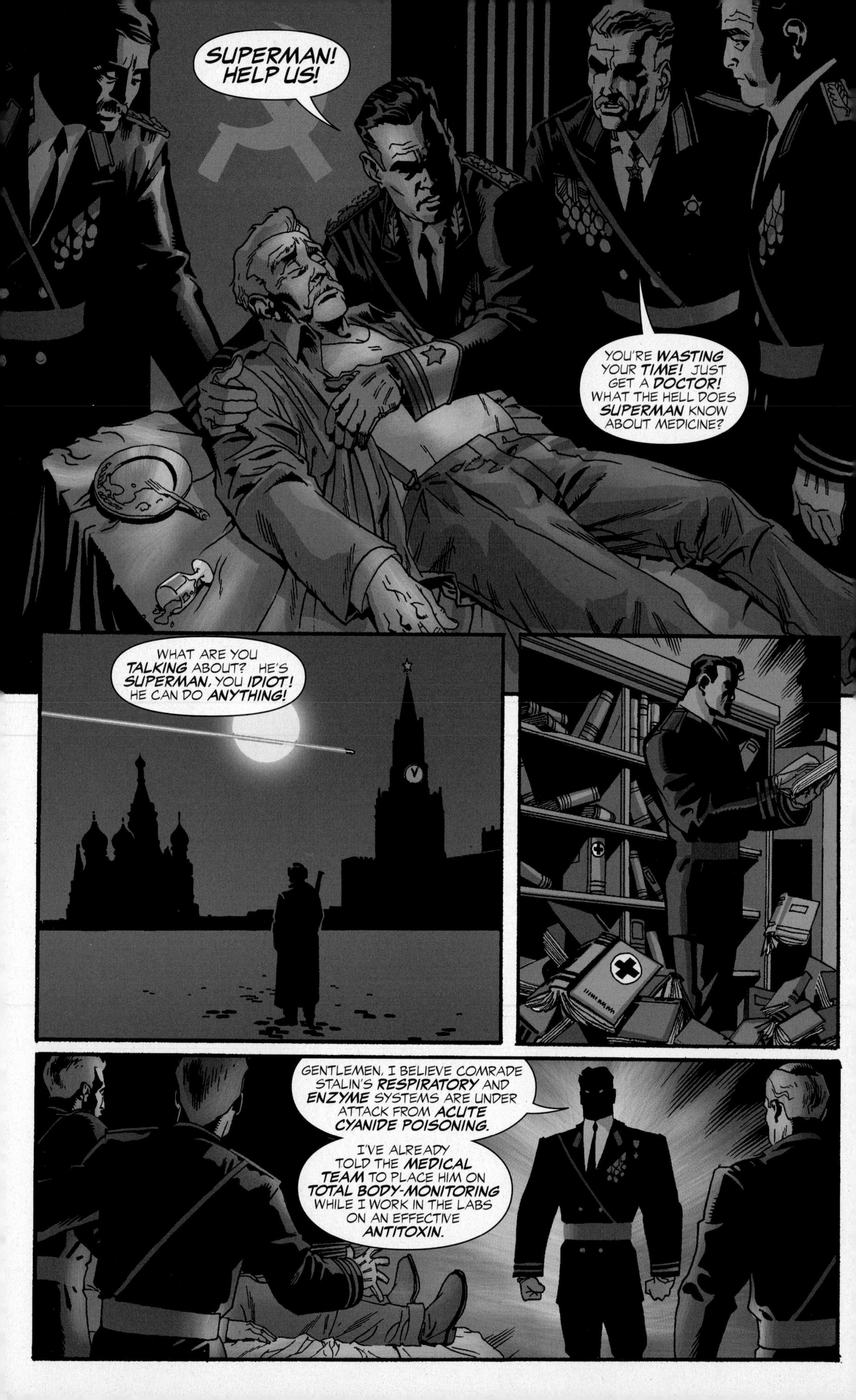
SUPERMAN! HELP US!
YOU'RE WASTING YOUR TIME! JUST GET A DOCTOR! WHAT THE HELL DOES SUPERMAN KNOW ABOUT MEDICINE?
WHAT ARE YOU TALKING ABOUT? HE'S SUPERMAN, YOU IDIOT! HE CAN DO ANYTHING!
GENTLEMEN, I BELIEVE COMRADE STALIN'S RESPIRATORY AND ENZYME SYSTEMS ARE UNDER ATTACK FROM ACUTE CYANIDE POISONING.
I'VE ALREADY TOLD THE MEDICAL TEAM TO PLACE HIM ON TOTAL BODY-MONITORING WHILE I WORK IN THE LABS ON AN EFFECTIVE ANTITOXIN.

S.T.A.R. LABS

THIS IS *UNBELIEVABLE*. I FEEL LIKE I'M ON THE SET OF A SCIENCE FICTION MOVIE OR SOMETHING.

HOW IS THIS *STUFF* YOU'VE BEEN BUILDING HERE EVEN *POSSIBLE*, FOR GOD'S SAKE?

BECAUSE THE WORLD AS WE KNOW IT BECOMES A LITTLE MORE IMPOSSIBLE *EVERY DAY*, AGENT OLSEN.

TECHNOLOGY CURVES STIPULATED THAT NONE OF THIS EQUIPMENT WOULD EVEN BE *INVENTED* FOR ANOTHER FIVE DECADES AND YET HERE WE ARE WITH SCIENCE STRAIGHT OUT OF *RAY BRADBURY HIMSELF*.

WHAT *IS* IT ABOUT THIS *MAN OF STEEL* THAT MAKES MY *HEAD* WORK SO MUCH FASTER, EH?

I *DON'T KNOW*, SIR, BUT WE'RE *NOT COMPLAINING*.

NORMAN ROCKWELL, APPLE PIE, *STARS AND STRIPES* AND *THE FOURTH OF JULY*, AGENT OLSEN.

THE PRESIDENT ASKED ME TO DESIGN A *FIGURE* WHO MIGHT *ENCAPSULATE* ALL THESE THINGS AND GIVE *AMERICA* BACK OUR MUCH-NEEDED *SWAGGER*.

HOLY SMOKES!

YOUNG MAN, I'D LIKE YOU TO MEET *SUPERMAN TWO*...

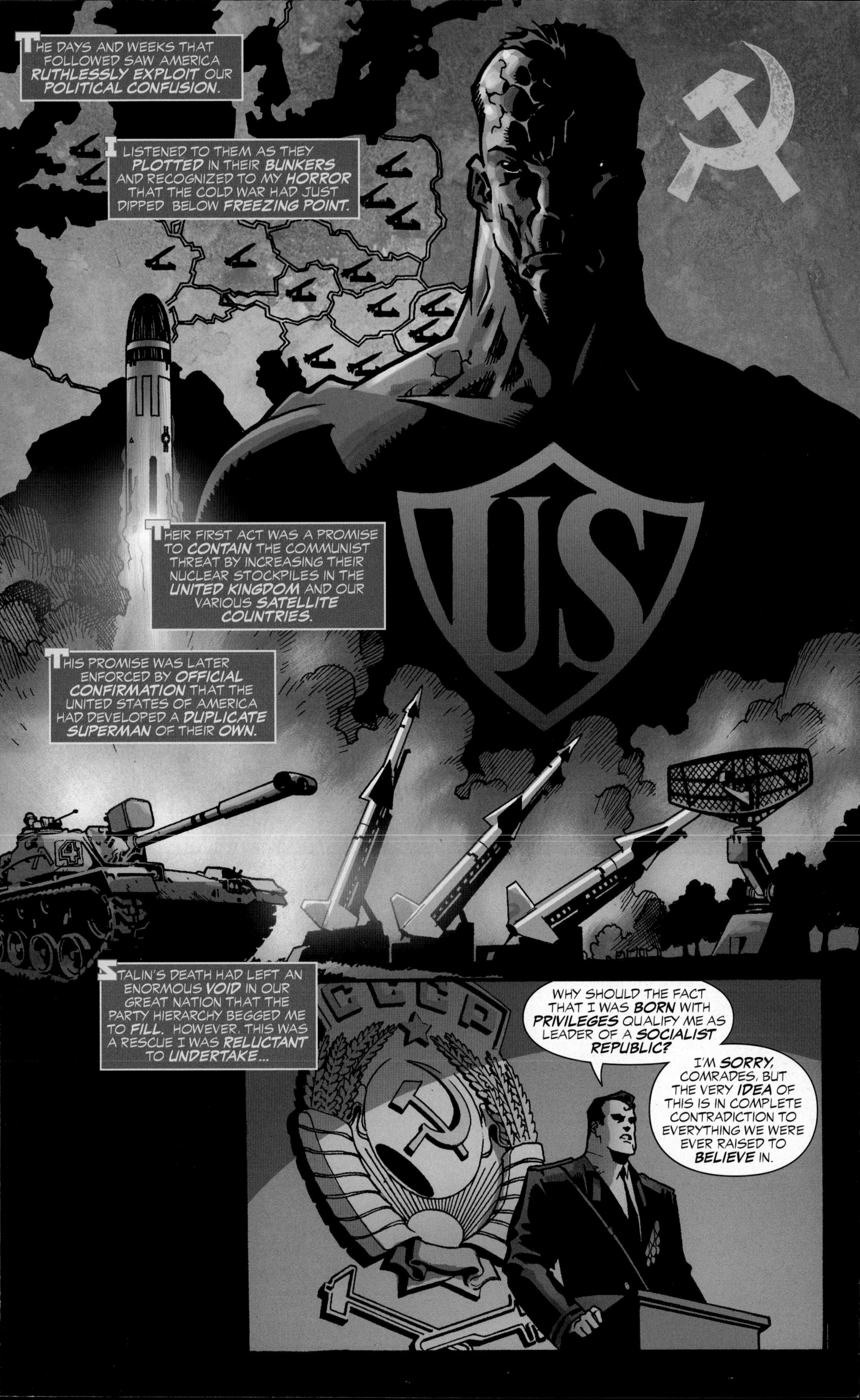
THE DAYS AND WEEKS THAT FOLLOWED SAW AMERICA RUTHLESSLY EXPLOIT OUR POLITICAL CONFUSION.
I LISTENED TO THEM AS THEY PLOTTED IN THEIR BUNKERS AND RECOGNIZED TO MY HORROR THAT THE COLD WAR HAD JUST DIPPED BELOW FREEZING POINT.
THEIR FIRST ACT WAS A PROMISE TO CONTAIN THE COMMUNIST THREAT BY INCREASING THEIR NUCLEAR STOCKPILES IN THE UNITED KINGDOM AND OUR VARIOUS SATELLITE COUNTRIES.
THIS PROMISE WAS LATER ENFORCED BY OFFICIAL CONFIRMATION THAT THE UNITED STATES OF AMERICA HAD DEVELOPED A DUPLICATE SUPERMAN OF THEIR OWN.
STALIN'S DEATH HAD LEFT AN ENORMOUS VOID IN OUR GREAT NATION THAT THE PARTY HIERARCHY BEGGED ME TO FILL. HOWEVER, THIS WAS A RESCUE I WAS RELUCTANT TO UNDERTAKE...
WHY SHOULD THE FACT THAT I WAS BORN WITH PRIVILEGES QUALIFY ME AS LEADER OF A SOCIALIST REPUBLIC?
I'M SORRY, COMRADES, BUT THE VERY IDEA OF THIS IS IN COMPLETE CONTRADICTION TO EVERYTHING WE WERE EVER RAISED TO BELIEVE IN.

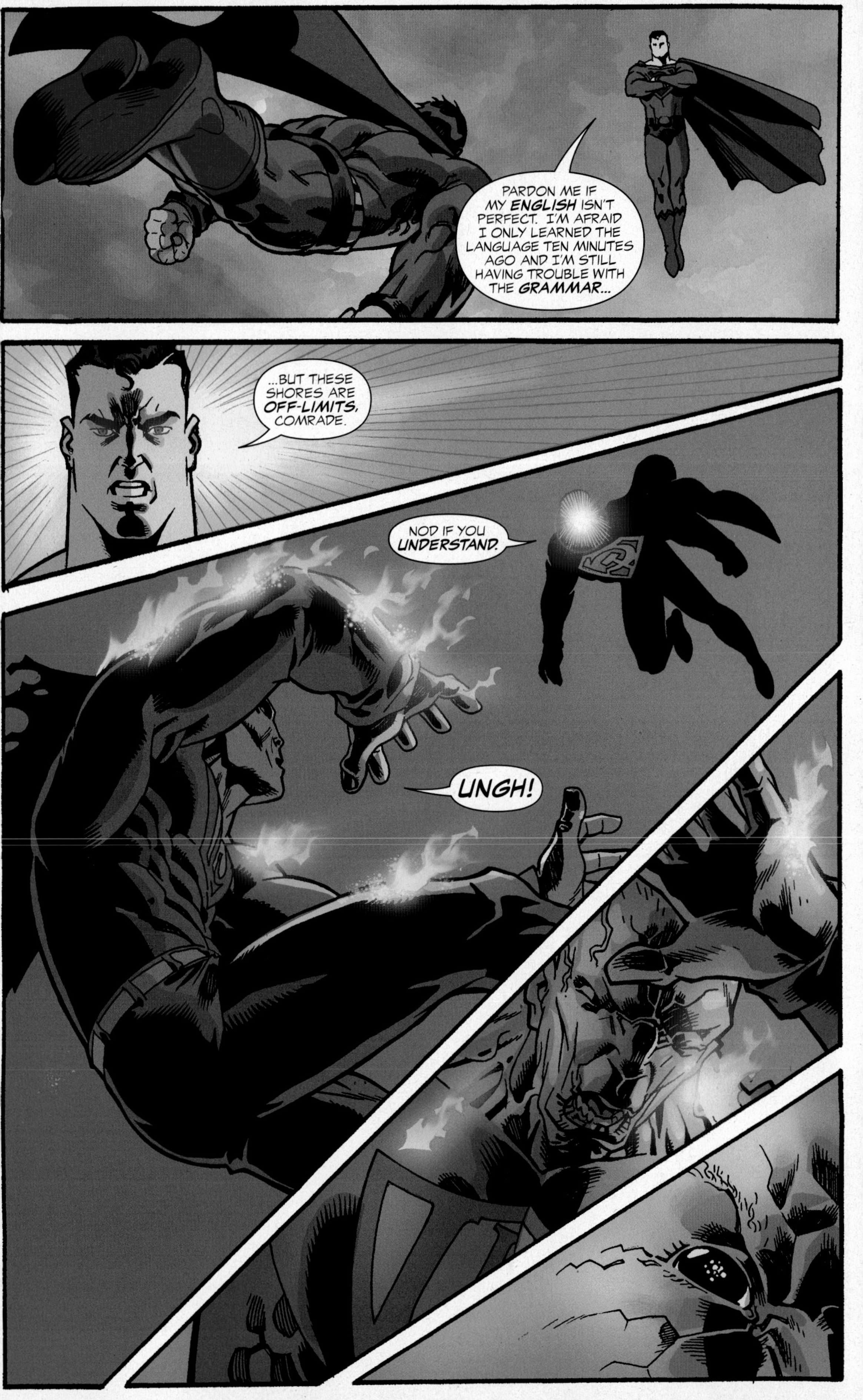
PARDON ME IF MY ENGLISH ISN'T PERFECT. I'M AFRAID I ONLY LEARNED THE LANGUAGE TEN MINUTES AGO AND I'M STILL HAVING TROUBLE WITH THE GRAMMAR...
...BUT THESE SHORES ARE OFF-LIMITS, COMRADE.
NOD IF YOU UNDERSTAND.
UNGH!

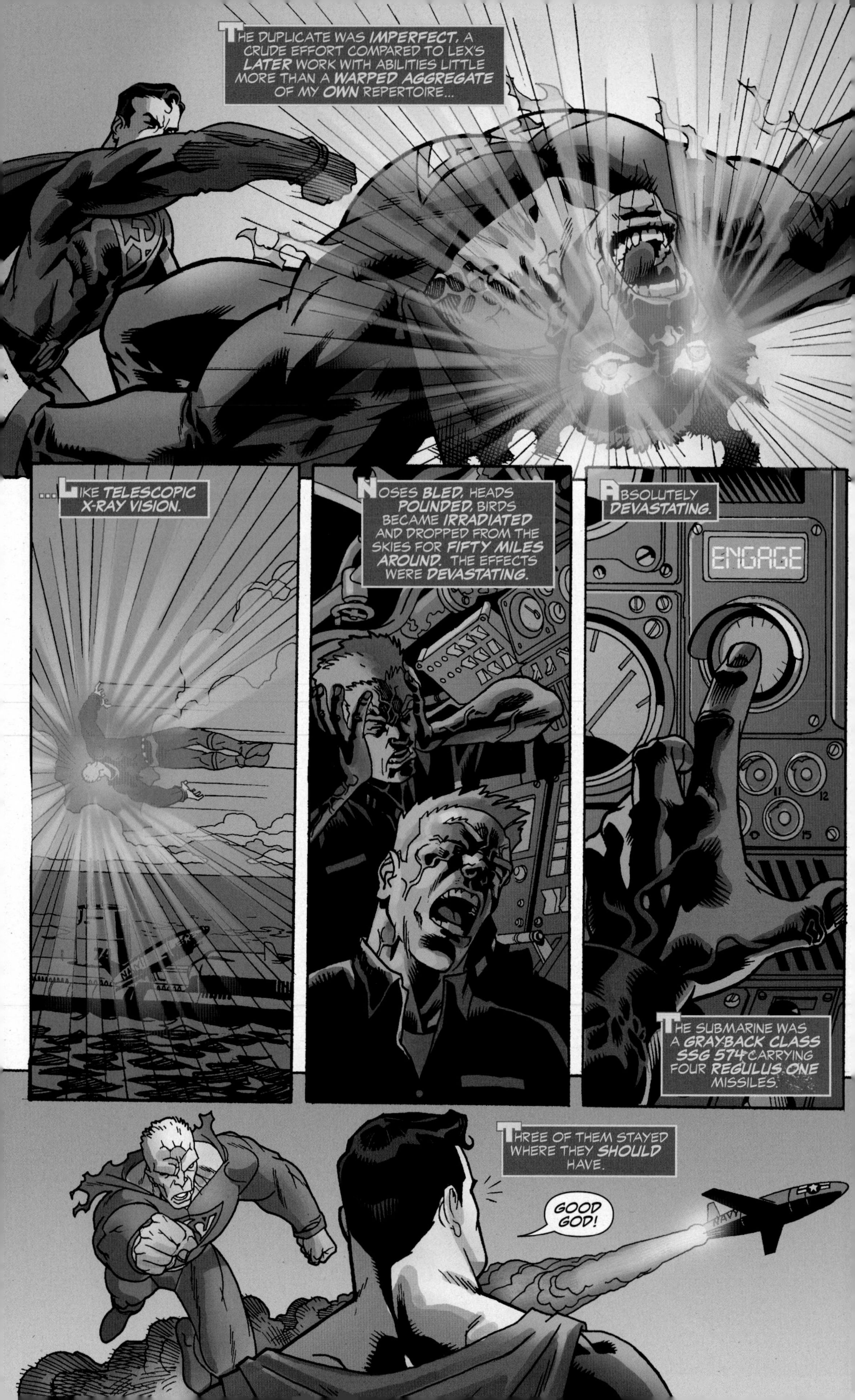
THE DUPLICATE WAS IMPERFECT, A CRUDE EFFORT COMPARED TO LEX'S LATER WORK WITH ABILITIES LITTLE MORE THAN A WARPED AGGREGATE OF MY OWN REPERTOIRE...
...LIKE TELESCOPIC X-RAY VISION.
NOSES BLED, HEADS POUNDED, BIRDS BECAME IRRADIATED AND DROPPED FROM THE SKIES FOR FIFTY MILES AROUND. THE EFFECTS WERE DEVASTATING.
ABSOLUTELY DEVASTATING.
ENGAGE
THE SUBMARINE WAS A GRAYBACK CLASS SSG 574 CARRYING FOUR REGULUS ONE MISSILES.
THREE OF THEM STAYED WHERE THEY SHOULD HAVE.
GOOD GOD!
NAVY

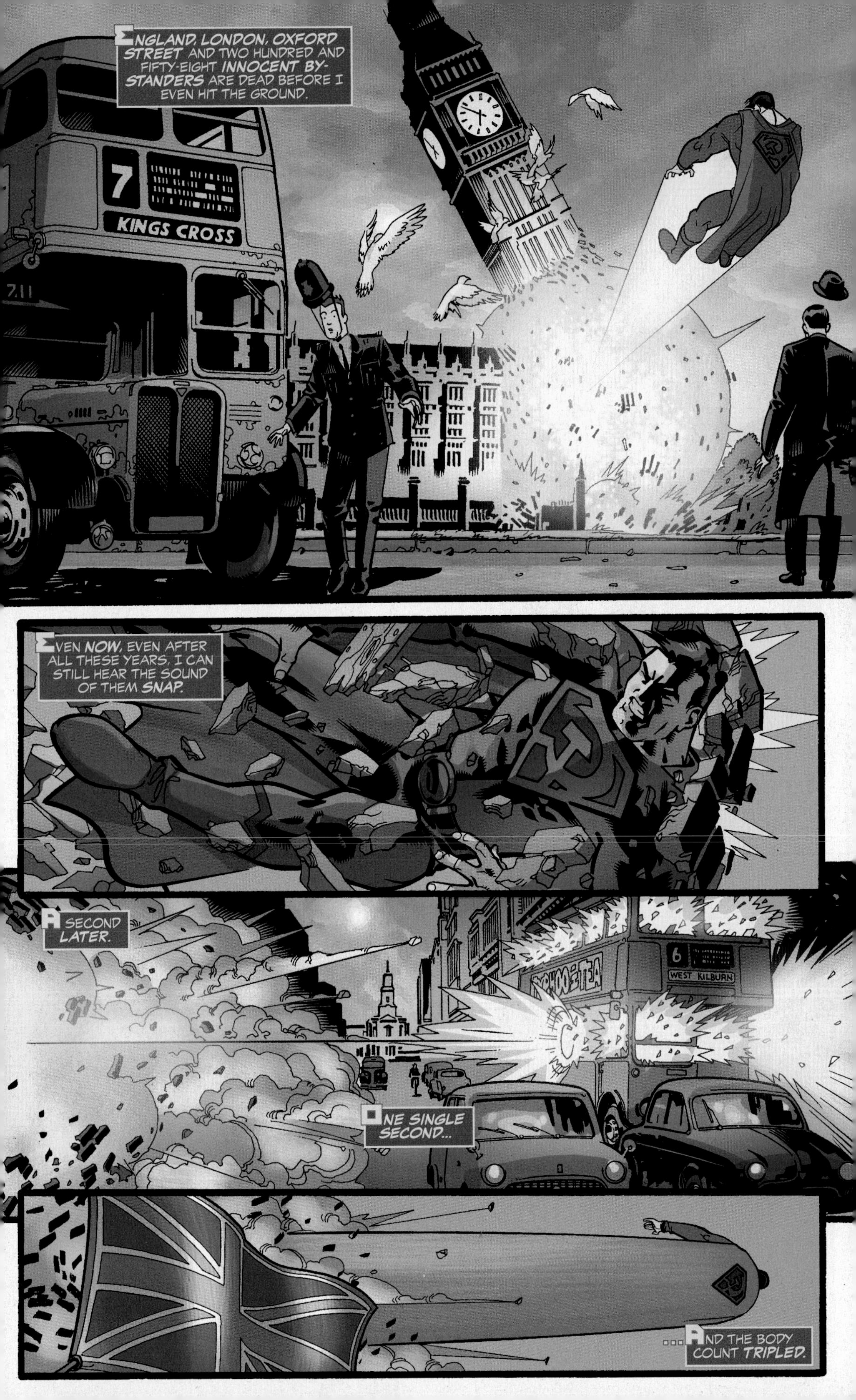
ENGLAND, LONDON, OXFORD STREET AND TWO HUNDRED AND FIFTY-EIGHT INNOCENT BY-STANDERS ARE DEAD BEFORE I EVEN HIT THE GROUND.
7
KINGS CROSS
EVEN NOW, EVEN AFTER ALL THESE YEARS, I CAN STILL HEAR THE SOUND OF THEM SNAP.
A SECOND LATER.
6
WEST KILBURN
ONE SINGLE SECOND...
...AND THE BODY COUNT TRIPLED.

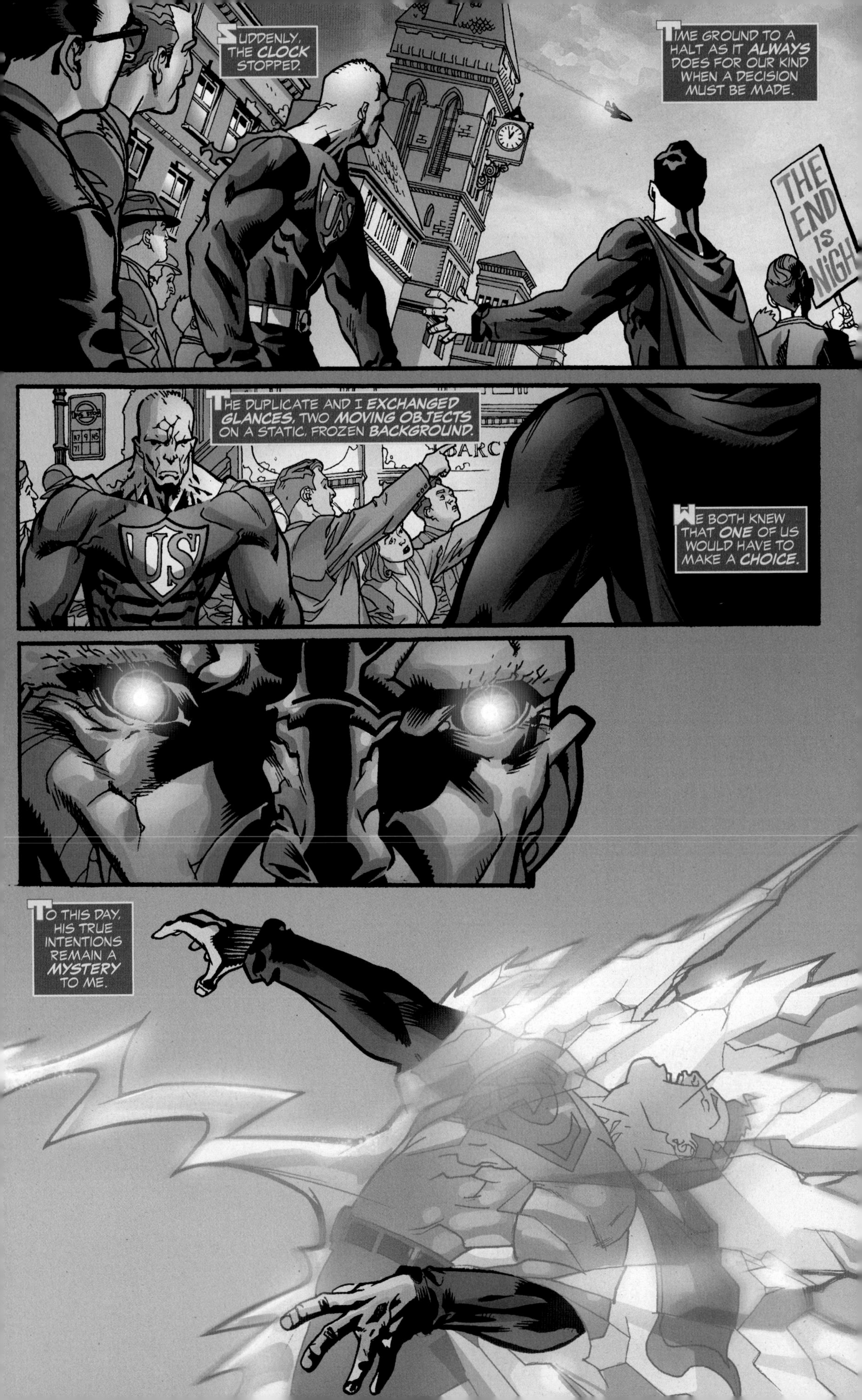
SUDDENLY, THE CLOCK STOPPED.
TIME GROUND TO A HALT AS IT ALWAYS DOES FOR OUR KIND WHEN A DECISION MUST BE MADE.
THE END IS NIGH
THE DUPLICATE AND I EXCHANGED GLANCES, TWO MOVING OBJECTS ON A STATIC, FROZEN BACKGROUND.
WE BOTH KNEW THAT ONE OF US WOULD HAVE TO MAKE A CHOICE.
TO THIS DAY, HIS TRUE INTENTIONS REMAIN A MYSTERY TO ME.

THE *MAN* OF *STEEL* IS *DEAD.*

ALL RISE FOR THE *NATIONAL ANTHEM.*

*J*OSEPH STALIN'S FUNERAL TOOK PLACE ON THE *THIRD TUESDAY* IN *NOVEMBER, NINETEEN FIFTY THREE.*

ЛЕНИН
СТАЛИН

*F*IVE MILLION MOURNERS HAD COME FROM ALL OVER RUSSIA TO PAY THEIR RESPECTS AS THE MOST FAMOUS MAN I HAD EVER KNOWN WAS LAID TO REST IN LENIN'S TOMB.

*F*IVE MILLION VOICES BOOMED OUR *GLORIOUS NATIONAL ANTHEM* BUT, BETWEEN THE *COUGHS* AND THE *PRAYERS* AND THE *SHUFFLING,* I COULD STILL *HEAR* HER...

...A UNIQUE, SOLITARY *VOICE PATTERN* FROM THE *RURAL COLLECTIVE* WHERE I WAS RAISED.

*T*HE SWEET RED-HEADED GIRL FROM MY *PAST.*

*T*HE *CORN-FIELDS* IN *THE UKRAINE* AND MY DEAR, SWEET PARENTS SEEMED SO FAR AWAY *EVEN THEN,* I REMEMBER.

*K*ING-MAKERS IN THE *PARTY* WERE *ALREADY CIRCLING,* EAGER TO ANOINT THIS *RELUCTANT SUCCESSOR...*

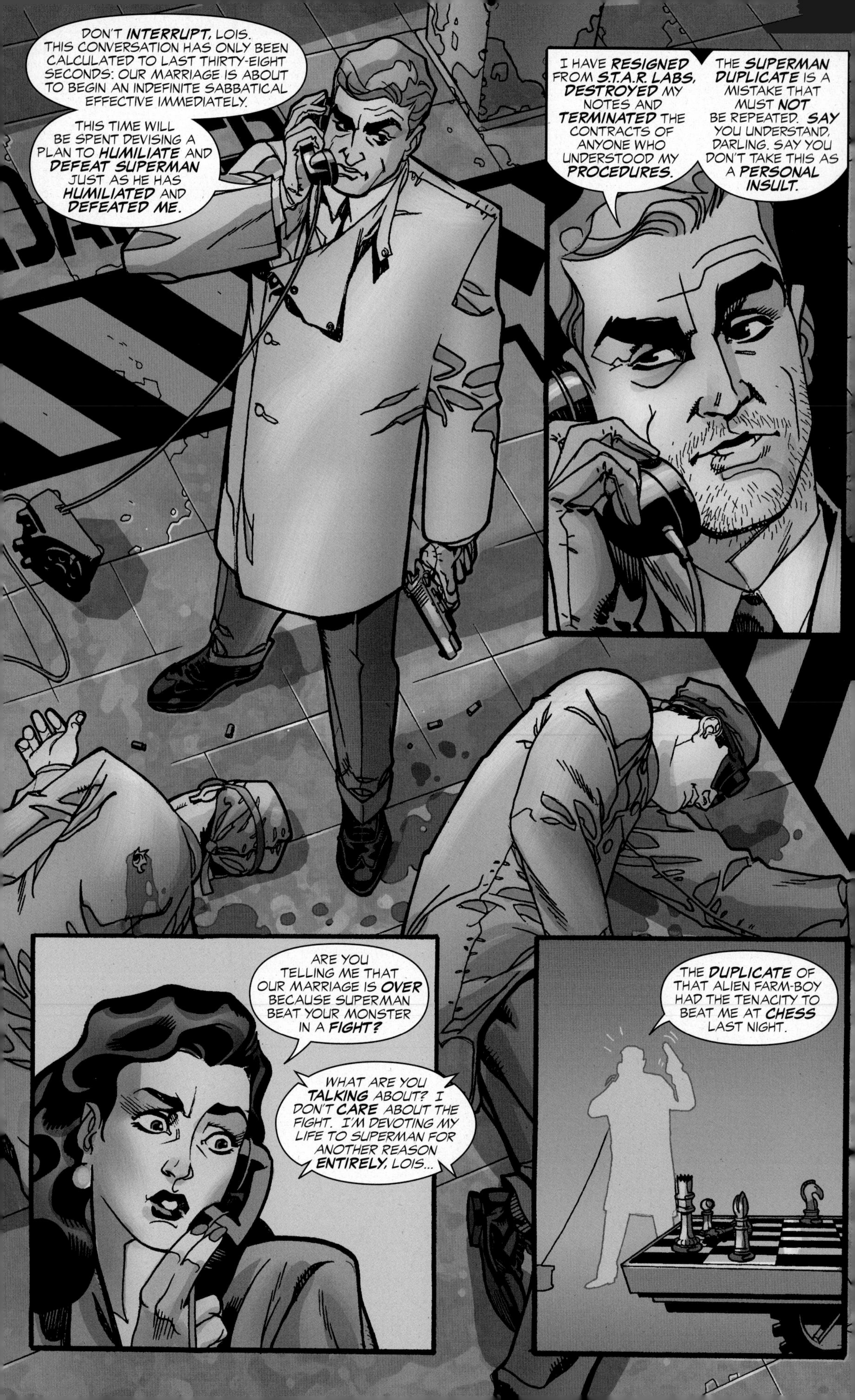
DON'T INTERRUPT, LOIS. THIS CONVERSATION HAS ONLY BEEN CALCULATED TO LAST THIRTY-EIGHT SECONDS: OUR MARRIAGE IS ABOUT TO BEGIN AN INDEFINITE SABBATICAL EFFECTIVE IMMEDIATELY.
THIS TIME WILL BE SPENT DEVISING A PLAN TO HUMILIATE AND DEFEAT SUPERMAN JUST AS HE HAS HUMILIATED AND DEFEATED ME.
I HAVE RESIGNED FROM S.T.A.R. LABS, DESTROYED MY NOTES AND TERMINATED THE CONTRACTS OF ANYONE WHO UNDERSTOOD MY PROCEDURES.
THE SUPERMAN DUPLICATE IS A MISTAKE THAT MUST NOT BE REPEATED. SAY YOU UNDERSTAND, DARLING. SAY YOU DON'T TAKE THIS AS A PERSONAL INSULT.
ARE YOU TELLING ME THAT OUR MARRIAGE IS OVER BECAUSE SUPERMAN BEAT YOUR MONSTER IN A FIGHT?
WHAT ARE YOU TALKING ABOUT? I DON'T CARE ABOUT THE FIGHT. I'M DEVOTING MY LIFE TO SUPERMAN FOR ANOTHER REASON ENTIRELY, LOIS...
THE DUPLICATE OF THAT ALIEN FARM-BOY HAD THE TENACITY TO BEAT ME AT CHESS LAST NIGHT.

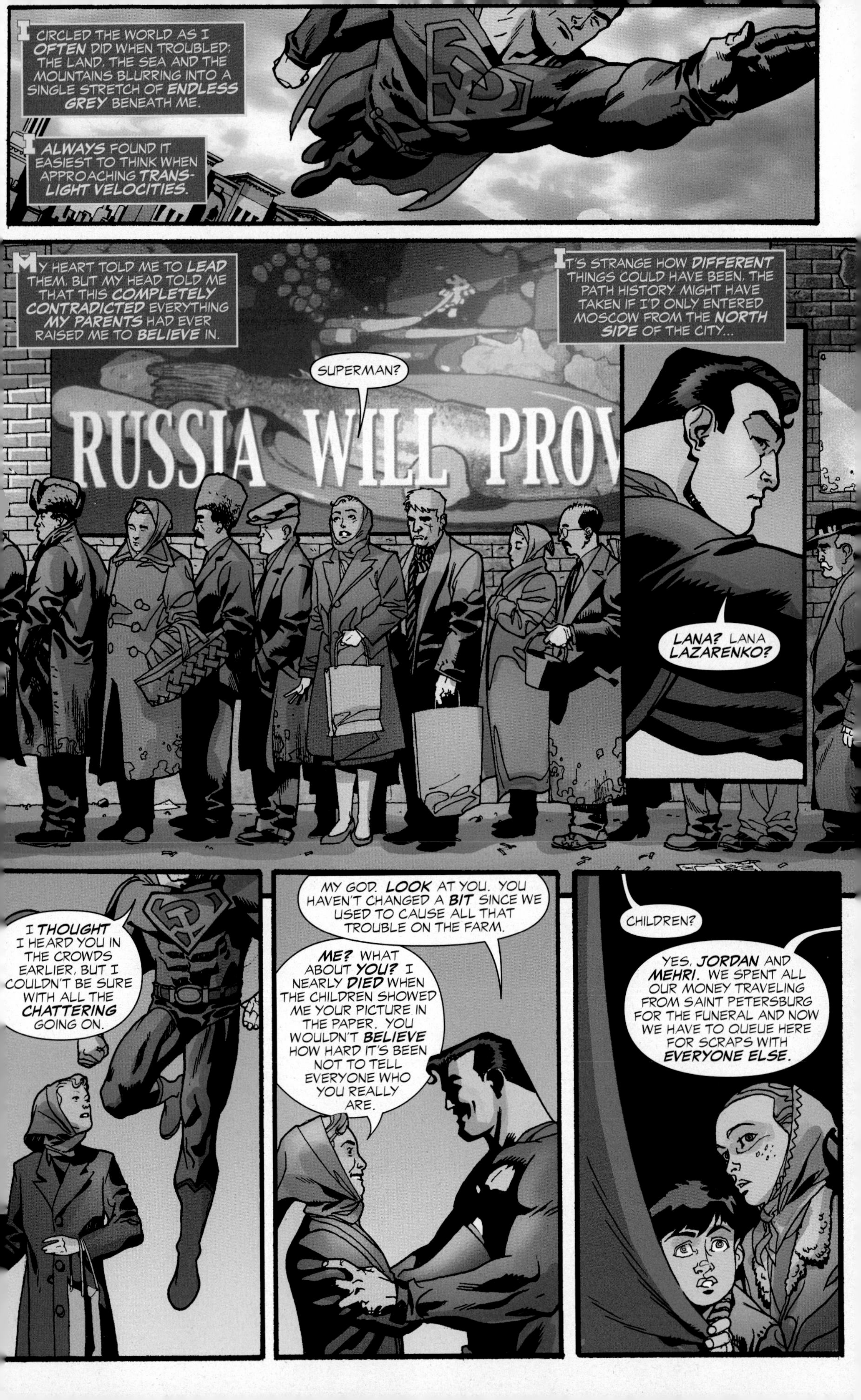
I CIRCLED THE WORLD AS I OFTEN DID WHEN TROUBLED; THE LAND, THE SEA AND THE MOUNTAINS BLURRING INTO A SINGLE STRETCH OF ENDLESS GREY BENEATH ME.
I ALWAYS FOUND IT EASIEST TO THINK WHEN APPROACHING TRANS-LIGHT VELOCITIES.
MY HEART TOLD ME TO LEAD THEM, BUT MY HEAD TOLD ME THAT THIS COMPLETELY CONTRADICTED EVERYTHING MY PARENTS HAD EVER RAISED ME TO BELIEVE IN.
IT'S STRANGE HOW DIFFERENT THINGS COULD HAVE BEEN, THE PATH HISTORY MIGHT HAVE TAKEN IF I'D ONLY ENTERED MOSCOW FROM THE NORTH SIDE OF THE CITY...
RUSSIA WILL PROV
SUPERMAN?
LANA? LANA LAZARENKO?
I THOUGHT I HEARD YOU IN THE CROWDS EARLIER, BUT I COULDN'T BE SURE WITH ALL THE CHATTERING GOING ON.
MY GOD. LOOK AT YOU. YOU HAVEN'T CHANGED A BIT SINCE WE USED TO CAUSE ALL THAT TROUBLE ON THE FARM.
ME? WHAT ABOUT YOU? I NEARLY DIED WHEN THE CHILDREN SHOWED ME YOUR PICTURE IN THE PAPER. YOU WOULDN'T BELIEVE HOW HARD IT'S BEEN NOT TO TELL EVERYONE WHO YOU REALLY ARE.
CHILDREN?
YES, JORDAN AND MEHRI. WE SPENT ALL OUR MONEY TRAVELING FROM SAINT PETERSBURG FOR THE FUNERAL AND NOW WE HAVE TO QUEUE HERE FOR SCRAPS WITH EVERYONE ELSE.

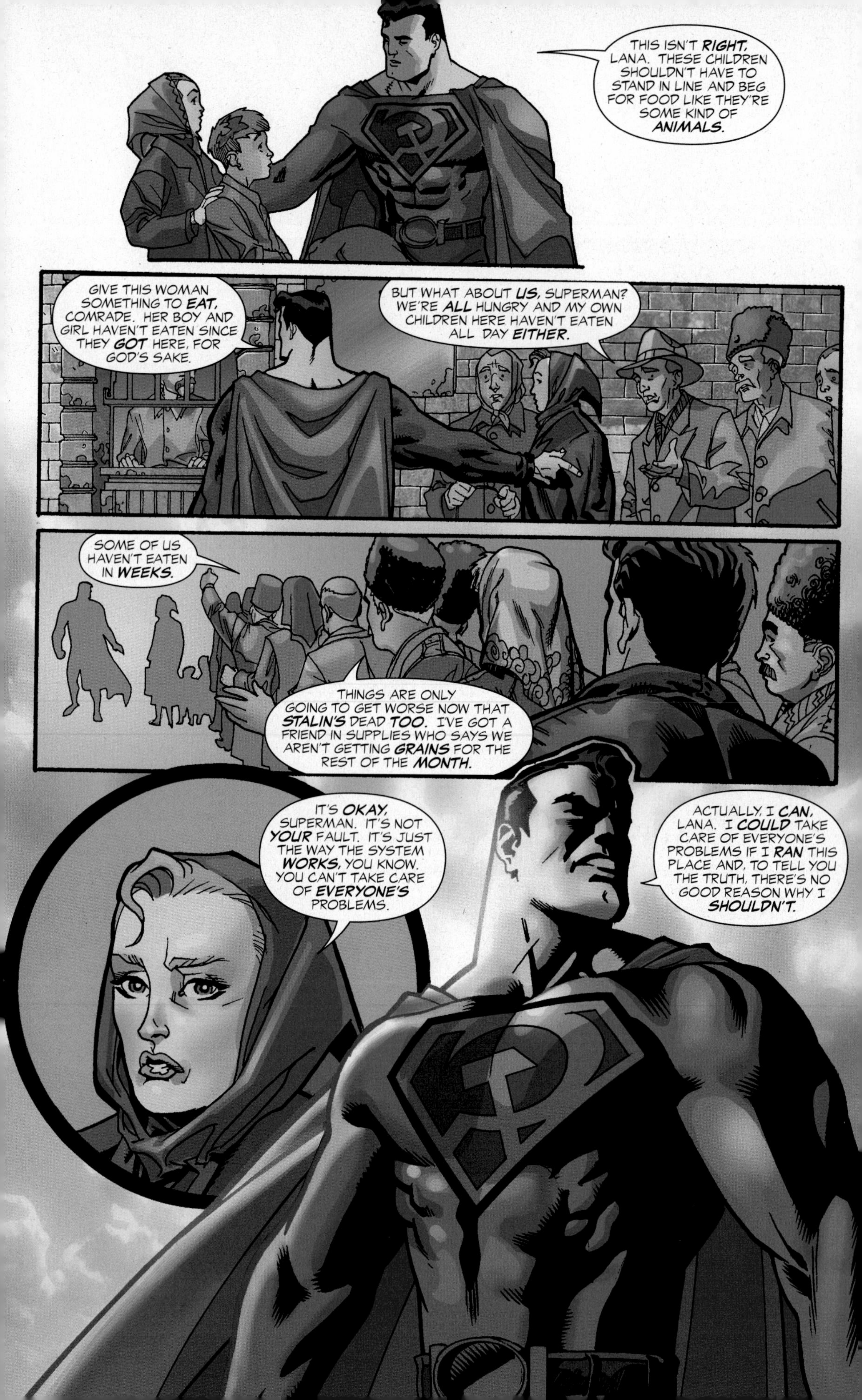

THIS ISN'T **RIGHT**, LANA. THESE CHILDREN SHOULDN'T HAVE TO STAND IN LINE AND BEG FOR FOOD LIKE THEY'RE SOME KIND OF **ANIMALS**.
GIVE THIS WOMAN SOMETHING TO **EAT**, COMRADE. HER BOY AND GIRL HAVEN'T EATEN SINCE THEY **GOT** HERE, FOR GOD'S SAKE.
BUT WHAT ABOUT **US**, SUPERMAN? WE'RE **ALL** HUNGRY AND MY OWN CHILDREN HERE HAVEN'T EATEN ALL DAY **EITHER**.
SOME OF US HAVEN'T EATEN IN **WEEKS**.
THINGS ARE ONLY GOING TO GET WORSE NOW THAT **STALIN'S** DEAD **TOO**. I'VE GOT A FRIEND IN SUPPLIES WHO SAYS WE AREN'T GETTING **GRAINS** FOR THE REST OF THE **MONTH**.
IT'S **OKAY**, SUPERMAN. IT'S NOT **YOUR** FAULT. IT'S JUST THE WAY THE SYSTEM **WORKS**, YOU KNOW. YOU CAN'T TAKE CARE OF **EVERYONE'S** PROBLEMS.
ACTUALLY, I **CAN**, LANA. I **COULD** TAKE CARE OF EVERYONE'S PROBLEMS IF I **RAN** THIS PLACE AND, TO TELL YOU THE TRUTH, THERE'S NO GOOD REASON WHY I **SHOULDN'T**.

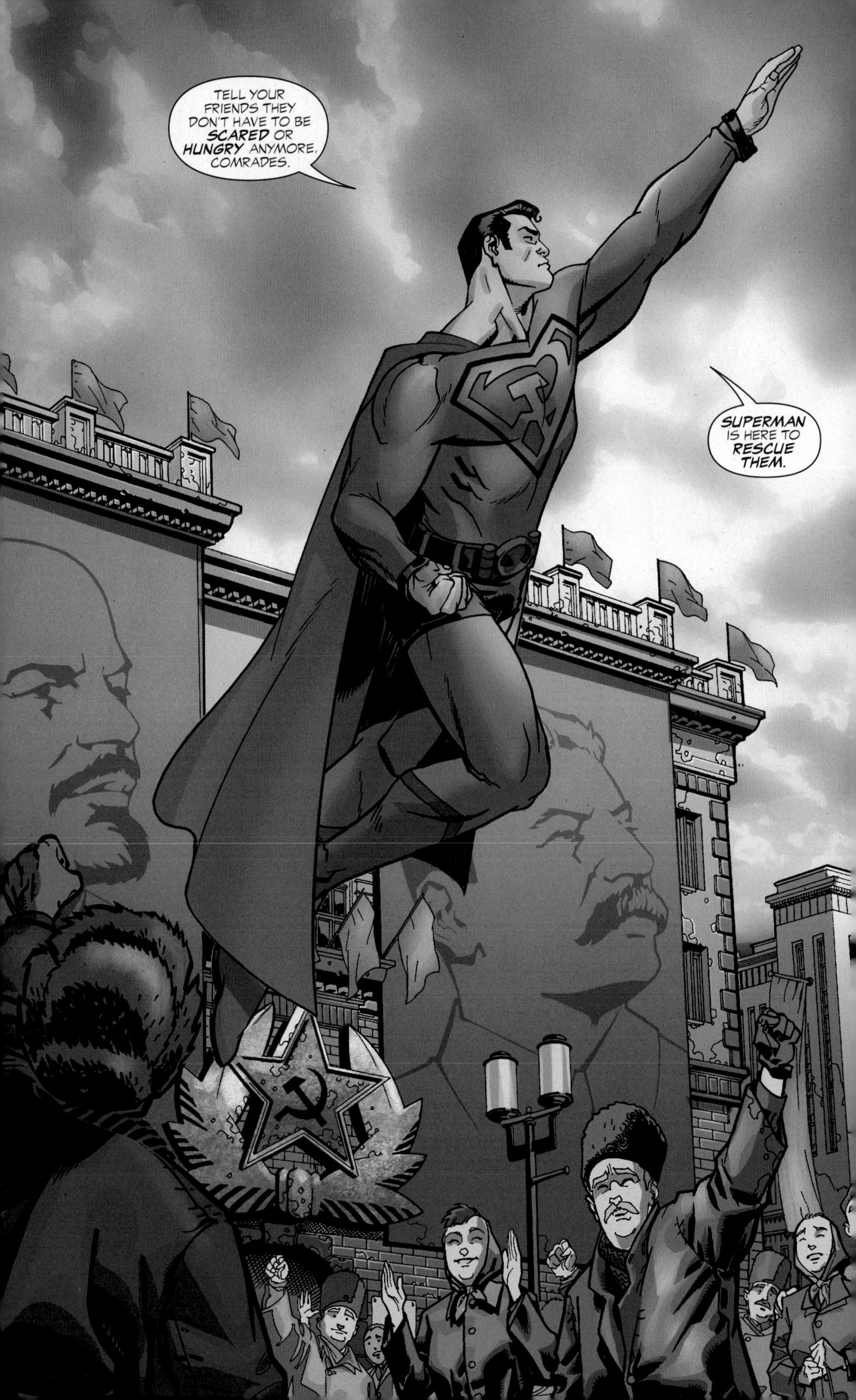
TELL YOUR FRIENDS THEY DON'T HAVE TO BE SCARED OR HUNGRY ANYMORE, COMRADES.
SUPERMAN IS HERE TO RESCUE THEM.

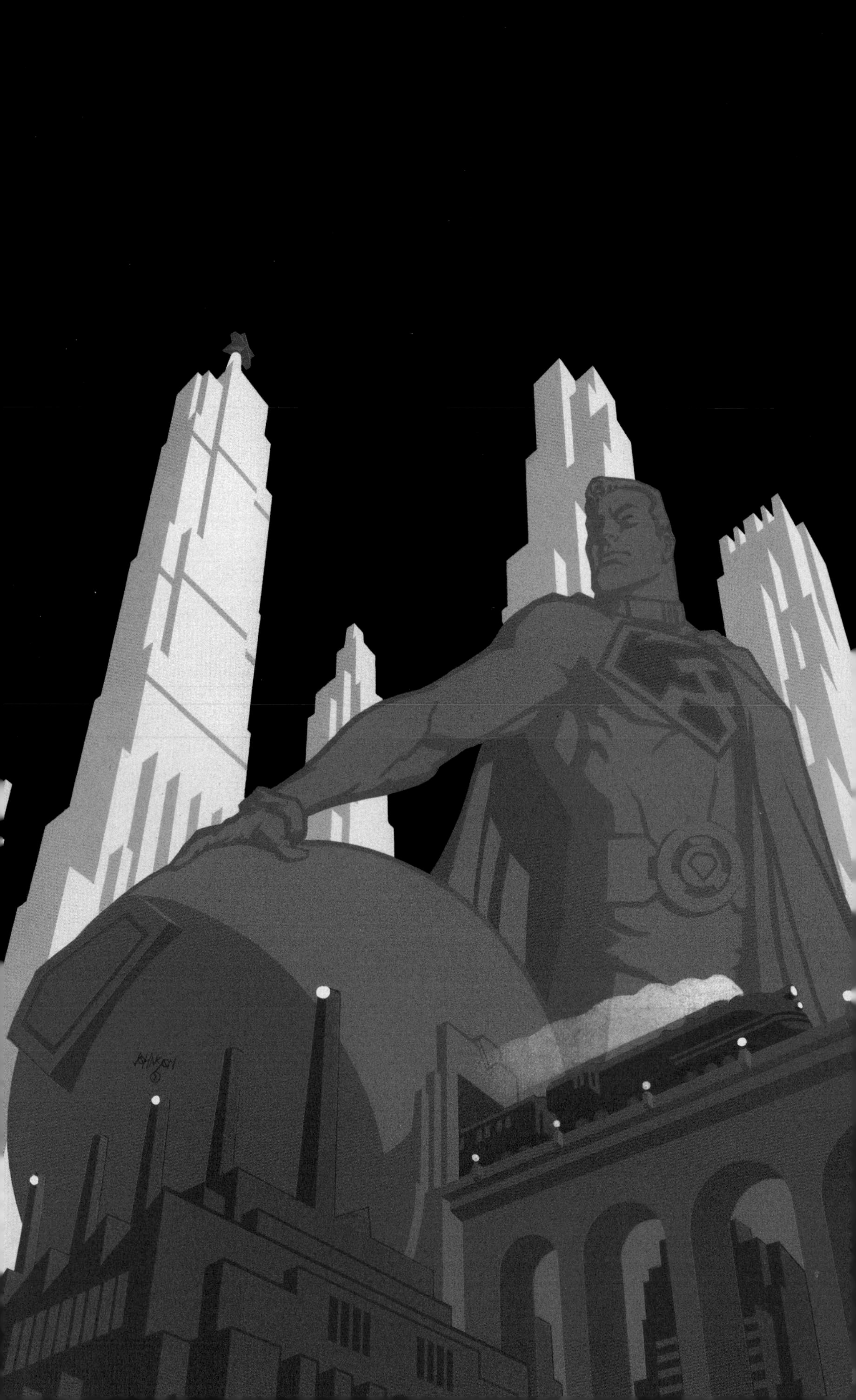

RED SON
ASCENDANT

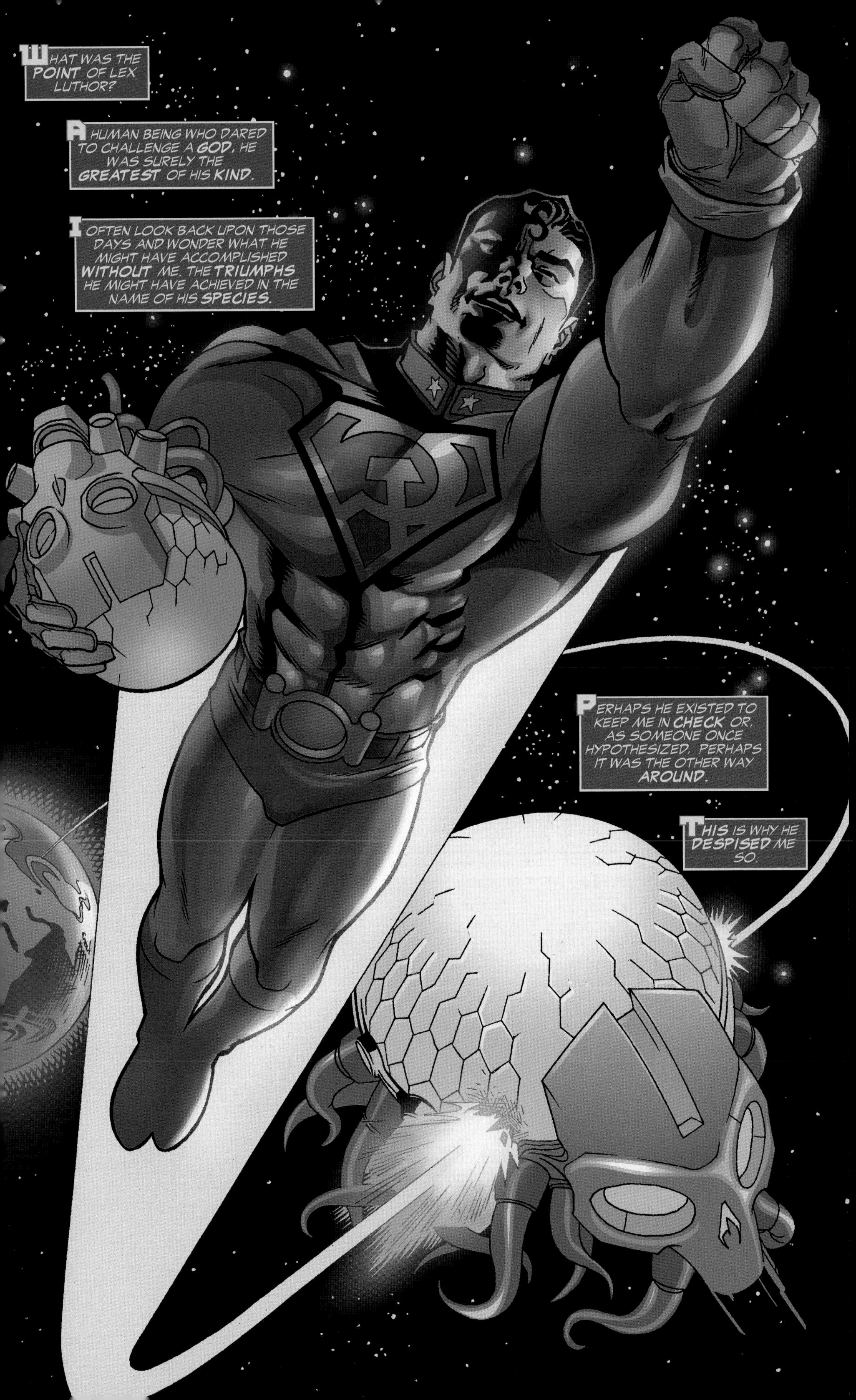
WHAT WAS THE POINT OF LEX LUTHOR?
A HUMAN BEING WHO DARED TO CHALLENGE A GOD, HE WAS SURELY THE GREATEST OF HIS KIND.
I OFTEN LOOK BACK UPON THOSE DAYS AND WONDER WHAT HE MIGHT HAVE ACCOMPLISHED WITHOUT ME. THE TRIUMPHS HE MIGHT HAVE ACHIEVED IN THE NAME OF HIS SPECIES.
PERHAPS HE EXISTED TO KEEP ME IN CHECK OR, AS SOMEONE ONCE HYPOTHESIZED, PERHAPS IT WAS THE OTHER WAY AROUND.
THIS IS WHY HE DESPISED ME SO.

GAME OVER, LUTHOR.

FIFTY-EIGHT SECONDS? YOU'RE *SLOWING DOWN*, SUPERMAN. BRAINIAC'S SHIP WAS ONLY FORTY-FIVE THOUSAND MILES AWAY.

SURELY ADVANCING MIDDLE AGE ISN'T CATCHING UP WITH RUSSIA'S MIGHTY *MAN OF TOMORROW?*

BRAINIAC'S *CENTRAL PROCESSING UNIT*, LEX. I USED IT TO ACCESS EVERY FILE IN THE SHIP'S DATABASE, BUT THERE ISN'T A *SHRED* OF *USEFUL INFORMATION.*

I CAN'T FIND *ANY MEANS* OF RETURNING *STALINGRAD* TO ITS *NATURAL SIZE.*

HARDLY SURPRISING WHEN BRAINIAC'S PRIME DIRECTIVE WAS *STORING* INFORMATION ON ALIEN CULTURES. I DON'T THINK HE EVER INTENDED GIVING ANY OF THESE CITIES *BACK*, YOU KNOW.

TELL YOU *WHAT.* I'M ALWAYS READING HOW *SMART* YOU ARE. HOW NOTHING WE *MORTALS* CAN IMAGINE IS BEYOND *PRESIDENT SUPERMAN'S* LIMITATIONS. CORRECT?

WELL, NOW'S YOUR CHANCE TO PROVE THEM *RIGHT*, ALIEN.

BEST OF LUCK.

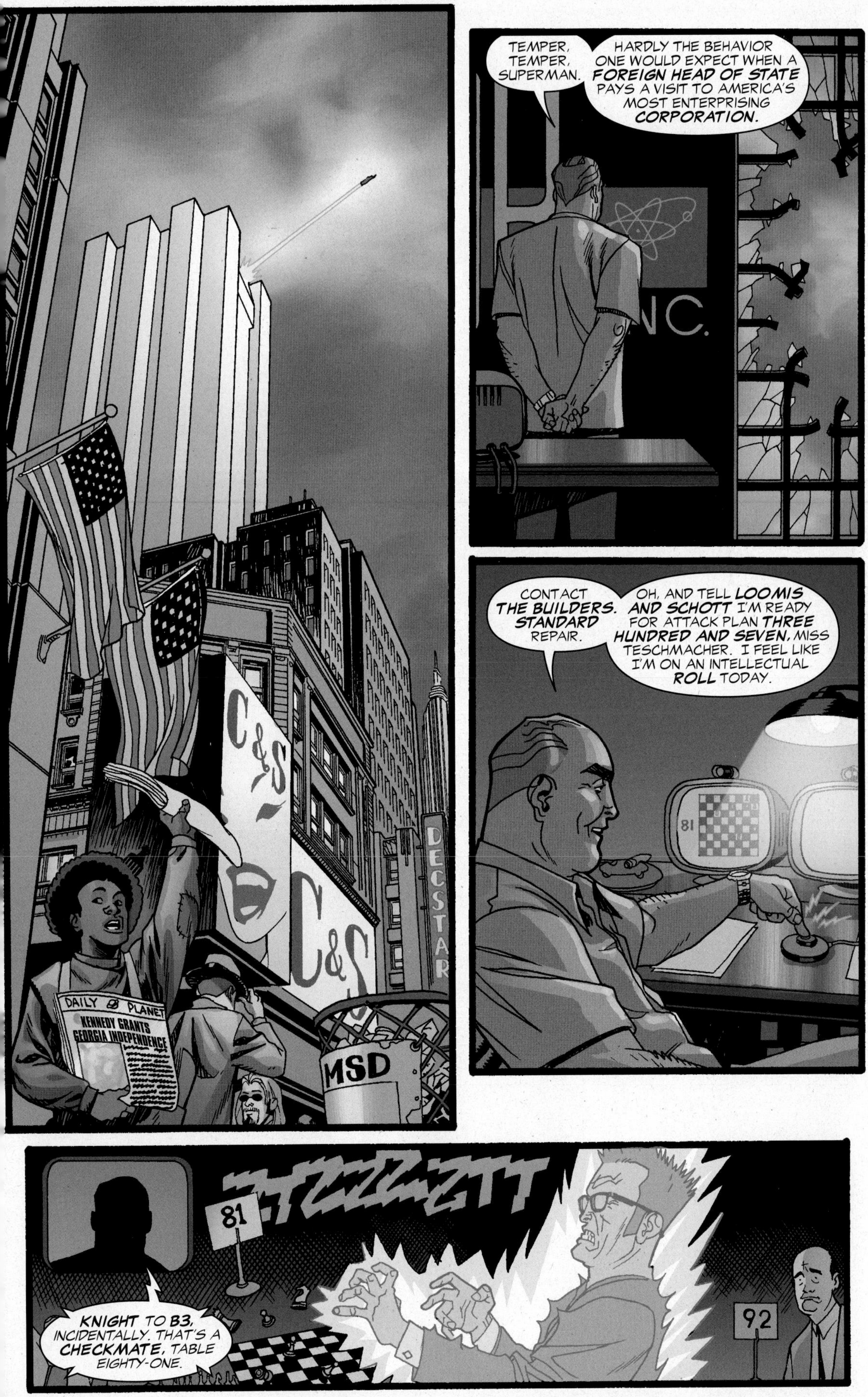
DAILY PLANET
KENNEDY GRANTS GEORGIA INDEPENDENCE
C&S
DECSTAR
MSD
TEMPER, TEMPER, SUPERMAN.
HARDLY THE BEHAVIOR ONE WOULD EXPECT WHEN A FOREIGN HEAD OF STATE PAYS A VISIT TO AMERICA'S MOST ENTERPRISING CORPORATION.
CONTACT THE BUILDERS. STANDARD REPAIR.
OH, AND TELL LOOMIS AND SCHOTT I'M READY FOR ATTACK PLAN THREE HUNDRED AND SEVEN, MISS TESCHMACHER. I FEEL LIKE I'M ON AN INTELLECTUAL ROLL TODAY.
81
ZZZZZTT
81
KNIGHT TO B3, INCIDENTALLY. THAT'S A CHECKMATE, TABLE EIGHTY-ONE.
92

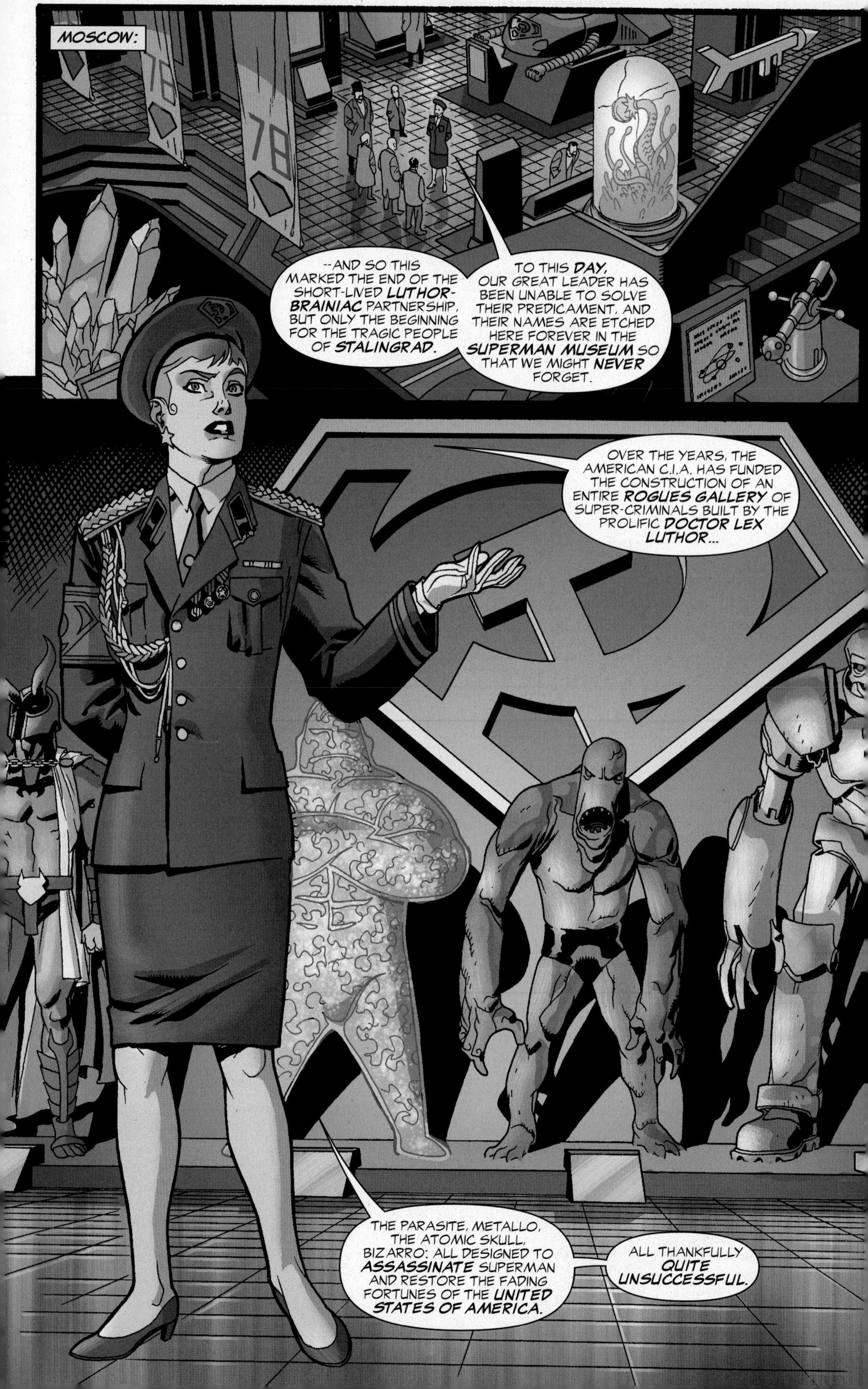
MOSCOW:
--AND SO THIS MARKED THE END OF THE SHORT-LIVED LUTHOR-BRAINIAC PARTNERSHIP, BUT ONLY THE BEGINNING FOR THE TRAGIC PEOPLE OF STALINGRAD.
TO THIS DAY, OUR GREAT LEADER HAS BEEN UNABLE TO SOLVE THEIR PREDICAMENT, AND THEIR NAMES ARE ETCHED HERE FOREVER IN THE SUPERMAN MUSEUM SO THAT WE MIGHT NEVER FORGET.
OVER THE YEARS, THE AMERICAN C.I.A. HAS FUNDED THE CONSTRUCTION OF AN ENTIRE ROGUES GALLERY OF SUPER-CRIMINALS BUILT BY THE PROLIFIC DOCTOR LEX LUTHOR...
THE PARASITE, METALLO, THE ATOMIC SKULL, BIZARRO: ALL DESIGNED TO ASSASSINATE SUPERMAN AND RESTORE THE FADING FORTUNES OF THE UNITED STATES OF AMERICA.
ALL THANKFULLY QUITE UNSUCCESSFUL.

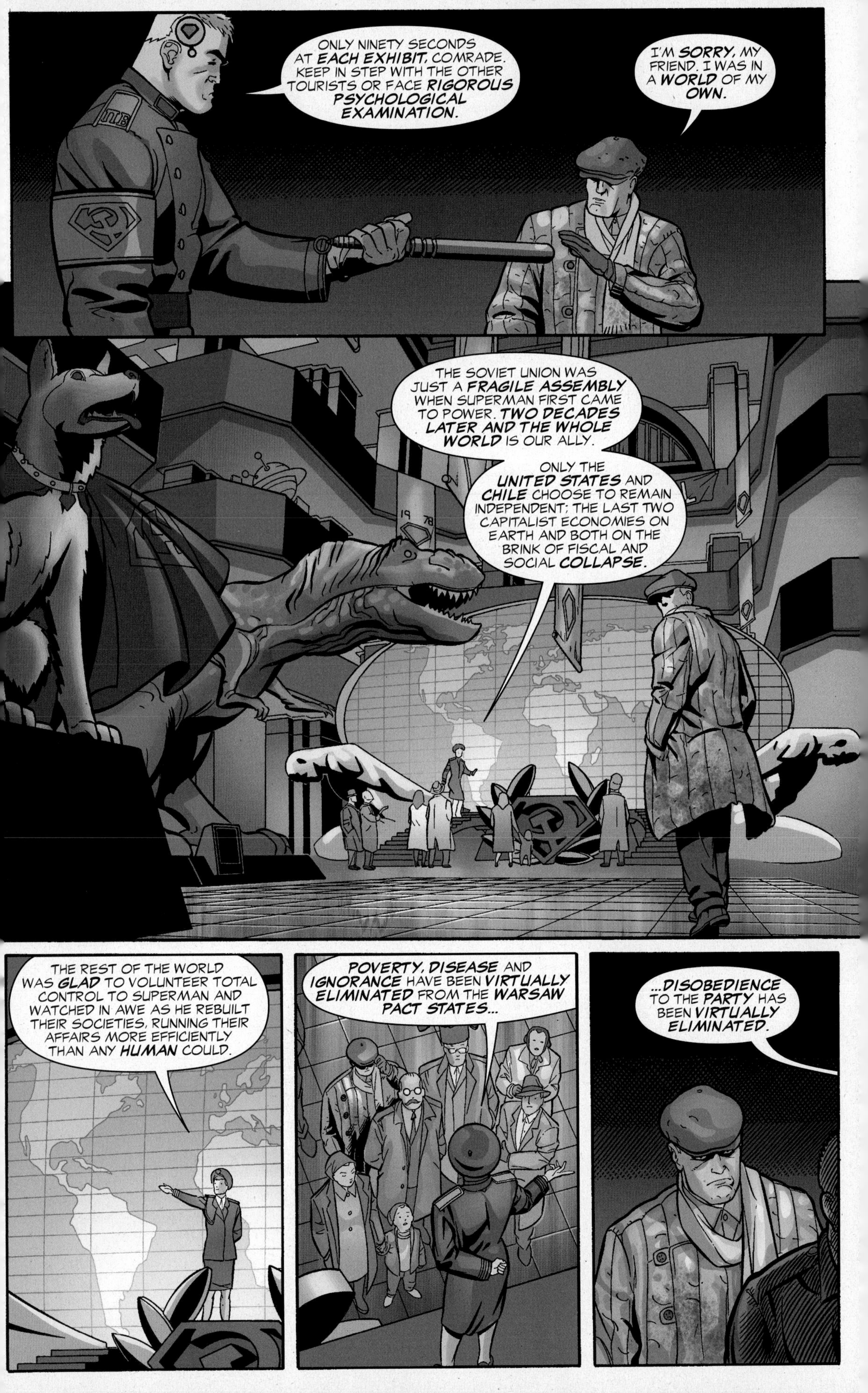

ONLY NINETY SECONDS AT EACH EXHIBIT, COMRADE. KEEP IN STEP WITH THE OTHER TOURISTS OR FACE RIGOROUS PSYCHOLOGICAL EXAMINATION.
I'M SORRY, MY FRIEND. I WAS IN A WORLD OF MY OWN.
THE SOVIET UNION WAS JUST A FRAGILE ASSEMBLY WHEN SUPERMAN FIRST CAME TO POWER. TWO DECADES LATER AND THE WHOLE WORLD IS OUR ALLY.
ONLY THE UNITED STATES AND CHILE CHOOSE TO REMAIN INDEPENDENT; THE LAST TWO CAPITALIST ECONOMIES ON EARTH AND BOTH ON THE BRINK OF FISCAL AND SOCIAL COLLAPSE.
19 78
THE REST OF THE WORLD WAS GLAD TO VOLUNTEER TOTAL CONTROL TO SUPERMAN AND WATCHED IN AWE AS HE REBUILT THEIR SOCIETIES, RUNNING THEIR AFFAIRS MORE EFFICIENTLY THAN ANY HUMAN COULD.
POVERTY, DISEASE AND IGNORANCE HAVE BEEN VIRTUALLY ELIMINATED FROM THE WARSAW PACT STATES...
...DISOBEDIENCE TO THE PARTY HAS BEEN VIRTUALLY ELIMINATED.

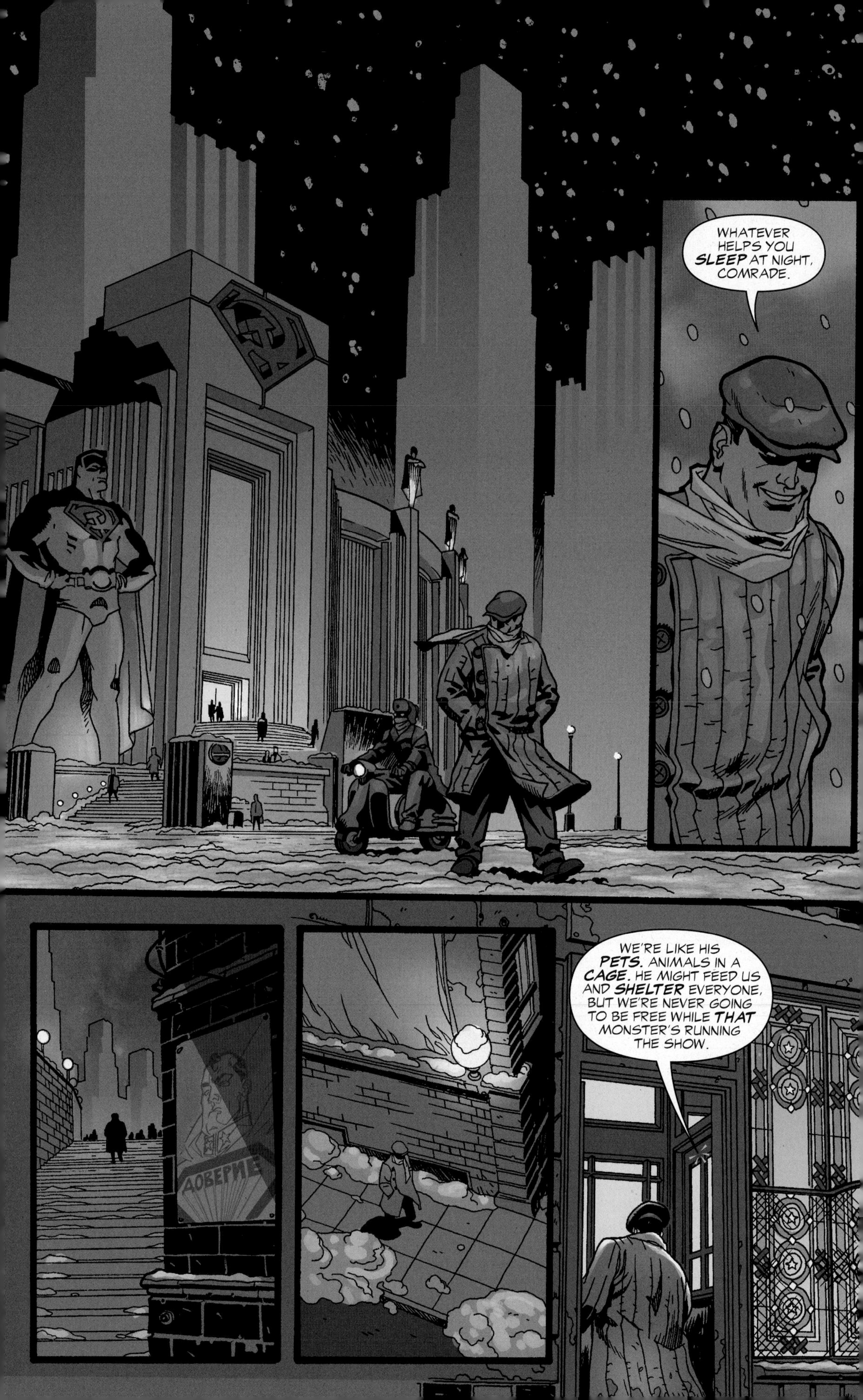

WHATEVER HELPS YOU SLEEP AT NIGHT, COMRADE.
ДОВЕРИЕ
WE'RE LIKE HIS PETS. ANIMALS IN A CAGE. HE MIGHT FEED US AND SHELTER EVERYONE, BUT WE'RE NEVER GOING TO BE FREE WHILE THAT MONSTER'S RUNNING THE SHOW.

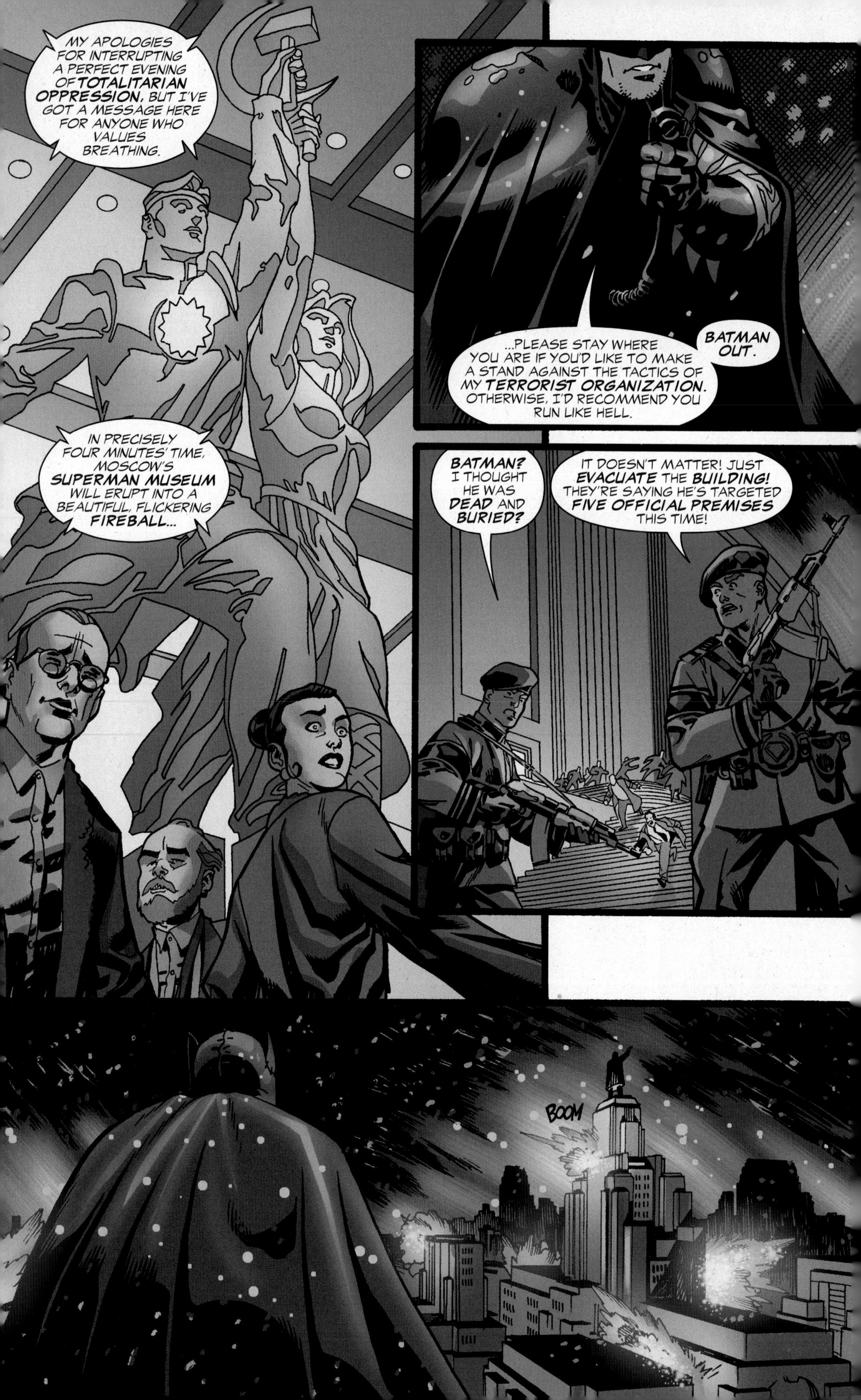
MY APOLOGIES FOR INTERRUPTING A PERFECT EVENING OF TOTALITARIAN OPPRESSION, BUT I'VE GOT A MESSAGE HERE FOR ANYONE WHO VALUES BREATHING.
IN PRECISELY FOUR MINUTES' TIME, MOSCOW'S SUPERMAN MUSEUM WILL ERUPT INTO A BEAUTIFUL, FLICKERING FIREBALL...
...PLEASE STAY WHERE YOU ARE IF YOU'D LIKE TO MAKE A STAND AGAINST THE TACTICS OF MY TERRORIST ORGANIZATION. OTHERWISE, I'D RECOMMEND YOU RUN LIKE HELL.
BATMAN OUT.
BATMAN? I THOUGHT HE WAS DEAD AND BURIED?
IT DOESN'T MATTER! JUST EVACUATE THE BUILDING! THEY'RE SAYING HE'S TARGETED FIVE OFFICIAL PREMISES THIS TIME!
BOOM

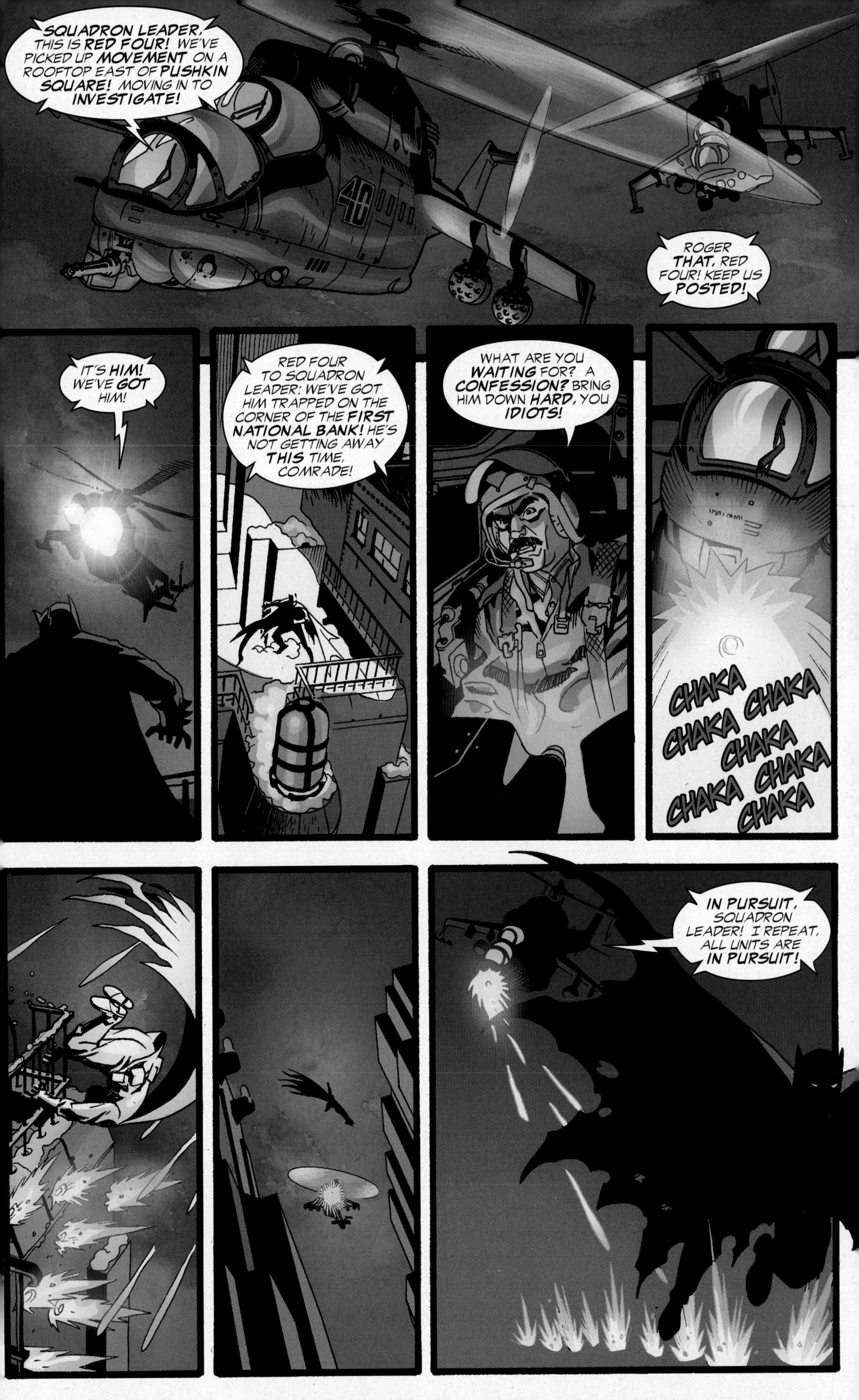
SQUADRON LEADER, THIS IS RED FOUR! WE'VE PICKED UP MOVEMENT ON A ROOFTOP EAST OF PUSHKIN SQUARE! MOVING IN TO INVESTIGATE!
ROGER THAT, RED FOUR! KEEP US POSTED!
IT'S HIM! WE'VE GOT HIM!
RED FOUR TO SQUADRON LEADER: WE'VE GOT HIM TRAPPED ON THE CORNER OF THE FIRST NATIONAL BANK! HE'S NOT GETTING AWAY THIS TIME, COMRADE!
WHAT ARE YOU WAITING FOR? A CONFESSION? BRING HIM DOWN HARD, YOU IDIOTS!
CHAKA CHAKA CHAKA CHAKA CHAKA CHAKA CHAKA
IN PURSUIT, SQUADRON LEADER! I REPEAT, ALL UNITS ARE IN PURSUIT!

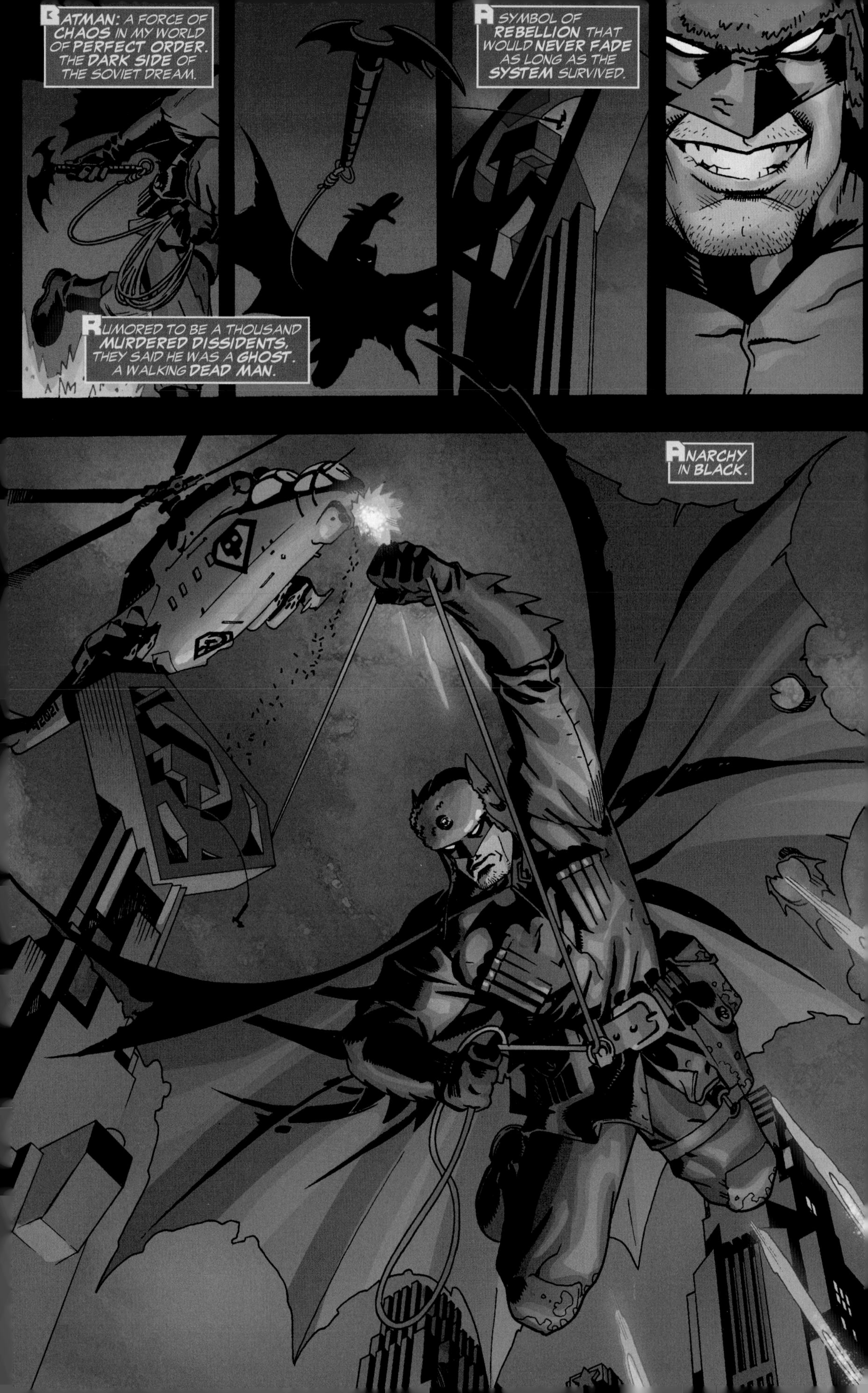
BATMAN: A FORCE OF CHAOS IN MY WORLD OF PERFECT ORDER. THE DARK SIDE OF THE SOVIET DREAM.
RUMORED TO BE A THOUSAND MURDERED DISSIDENTS. THEY SAID HE WAS A GHOST. A WALKING DEAD MAN.
A SYMBOL OF REBELLION THAT WOULD NEVER FADE AS LONG AS THE SYSTEM SURVIVED.
ANARCHY IN BLACK.

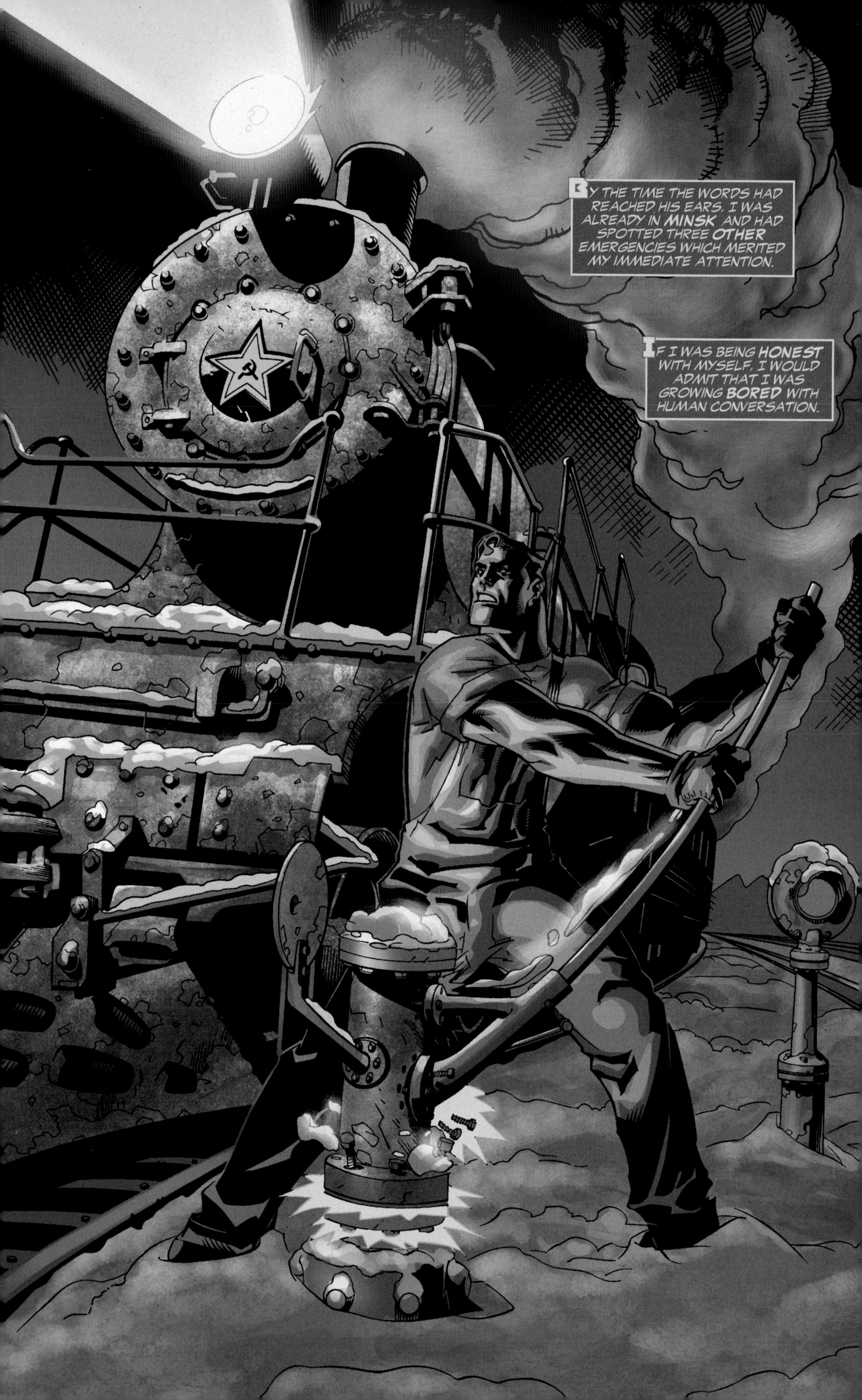
BY THE TIME THE WORDS HAD REACHED HIS EARS, I WAS ALREADY IN MINSK AND HAD SPOTTED THREE OTHER EMERGENCIES WHICH MERITED MY IMMEDIATE ATTENTION.
IF I WAS BEING HONEST WITH MYSELF, I WOULD ADMIT THAT I WAS GROWING BORED WITH HUMAN CONVERSATION.

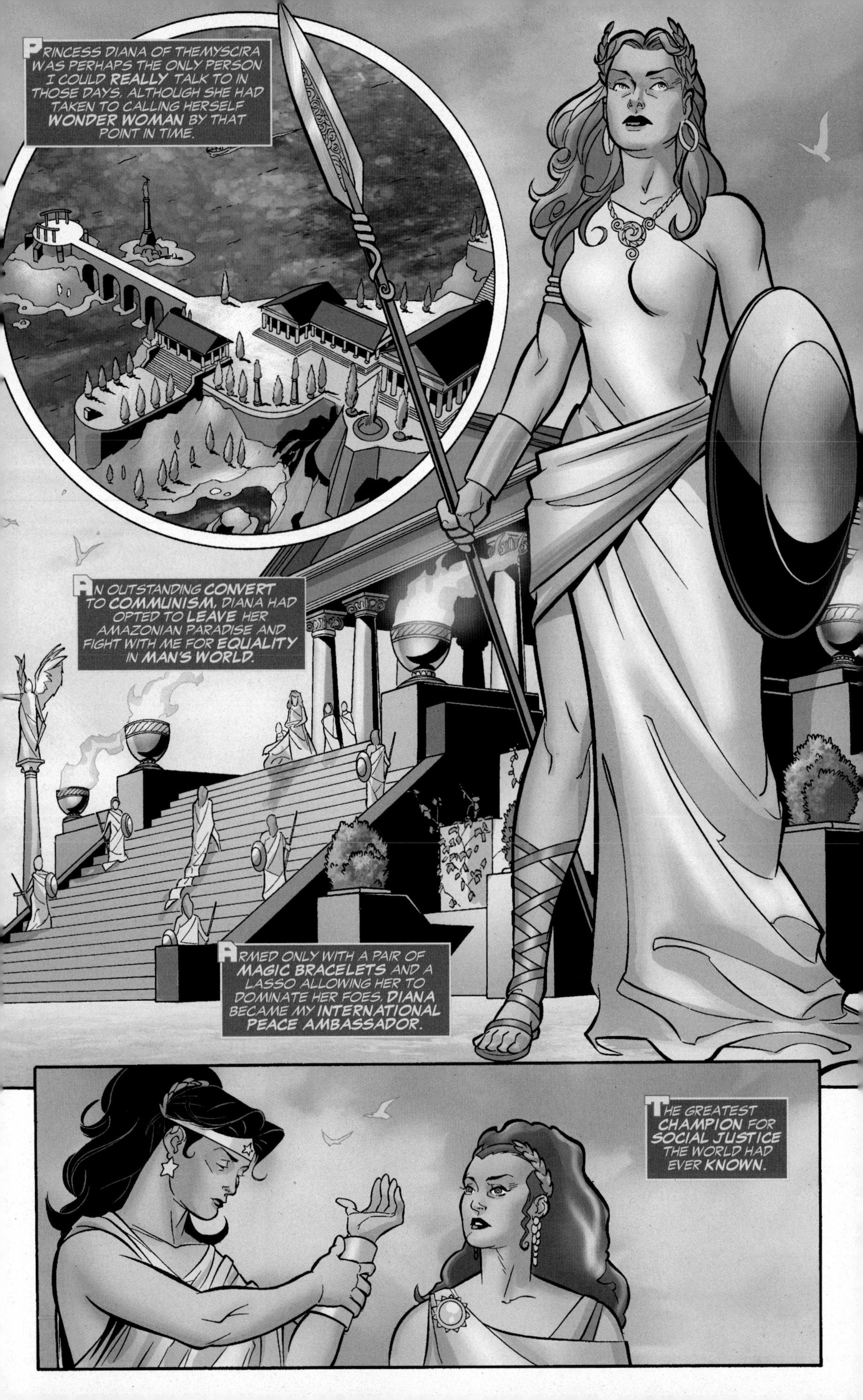

PRINCESS DIANA OF THEMYSCIRA WAS PERHAPS THE ONLY PERSON I COULD REALLY TALK TO IN THOSE DAYS, ALTHOUGH SHE HAD TAKEN TO CALLING HERSELF WONDER WOMAN BY THAT POINT IN TIME.
AN OUTSTANDING CONVERT TO COMMUNISM, DIANA HAD OPTED TO LEAVE HER AMAZONIAN PARADISE AND FIGHT WITH ME FOR EQUALITY IN MAN'S WORLD.
ARMED ONLY WITH A PAIR OF MAGIC BRACELETS AND A LASSO ALLOWING HER TO DOMINATE HER FOES, DIANA BECAME MY INTERNATIONAL PEACE AMBASSADOR.
THE GREATEST CHAMPION FOR SOCIAL JUSTICE THE WORLD HAD EVER KNOWN.

FOOOSH

YOU'RE SUCH A *SHOWOFF.* YOU *KNOW* THAT?

SOMETIMES I WONDER IF LUTHOR AND THE AMERICANS ARE *RIGHT,* DIANA. PERHAPS WE *DO* INTERFERE WITH HUMANITY TOO MUCH.

NOBODY WEARS A *SEATBELT* ANYMORE. SHIPS HAVE EVEN STOPPED CARRYING *LIFEJACKETS.* I DON'T LIKE THIS UNHEALTHY NEW WAY THAT PEOPLE ARE *BEHAVING.*

THERE'S NOTHING WRONG WITH *HELPING* PEOPLE, SUPERMAN. YOU CAN'T JUST SIT BACK AND WATCH THEM DIE WITH YOUR *TELESCOPIC VISION.* YOU'RE BEING *IRRATIONAL.*

OH, THE PEOPLE *LOVE* YOU, SUPERMAN.

SOME MORE THAN YOU'D EVER *BELIEVE.*

THE K.G.B. ARE ALWAYS PUSHING ME TO TAKE MORE AND MORE CONTROL, BUT I *ALREADY* FEEL LIKE I'M HOLDING ON TOO TIGHT. SOMETIMES I WORRY THE PEOPLE DON'T EVEN *LIKE* ME.

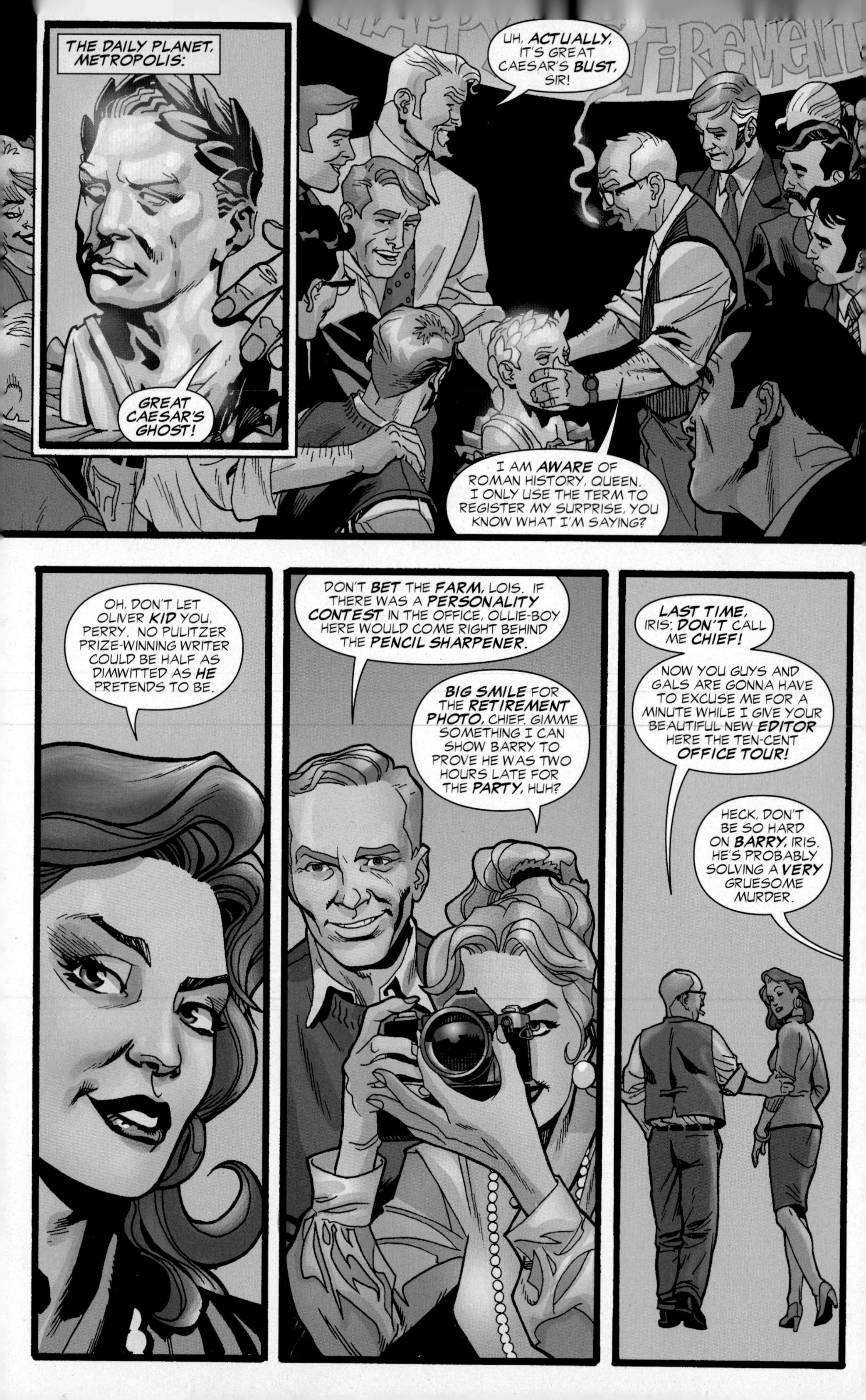
THE DAILY PLANET, METROPOLIS:
GREAT CAESAR'S GHOST!
UH, ACTUALLY, IT'S GREAT CAESAR'S BUST, SIR!
I AM AWARE OF ROMAN HISTORY, QUEEN. I ONLY USE THE TERM TO REGISTER MY SURPRISE, YOU KNOW WHAT I'M SAYING?
OH, DON'T LET OLIVER KID YOU, PERRY. NO PULITZER PRIZE-WINNING WRITER COULD BE HALF AS DIMWITTED AS HE PRETENDS TO BE.
DON'T BET THE FARM, LOIS. IF THERE WAS A PERSONALITY CONTEST IN THE OFFICE, OLLIE-BOY HERE WOULD COME RIGHT BEHIND THE PENCIL SHARPENER.
BIG SMILE FOR THE RETIREMENT PHOTO, CHIEF. GIMME SOMETHING I CAN SHOW BARRY TO PROVE HE WAS TWO HOURS LATE FOR THE PARTY, HUH?
LAST TIME, IRIS: DON'T CALL ME CHIEF!
NOW YOU GUYS AND GALS ARE GONNA HAVE TO EXCUSE ME FOR A MINUTE WHILE I GIVE YOUR BEAUTIFUL NEW EDITOR HERE THE TEN-CENT OFFICE TOUR!
HECK, DON'T BE SO HARD ON BARRY, IRIS. HE'S PROBABLY SOLVING A VERY GRUESOME MURDER.

WHO WAS THAT RED-HEADED GUY I JUST PASSED IN THE HALL? HE LOOKED KIND OF *FAMILIAR*.

WELL, HE *SHOULDN'T* HAVE. THAT WAS MISTER *JAMES OLSEN*, THE PENTAGON'S *ANTI-SUPERMAN ADVISOR* AND PROBABLY THE NEXT DIRECTOR OF THE C.I.A.

DOOR CLOSING

OLSEN COMMISSIONED *LEXCORP* TO DEVELOP WHAT WE THINK COULD BE THE MOST EFFECTIVE ANTI-SUPERMAN DETERRENT YET, USING INFORMATION HE RECEIVED FROM SYMPATHIZERS IN THE KREMLIN.

IS THAT WHAT YOU'RE WORKING ON *NOW*?

SPEAKING OF WHICH, *J.F.K.* AND *NORMA JEAN* ARE JOINING US FOR DINNER TONIGHT. APPARENTLY, JACK'S GOT SOME *U.F.O.* BUSINESS HE SAID I'D BE INTERESTED IN.

I'M *SORRY*, DARLING, BUT I'M AFRAID THAT'S *CLASSIFIED INFORMATION*.

OH, LEX. DON'T YOU EVER *STOP*? THIS WAS SUPPOSED TO BE THE ONE NIGHT OF THE YEAR WE ALWAYS GUARANTEE WE'RE GOING TO SPEND SOME *TIME* TOGETHER.

YOU DON'T *UNDERSTAND*, LOIS. JACK TELLS ME BRAINIAC AND SUPERMAN AREN'T THE *ONLY* ALIENS WHO'VE VISITED EARTH.

IT SEEMS *ANOTHER* ALIEN CRASHED IN ROSWELL, NEW MEXICO, BACK IN 1947 AND THE UNITED STATES OF AMERICA HAVE AN *EXTRA TERRESTRIAL* OF OUR VERY OWN.

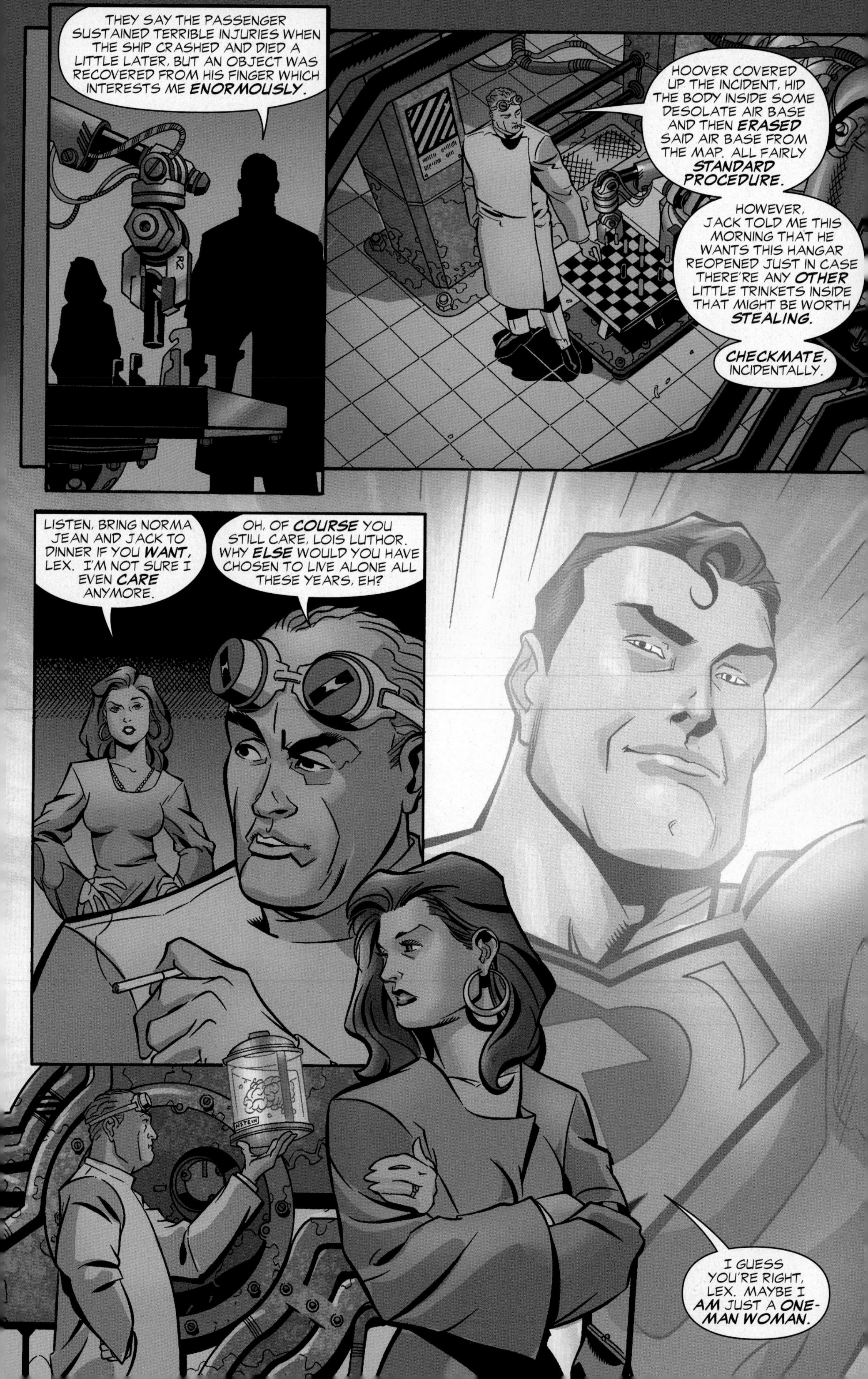
THEY SAY THE PASSENGER SUSTAINED TERRIBLE INJURIES WHEN THE SHIP CRASHED AND DIED A LITTLE LATER, BUT AN OBJECT WAS RECOVERED FROM HIS FINGER WHICH INTERESTS ME ENORMOUSLY.
R2
HOOVER COVERED UP THE INCIDENT, HID THE BODY INSIDE SOME DESOLATE AIR BASE AND THEN ERASED SAID AIR BASE FROM THE MAP. ALL FAIRLY STANDARD PROCEDURE.
HOWEVER, JACK TOLD ME THIS MORNING THAT HE WANTS THIS HANGAR REOPENED JUST IN CASE THERE'RE ANY OTHER LITTLE TRINKETS INSIDE THAT MIGHT BE WORTH STEALING.
CHECKMATE, INCIDENTALLY.
LISTEN, BRING NORMA JEAN AND JACK TO DINNER IF YOU WANT, LEX. I'M NOT SURE I EVEN CARE ANYMORE.
OH, OF COURSE YOU STILL CARE, LOIS LUTHOR. WHY ELSE WOULD YOU HAVE CHOSEN TO LIVE ALONE ALL THESE YEARS, EH?
NSTEIN
I GUESS YOU'RE RIGHT, LEX. MAYBE I AM JUST A ONE-MAN WOMAN.

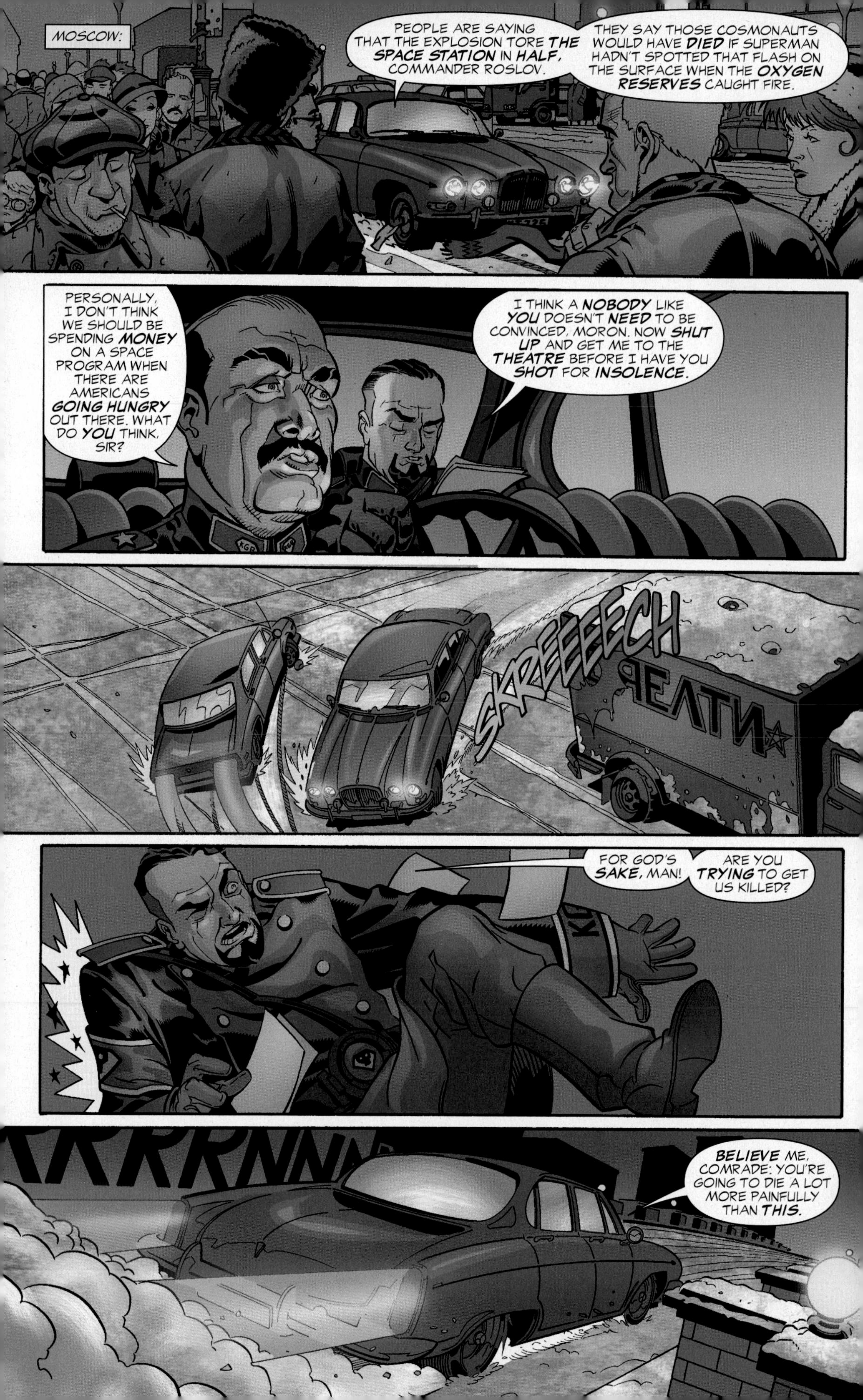

MOSCOW:
PEOPLE ARE SAYING THAT THE EXPLOSION TORE THE SPACE STATION IN HALF, COMMANDER ROSLOV.
THEY SAY THOSE COSMONAUTS WOULD HAVE DIED IF SUPERMAN HADN'T SPOTTED THAT FLASH ON THE SURFACE WHEN THE OXYGEN RESERVES CAUGHT FIRE.
PERSONALLY, I DON'T THINK WE SHOULD BE SPENDING MONEY ON A SPACE PROGRAM WHEN THERE ARE AMERICANS GOING HUNGRY OUT THERE. WHAT DO YOU THINK, SIR?
I THINK A NOBODY LIKE YOU DOESN'T NEED TO BE CONVINCED, MORON. NOW SHUT UP AND GET ME TO THE THEATRE BEFORE I HAVE YOU SHOT FOR INSOLENCE.
SKREEEECH
ТЕАТР
FOR GOD'S SAKE, MAN!
ARE YOU TRYING TO GET US KILLED?
RRRRNNN
BELIEVE ME, COMRADE: YOU'RE GOING TO DIE A LOT MORE PAINFULLY THAN THIS.

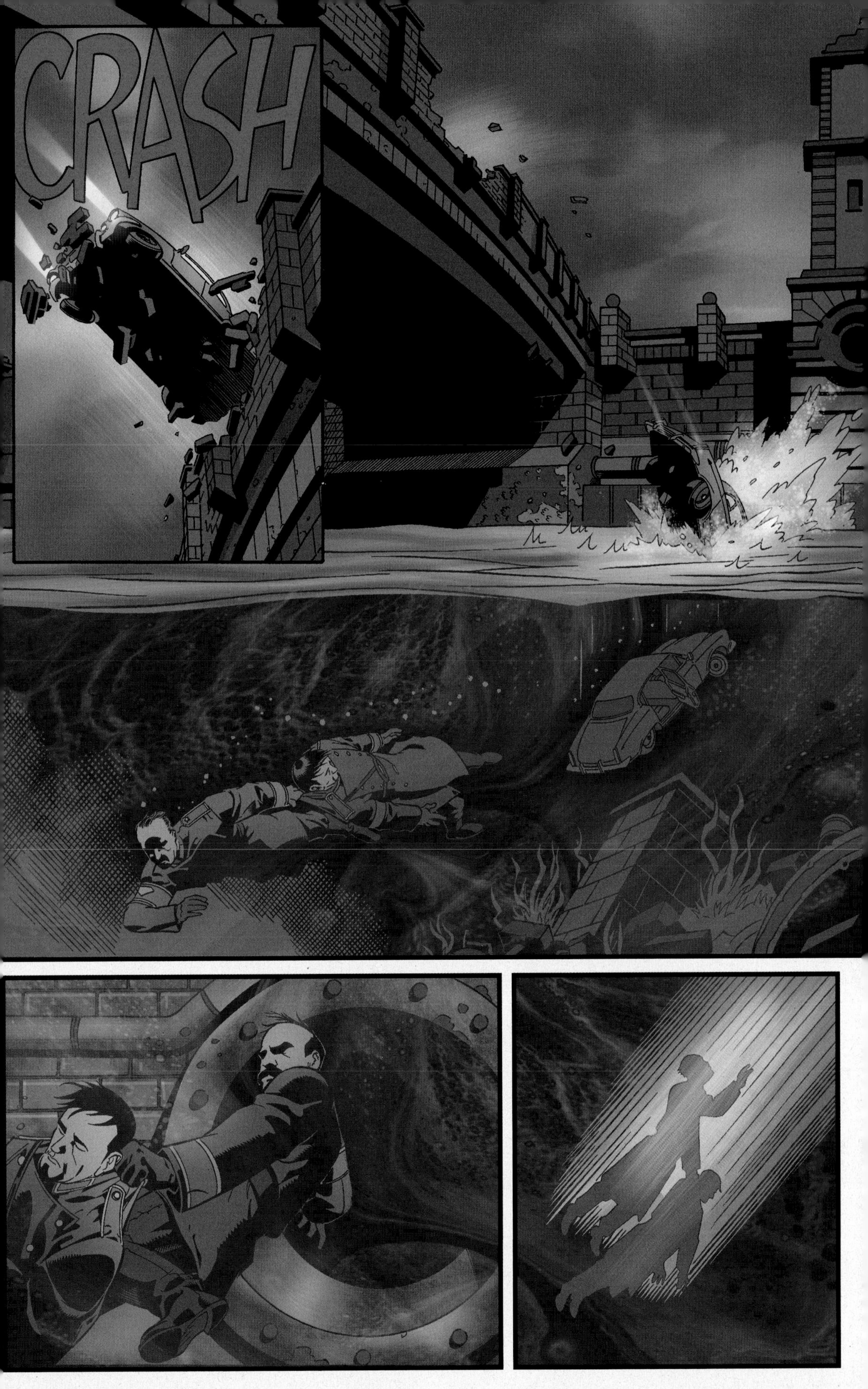
CRASH

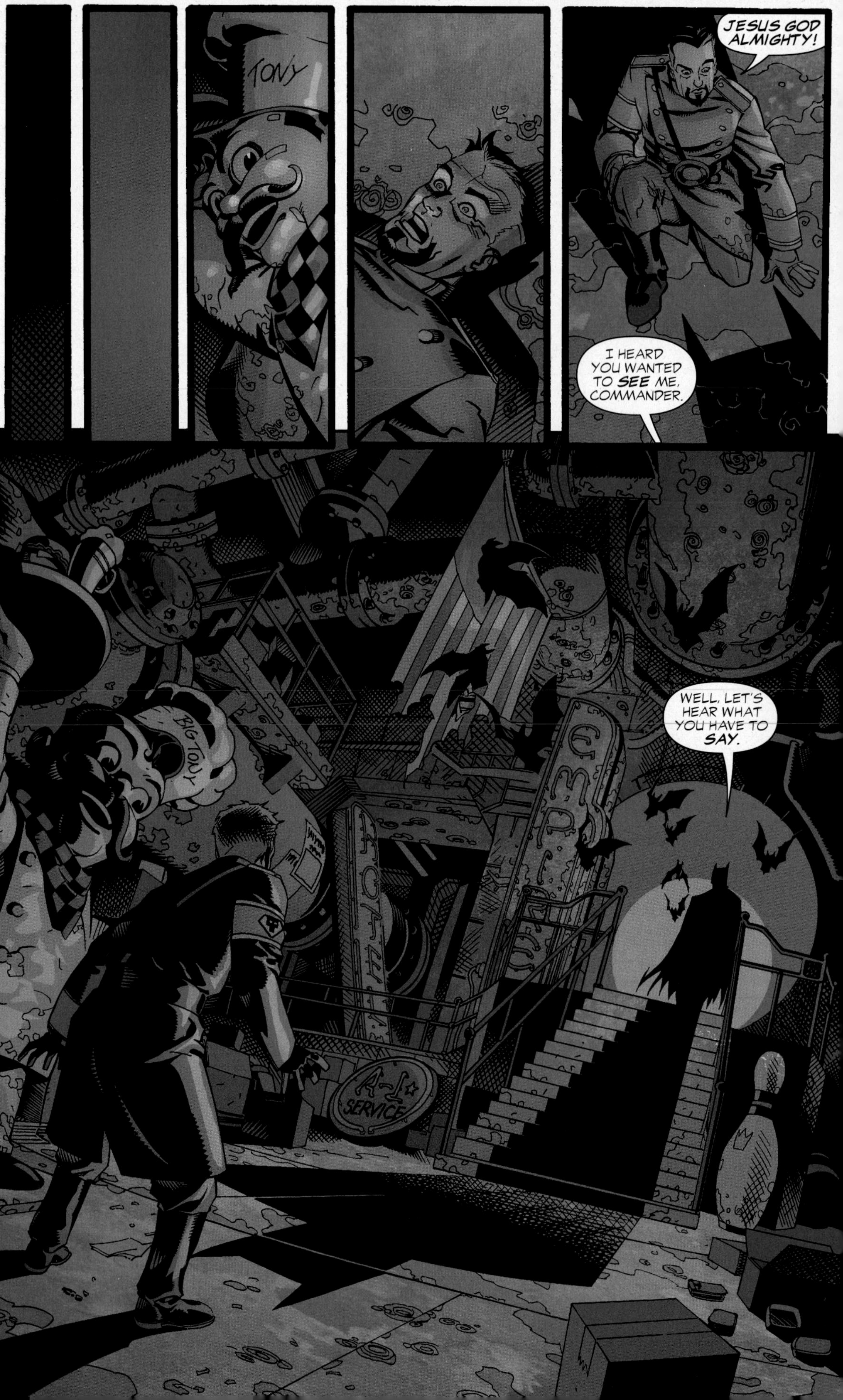

TONY
JESUS GOD ALMIGHTY!
I HEARD YOU WANTED TO **SEE** ME, COMMANDER.
BIG TONY
WELL, LET'S HEAR WHAT YOU HAVE TO **SAY**.
A-1 SERVICE

WHAT? HOW **DARE** YOU SPEAK TO ME LIKE THAT? DO YOU REALIZE WHO I **AM**?

YOU'RE A **VAIN** MAN, A **CRUEL** MAN AND OBSESSIVELY JEALOUS OF **SUPERMAN**. IT'S NO SECRET THAT YOU HARBOR **POLITICAL AMBITIONS** OF YOUR **OWN**.

YOUR NAME IS **PYOTR IOSIF ROSLOV**: ILLEGITIMATE SON OF THE LATE **JOSEPH STALIN** AND CURRENTLY HEAD OF THE **SECURITY SERVICES**.

WHO YOU ARE IS **MEANINGLESS**. THE QUESTION IS WHY YOU'RE PUTTING THE **WORD** AROUND THAT YOU WANT TO TALK TO **ME**.

I TAKE IT, AH...THAT IT'S **SAFE** TO **SPEAK** DOWN HERE?

NATURALLY, COMMANDER. ALL MY CAVES ARE SOUNDPROOFED AND CLOAKED USING THE CUTTING EDGE OF MILITARY TECHNOLOGY; ALL STOLEN FROM YOUR **BASES**, OF COURSE.

THEN I'LL GET STRAIGHT TO THE POINT: LEX LUTHOR AND HIS FRIENDS IN THE C.I.A. HAVE AN INTERESTING PROPOSITION FOR YOU, BATMAN.

THEY WANT YOU TO KILL **SUPERMAN**, AND GUARANTEE THEY NOW HAVE THE **MEANS** TO FINISH HIM OFF **PROPERLY**.

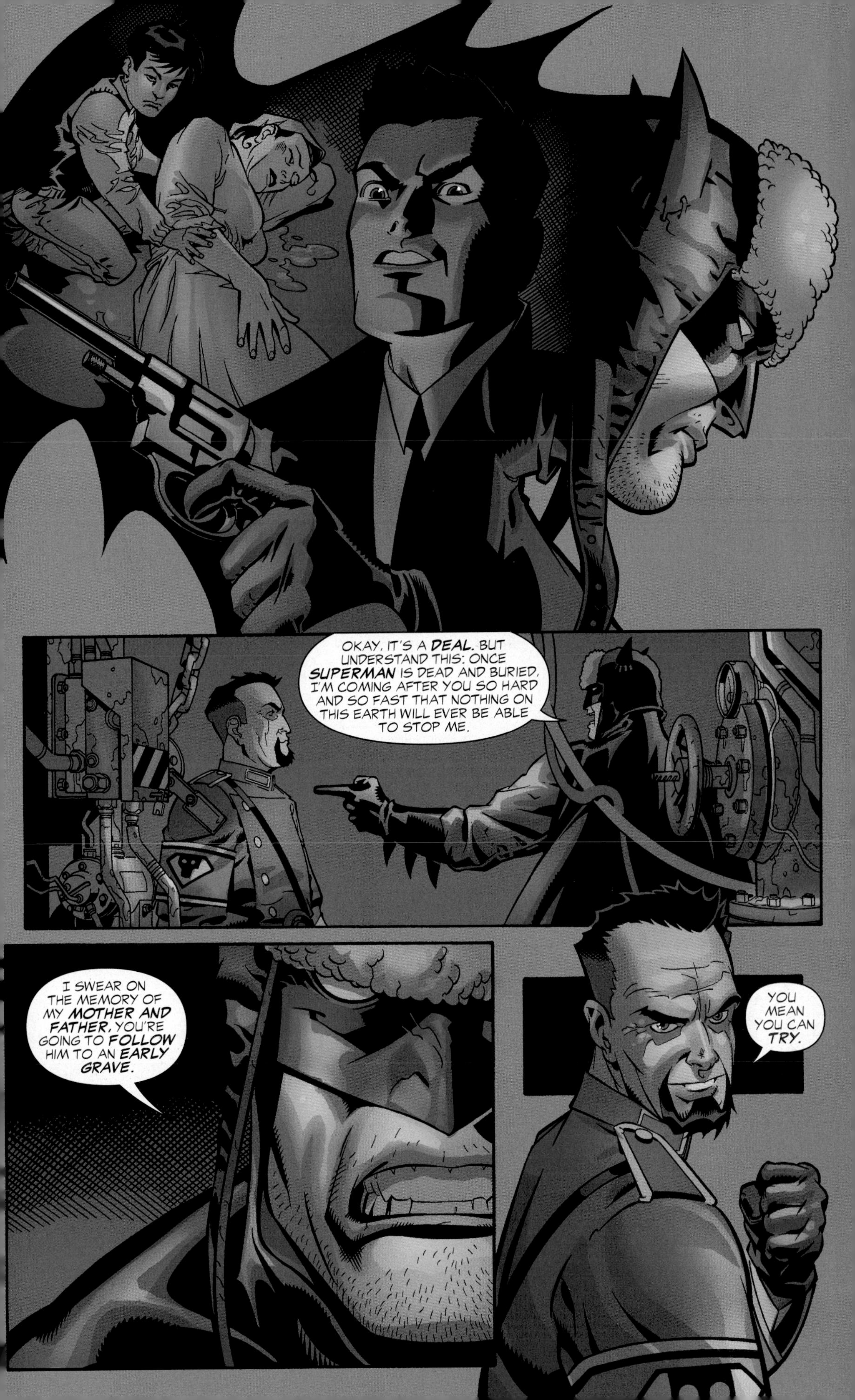

OKAY, IT'S A DEAL. BUT UNDERSTAND THIS: ONCE SUPERMAN IS DEAD AND BURIED, I'M COMING AFTER YOU SO HARD AND SO FAST THAT NOTHING ON THIS EARTH WILL EVER BE ABLE TO STOP ME.
I SWEAR ON THE MEMORY OF MY MOTHER AND FATHER, YOU'RE GOING TO FOLLOW HIM TO AN EARLY GRAVE.
YOU MEAN YOU CAN TRY.

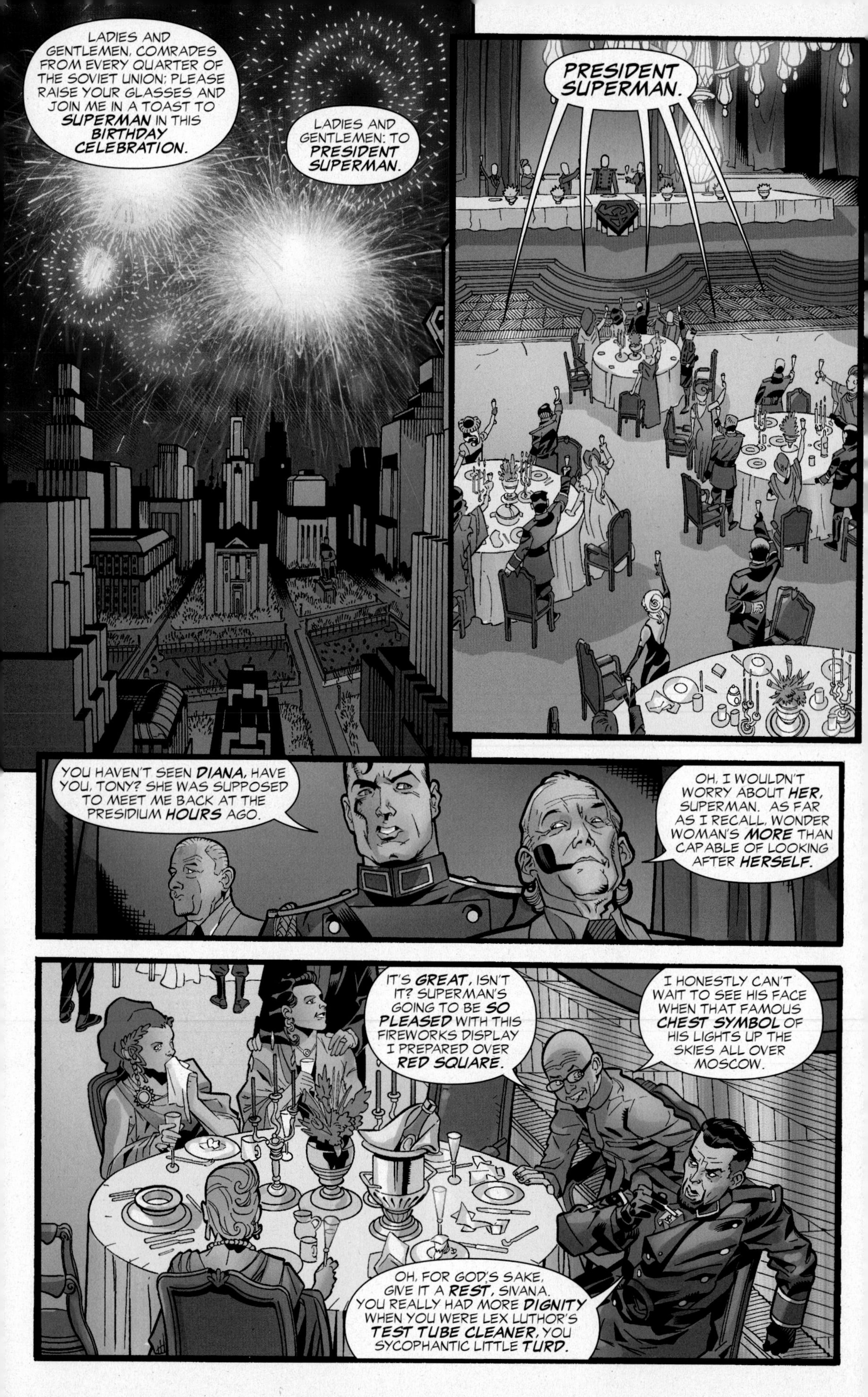
LADIES AND GENTLEMEN, COMRADES FROM EVERY QUARTER OF THE SOVIET UNION; PLEASE RAISE YOUR GLASSES AND JOIN ME IN A TOAST TO SUPERMAN IN THIS BIRTHDAY CELEBRATION.
LADIES AND GENTLEMEN: TO PRESIDENT SUPERMAN.
PRESIDENT SUPERMAN.
YOU HAVEN'T SEEN DIANA, HAVE YOU, TONY? SHE WAS SUPPOSED TO MEET ME BACK AT THE PRESIDIUM HOURS AGO.
OH, I WOULDN'T WORRY ABOUT HER, SUPERMAN. AS FAR AS I RECALL, WONDER WOMAN'S MORE THAN CAPABLE OF LOOKING AFTER HERSELF.
IT'S GREAT, ISN'T IT? SUPERMAN'S GOING TO BE SO PLEASED WITH THIS FIREWORKS DISPLAY I PREPARED OVER RED SQUARE.
I HONESTLY CAN'T WAIT TO SEE HIS FACE WHEN THAT FAMOUS CHEST SYMBOL OF HIS LIGHTS UP THE SKIES ALL OVER MOSCOW.
OH, FOR GOD'S SAKE, GIVE IT A REST, SIVANA. YOU REALLY HAD MORE DIGNITY WHEN YOU WERE LEX LUTHOR'S TEST TUBE CLEANER, YOU SYCOPHANTIC LITTLE TURD.

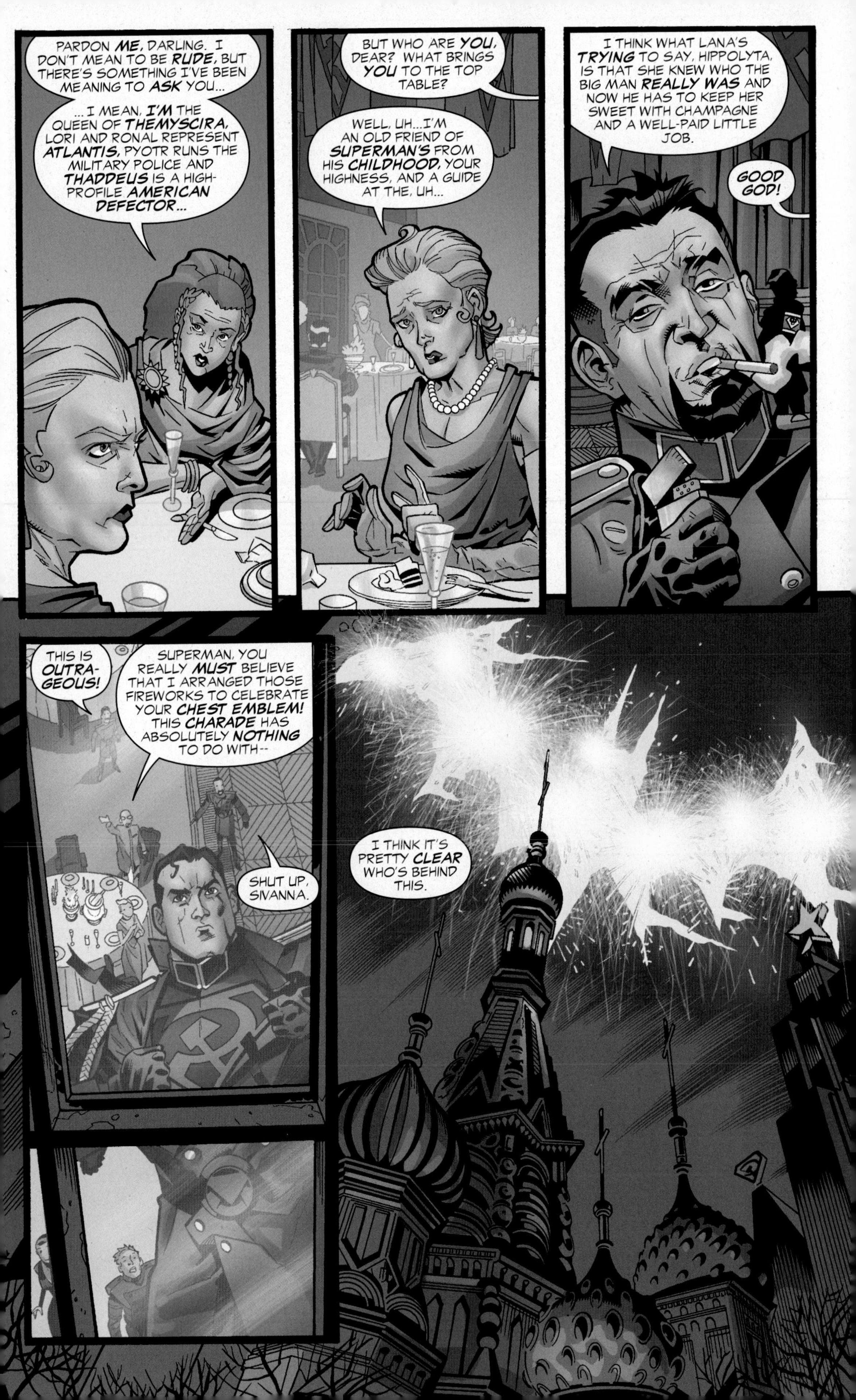
PARDON ME, DARLING. I DON'T MEAN TO BE RUDE, BUT THERE'S SOMETHING I'VE BEEN MEANING TO ASK YOU...
... I MEAN, I'M THE QUEEN OF THEMYSCIRA, LORI AND RONAL REPRESENT ATLANTIS, PYOTR RUNS THE MILITARY POLICE AND THADDEUS IS A HIGH-PROFILE AMERICAN DEFECTOR...
BUT WHO ARE YOU, DEAR? WHAT BRINGS YOU TO THE TOP TABLE?
WELL, UH...I'M AN OLD FRIEND OF SUPERMAN'S FROM HIS CHILDHOOD, YOUR HIGHNESS, AND A GUIDE AT THE, UH...
I THINK WHAT LANA'S TRYING TO SAY, HIPPOLYTA, IS THAT SHE KNEW WHO THE BIG MAN REALLY WAS AND NOW HE HAS TO KEEP HER SWEET WITH CHAMPAGNE AND A WELL-PAID LITTLE JOB.
GOOD GOD!
THIS IS OUTRA-GEOUS!
SUPERMAN, YOU REALLY MUST BELIEVE THAT I ARRANGED THOSE FIREWORKS TO CELEBRATE YOUR CHEST EMBLEM! THIS CHARADE HAS ABSOLUTELY NOTHING TO DO WITH--
SHUT UP, SIVANNA.
I THINK IT'S PRETTY CLEAR WHO'S BEHIND THIS.

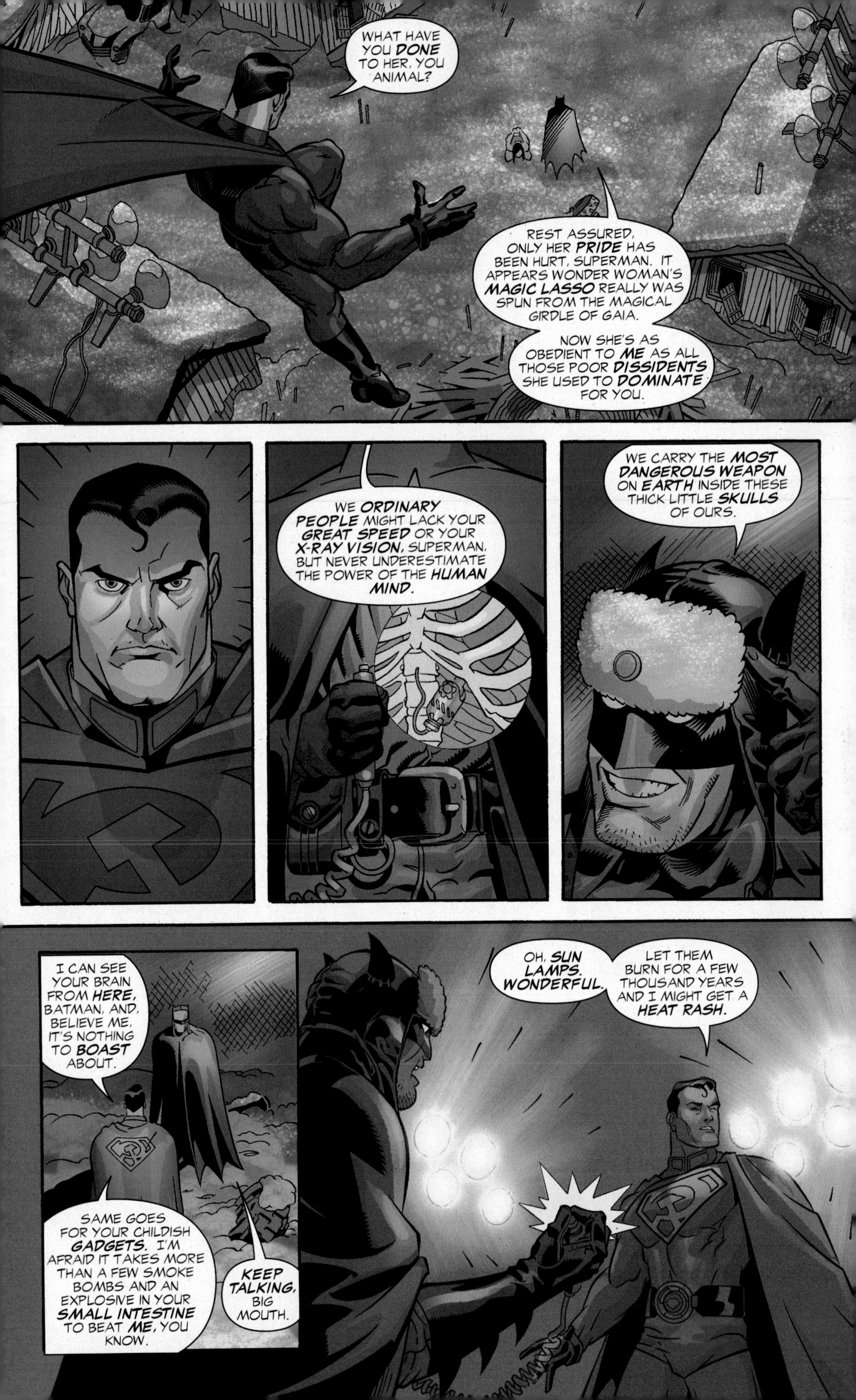
WHAT HAVE YOU DONE TO HER, YOU ANIMAL?
REST ASSURED, ONLY HER PRIDE HAS BEEN HURT, SUPERMAN. IT APPEARS WONDER WOMAN'S MAGIC LASSO REALLY WAS SPUN FROM THE MAGICAL GIRDLE OF GAIA.
NOW SHE'S AS OBEDIENT TO ME AS ALL THOSE POOR DISSIDENTS SHE USED TO DOMINATE FOR YOU.
WE ORDINARY PEOPLE MIGHT LACK YOUR GREAT SPEED OR YOUR X-RAY VISION, SUPERMAN, BUT NEVER UNDERESTIMATE THE POWER OF THE HUMAN MIND.
WE CARRY THE MOST DANGEROUS WEAPON ON EARTH INSIDE THESE THICK LITTLE SKULLS OF OURS.
I CAN SEE YOUR BRAIN FROM HERE, BATMAN, AND, BELIEVE ME, IT'S NOTHING TO BOAST ABOUT.
SAME GOES FOR YOUR CHILDISH GADGETS. I'M AFRAID IT TAKES MORE THAN A FEW SMOKE BOMBS AND AN EXPLOSIVE IN YOUR SMALL INTESTINE TO BEAT ME, YOU KNOW.
KEEP TALKING, BIG MOUTH.
OH, SUN LAMPS. WONDERFUL.
LET THEM BURN FOR A FEW THOUSAND YEARS AND I MIGHT GET A HEAT RASH.

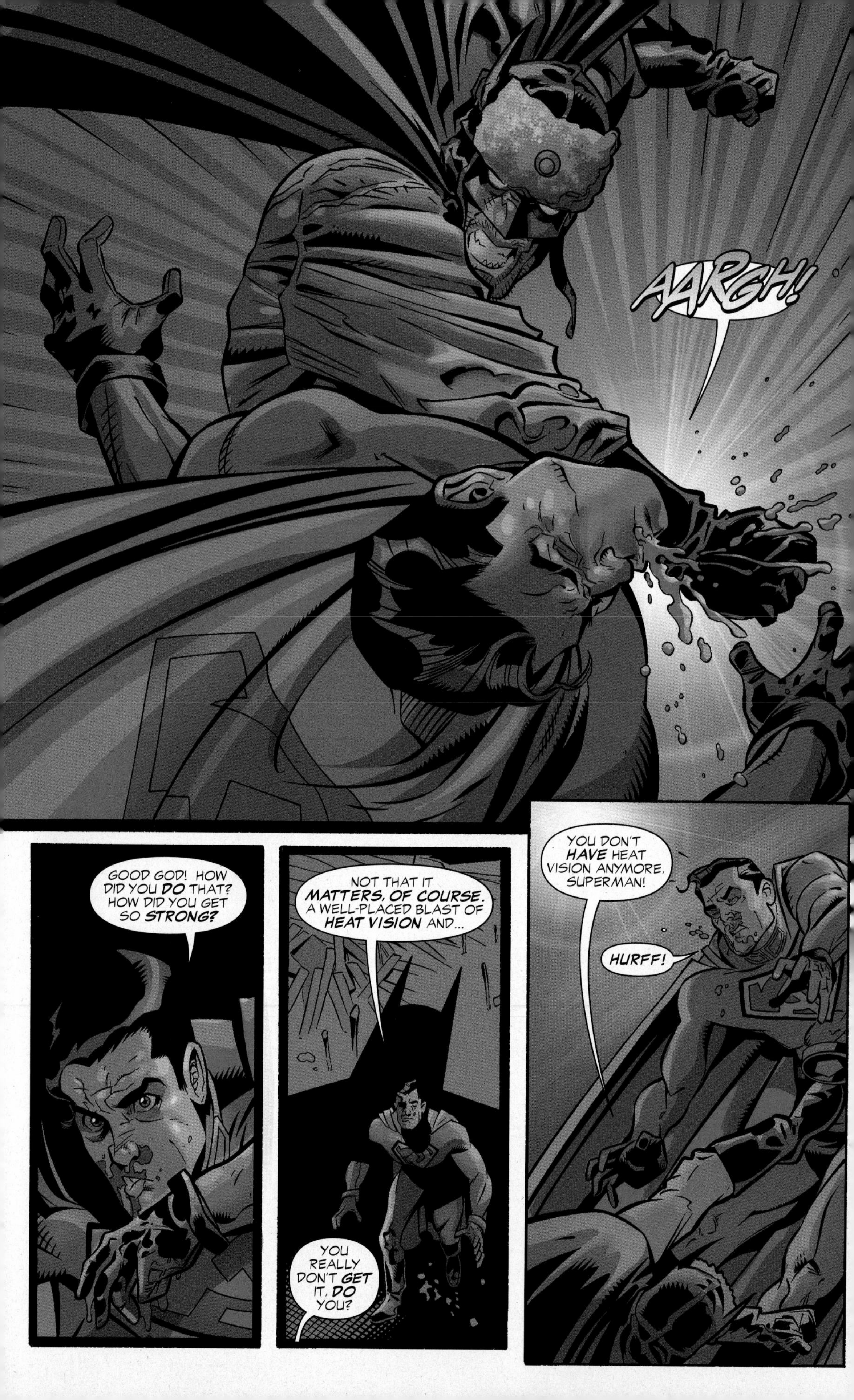
AARGH!
GOOD GOD! HOW DID YOU DO THAT? HOW DID YOU GET SO STRONG?
NOT THAT IT MATTERS, OF COURSE. A WELL-PLACED BLAST OF HEAT VISION AND...
YOU REALLY DON'T GET IT, DO YOU?
YOU DON'T HAVE HEAT VISION ANYMORE, SUPERMAN!
HURFF!

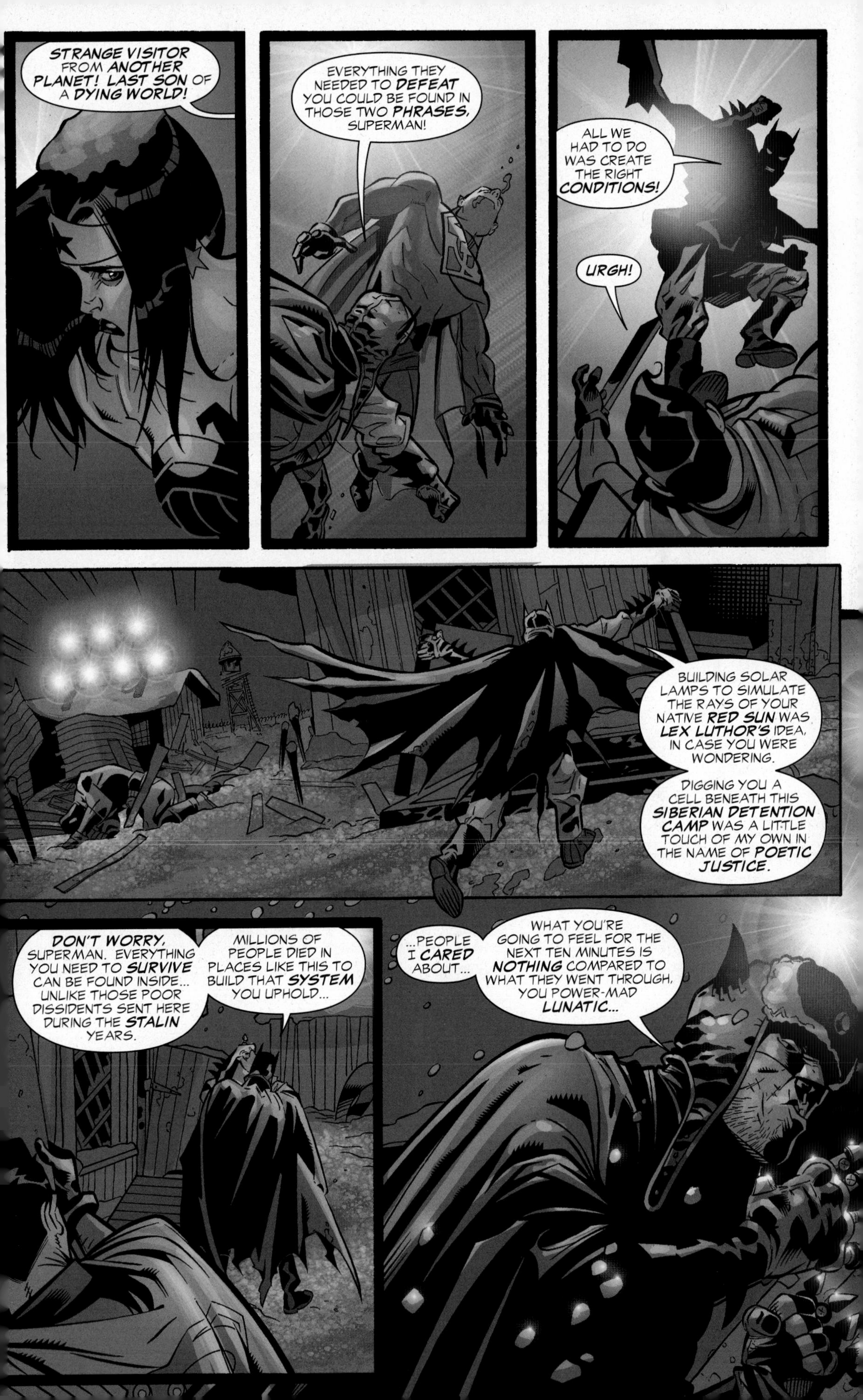
STRANGE VISITOR FROM ANOTHER PLANET! LAST SON OF A DYING WORLD!
EVERYTHING THEY NEEDED TO DEFEAT YOU COULD BE FOUND IN THOSE TWO PHRASES, SUPERMAN!
ALL WE HAD TO DO WAS CREATE THE RIGHT CONDITIONS!
URGH!
BUILDING SOLAR LAMPS TO SIMULATE THE RAYS OF YOUR NATIVE RED SUN WAS LEX LUTHOR'S IDEA, IN CASE YOU WERE WONDERING.
DIGGING YOU A CELL BENEATH THIS SIBERIAN DETENTION CAMP WAS A LITTLE TOUCH OF MY OWN IN THE NAME OF POETIC JUSTICE.
DON'T WORRY, SUPERMAN. EVERYTHING YOU NEED TO SURVIVE CAN BE FOUND INSIDE... UNLIKE THOSE POOR DISSIDENTS SENT HERE DURING THE STALIN YEARS.
MILLIONS OF PEOPLE DIED IN PLACES LIKE THIS TO BUILD THAT SYSTEM YOU UPHOLD...
...PEOPLE I CARED ABOUT...
WHAT YOU'RE GOING TO FEEL FOR THE NEXT TEN MINUTES IS NOTHING COMPARED TO WHAT THEY WENT THROUGH, YOU POWER-MAD LUNATIC...

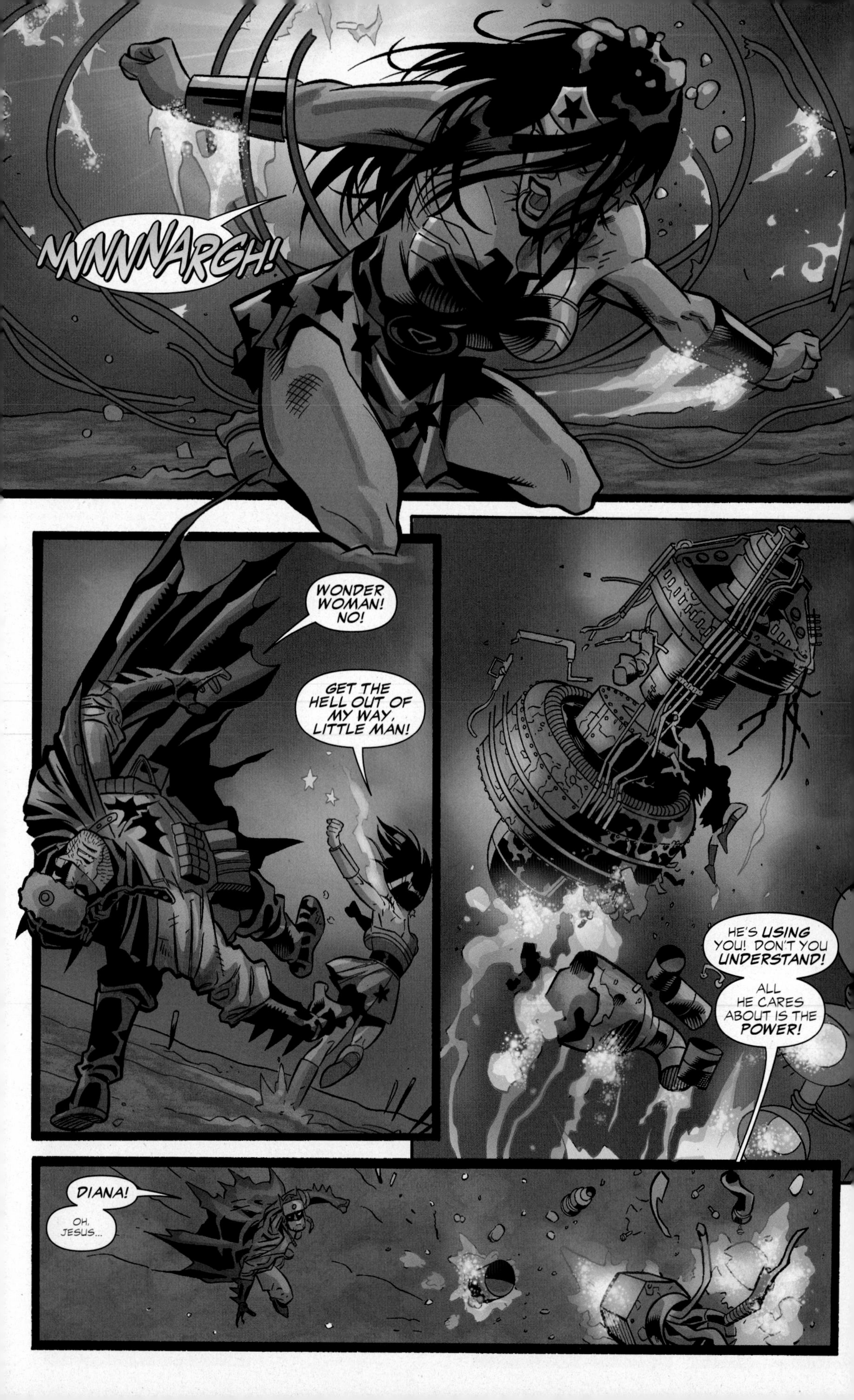
NNNNNARGH!
WONDER WOMAN! NO!
GET THE HELL OUT OF MY WAY, LITTLE MAN!
HE'S USING YOU! DON'T YOU UNDERSTAND!
ALL HE CARES ABOUT IS THE POWER!
DIANA!
OH, JESUS...

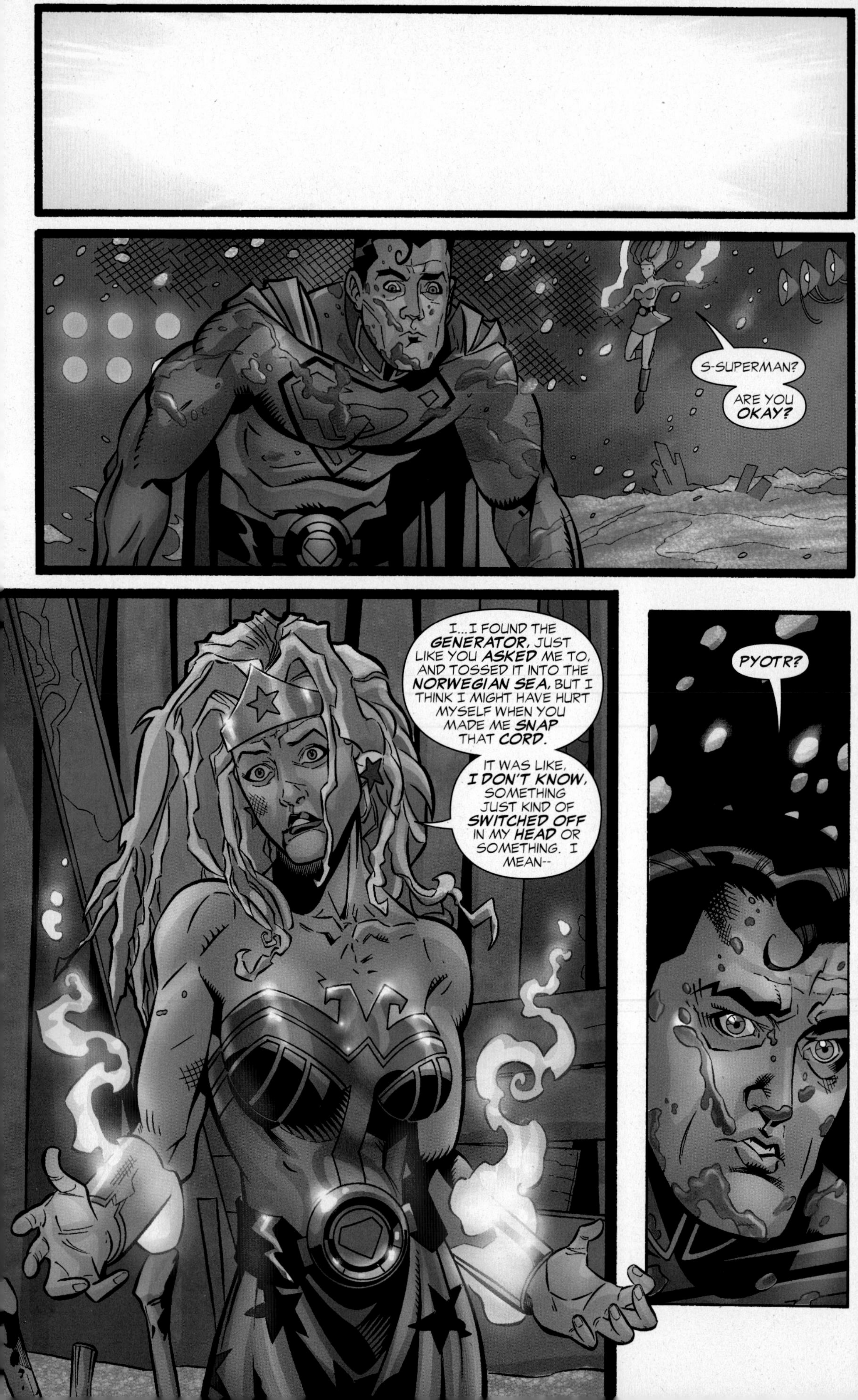
S-SUPERMAN?
ARE YOU OKAY?
I...I FOUND THE GENERATOR, JUST LIKE YOU ASKED ME TO, AND TOSSED IT INTO THE NORWEGIAN SEA, BUT I THINK I MIGHT HAVE HURT MYSELF WHEN YOU MADE ME SNAP THAT CORD.
IT WAS LIKE, I DON'T KNOW, SOMETHING JUST KIND OF SWITCHED OFF IN MY HEAD OR SOMETHING. I MEAN--
PYOTR?

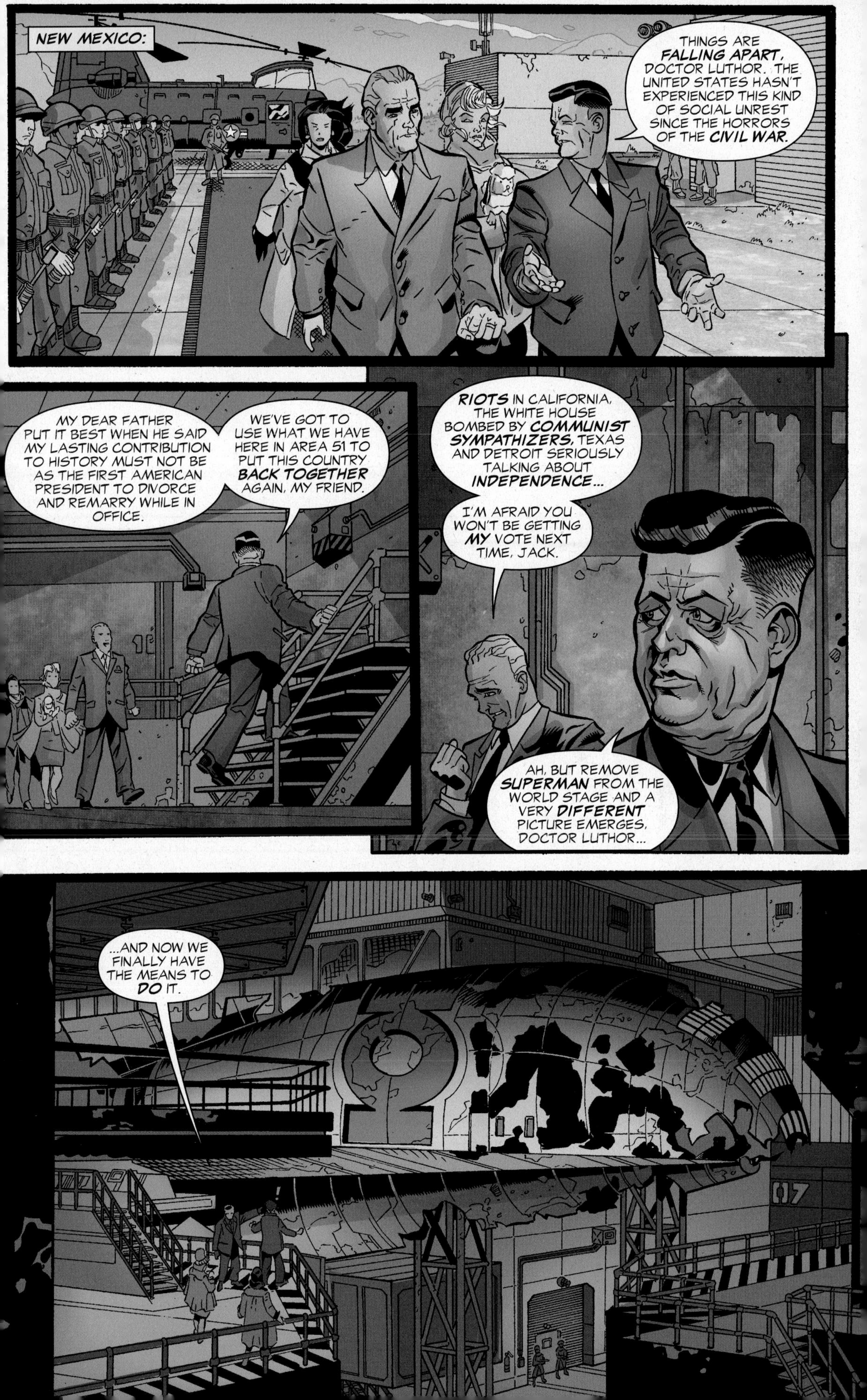
NEW MEXICO:
THINGS ARE FALLING APART, DOCTOR LUTHOR. THE UNITED STATES HASN'T EXPERIENCED THIS KIND OF SOCIAL UNREST SINCE THE HORRORS OF THE CIVIL WAR.
RIOTS IN CALIFORNIA, THE WHITE HOUSE BOMBED BY COMMUNIST SYMPATHIZERS, TEXAS AND DETROIT SERIOUSLY TALKING ABOUT INDEPENDENCE...
I'M AFRAID YOU WON'T BE GETTING MY VOTE NEXT TIME, JACK.
AH, BUT REMOVE SUPERMAN FROM THE WORLD STAGE AND A VERY DIFFERENT PICTURE EMERGES, DOCTOR LUTHOR...
MY DEAR FATHER PUT IT BEST WHEN HE SAID MY LASTING CONTRIBUTION TO HISTORY MUST NOT BE AS THE FIRST AMERICAN PRESIDENT TO DIVORCE AND REMARRY WHILE IN OFFICE.
WE'VE GOT TO USE WHAT WE HAVE HERE IN AREA 51 TO PUT THIS COUNTRY BACK TOGETHER AGAIN, MY FRIEND.
...AND NOW WE FINALLY HAVE THE MEANS TO DO IT.
07

TIME PASSED AND MY GRIP GREW **TIGHTER**.

BARELY A DECISION WAS MADE ACROSS THE LENGTH AND BREADTH OF THE SOVIET UNION WITHOUT MY PERMISSION IN **SOME** FORM OR ANOTHER.

MY DESIRE FOR **ORDER AND PERFECTION** WAS MATCHED ONLY BY THEIR DREAMS OF **VIOLENCE AND CHAOS.**

THE POPULATION WAS LARGELY **GRATEFUL** AND **OBEDIENT** BUT THE FREEDOM FIGHTERS, INSPIRED BY THE DEATH OF BATMAN, REMAINED SOMETHING OF A **PROBLEM.**

I OFFERED THEM **UTOPIA,** BUT THEY FOUGHT FOR THE RIGHT TO LIVE IN **HELL.**

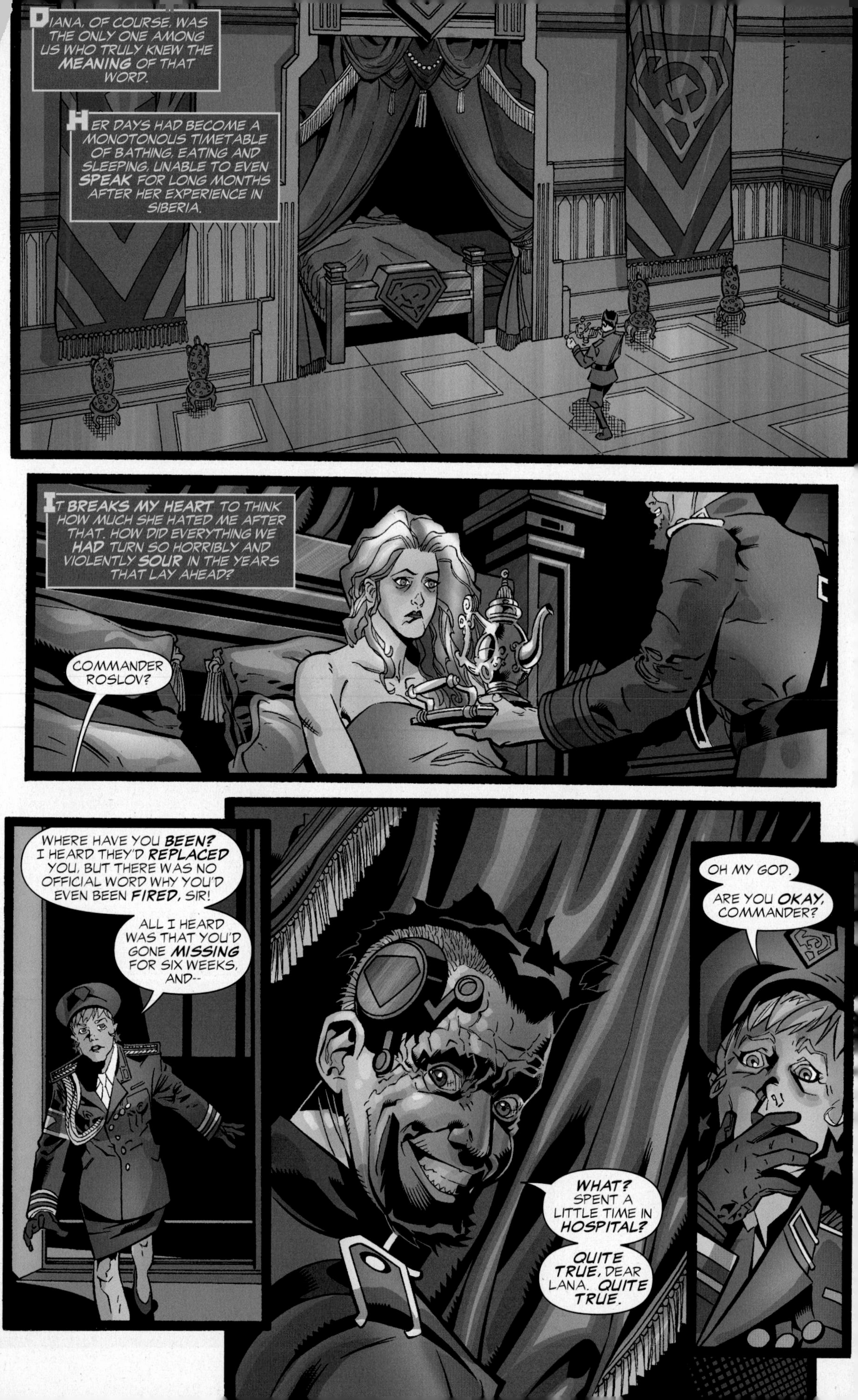
DIANA, OF COURSE, WAS THE ONLY ONE AMONG US WHO TRULY KNEW THE MEANING OF THAT WORD.
HER DAYS HAD BECOME A MONOTONOUS TIMETABLE OF BATHING, EATING AND SLEEPING, UNABLE TO EVEN SPEAK FOR LONG MONTHS AFTER HER EXPERIENCE IN SIBERIA.
IT BREAKS MY HEART TO THINK HOW MUCH SHE HATED ME AFTER THAT. HOW DID EVERYTHING WE HAD TURN SO HORRIBLY AND VIOLENTLY SOUR IN THE YEARS THAT LAY AHEAD?
COMMANDER ROSLOV?
WHERE HAVE YOU BEEN? I HEARD THEY'D REPLACED YOU, BUT THERE WAS NO OFFICIAL WORD WHY YOU'D EVEN BEEN FIRED, SIR!
ALL I HEARD WAS THAT YOU'D GONE MISSING FOR SIX WEEKS, AND--
OH MY GOD.
ARE YOU OKAY, COMMANDER?
WHAT? SPENT A LITTLE TIME IN HOSPITAL?
QUITE TRUE, DEAR LANA. QUITE TRUE.

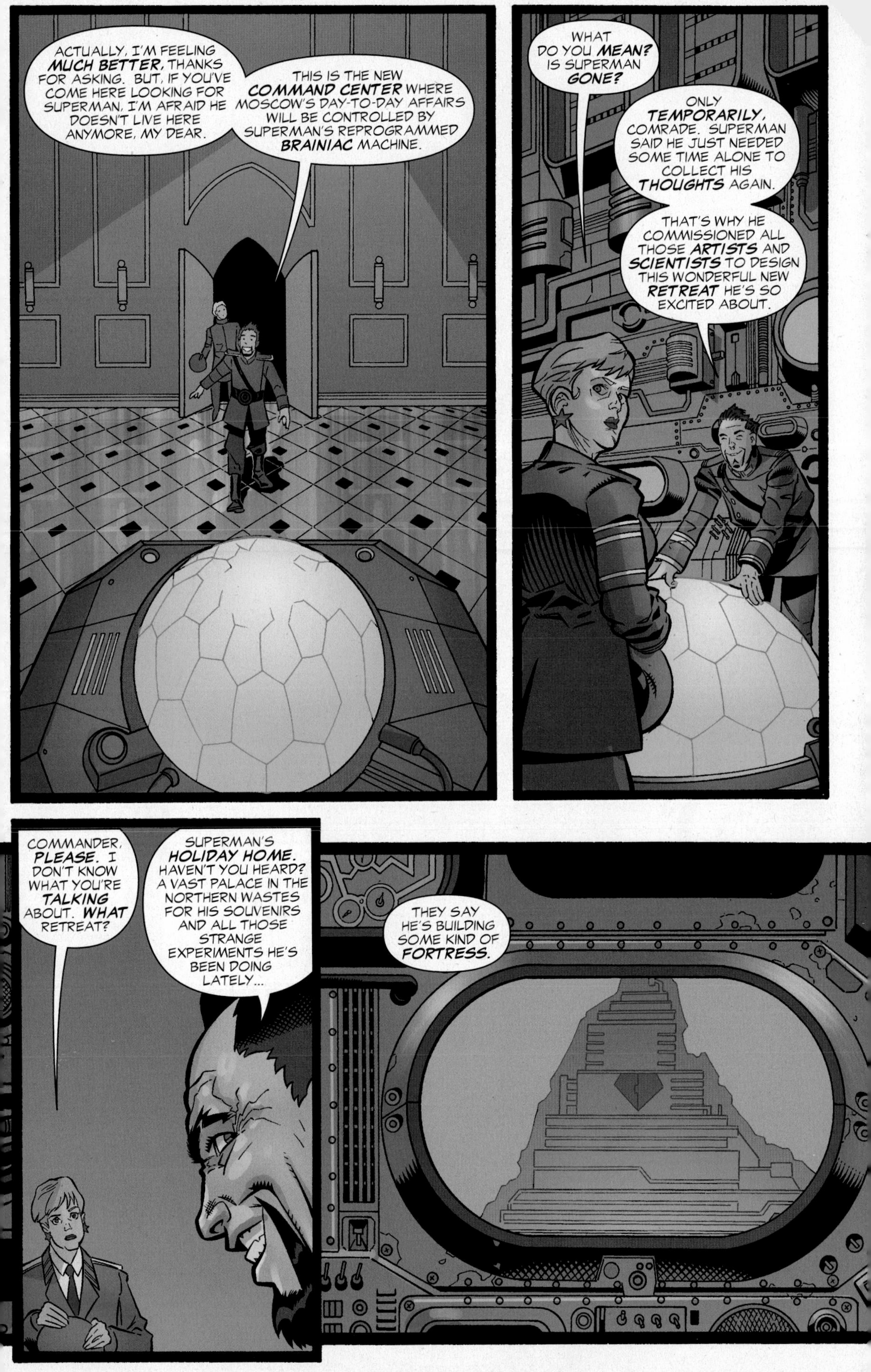
ACTUALLY, I'M FEELING MUCH BETTER, THANKS FOR ASKING. BUT, IF YOU'VE COME HERE LOOKING FOR SUPERMAN, I'M AFRAID HE DOESN'T LIVE HERE ANYMORE, MY DEAR.
THIS IS THE NEW COMMAND CENTER WHERE MOSCOW'S DAY-TO-DAY AFFAIRS WILL BE CONTROLLED BY SUPERMAN'S REPROGRAMMED BRAINIAC MACHINE.
WHAT DO YOU MEAN? IS SUPERMAN GONE?
ONLY TEMPORARILY, COMRADE. SUPERMAN SAID HE JUST NEEDED SOME TIME ALONE TO COLLECT HIS THOUGHTS AGAIN.
THAT'S WHY HE COMMISSIONED ALL THOSE ARTISTS AND SCIENTISTS TO DESIGN THIS WONDERFUL NEW RETREAT HE'S SO EXCITED ABOUT.
COMMANDER, PLEASE. I DON'T KNOW WHAT YOU'RE TALKING ABOUT. WHAT RETREAT?
SUPERMAN'S HOLIDAY HOME. HAVEN'T YOU HEARD? A VAST PALACE IN THE NORTHERN WASTES FOR HIS SOUVENIRS AND ALL THOSE STRANGE EXPERIMENTS HE'S BEEN DOING LATELY...
THEY SAY HE'S BUILDING SOME KIND OF FORTRESS.

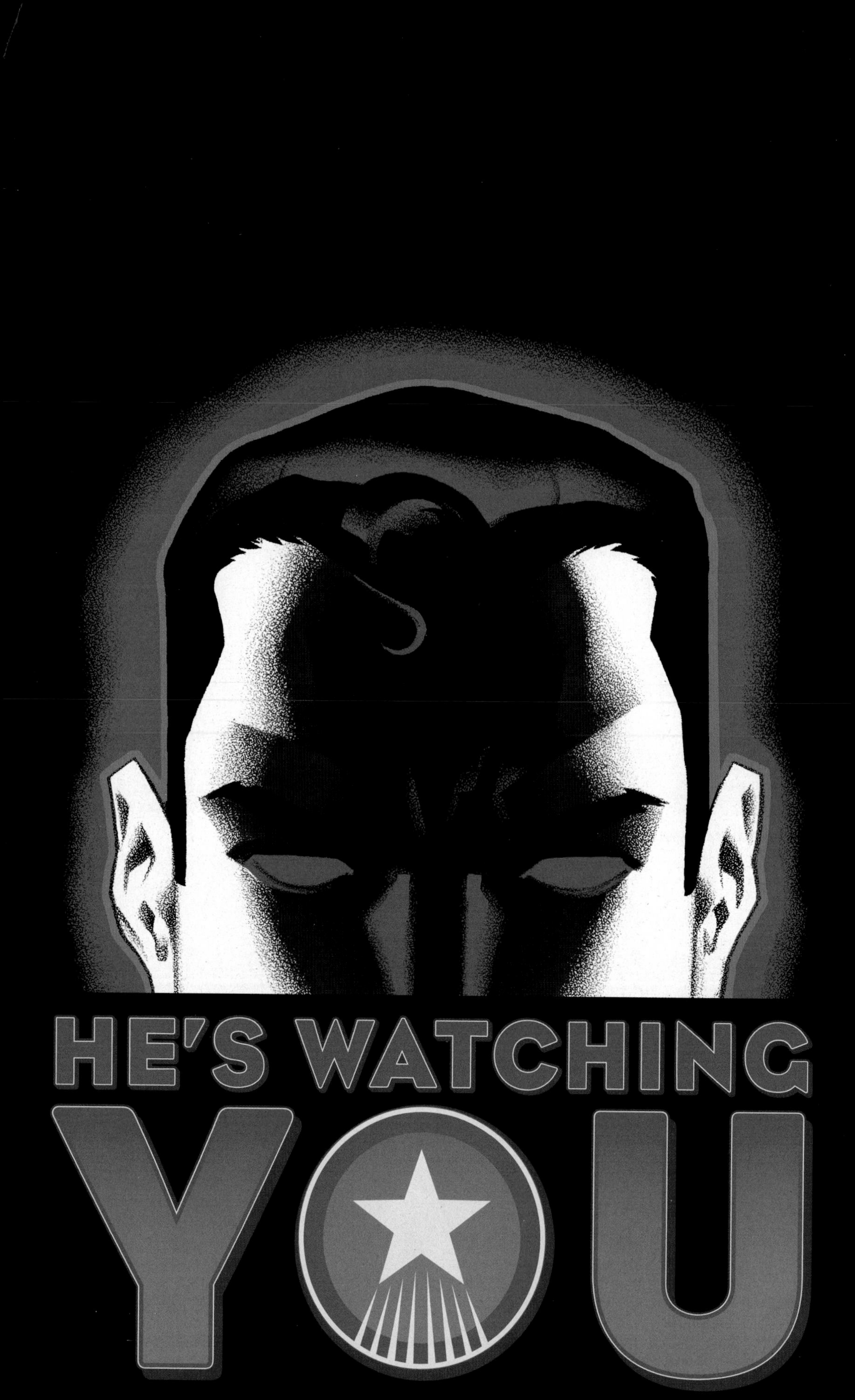
HE'S WATCHING
YOU

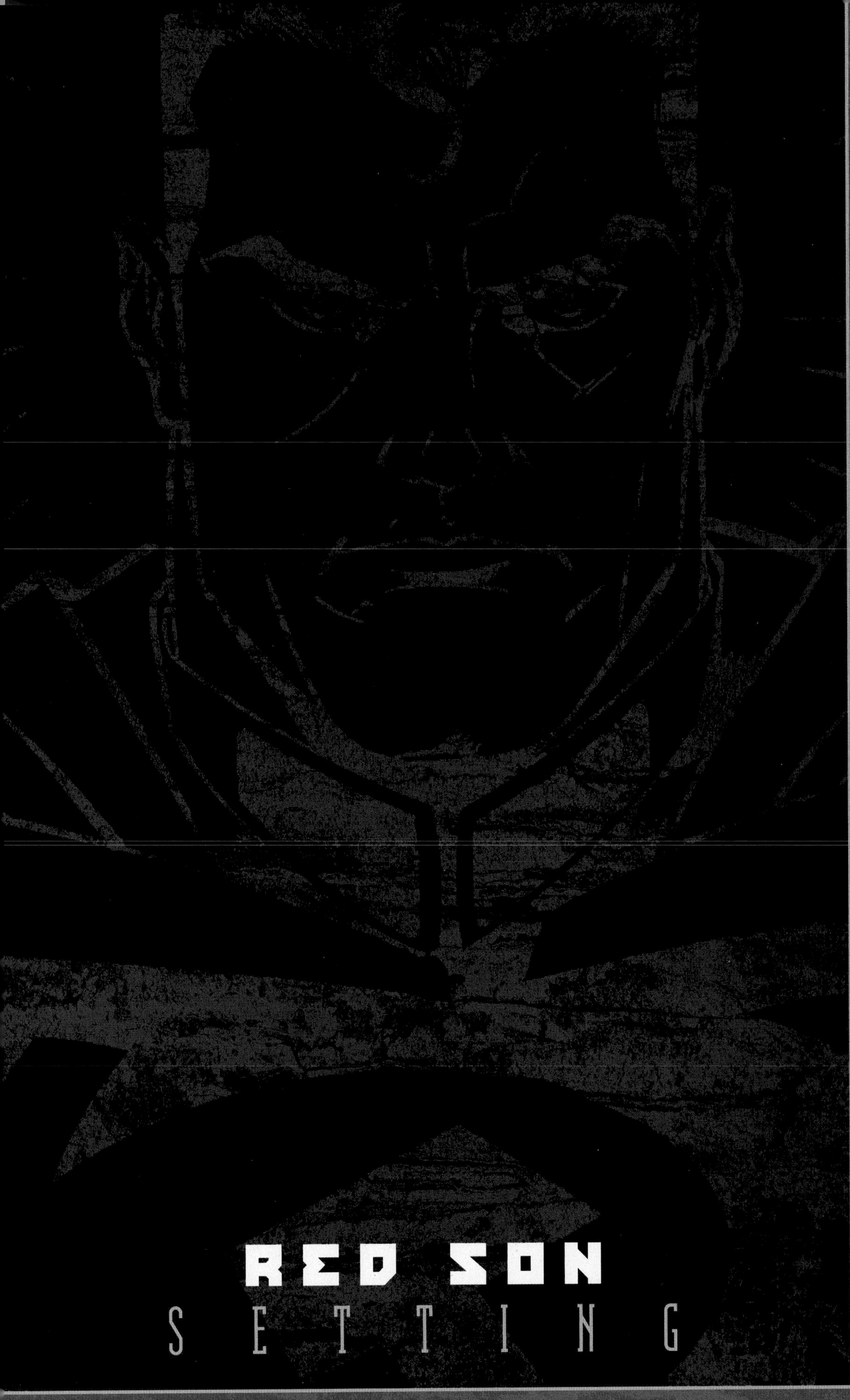

RED SON
SETTING

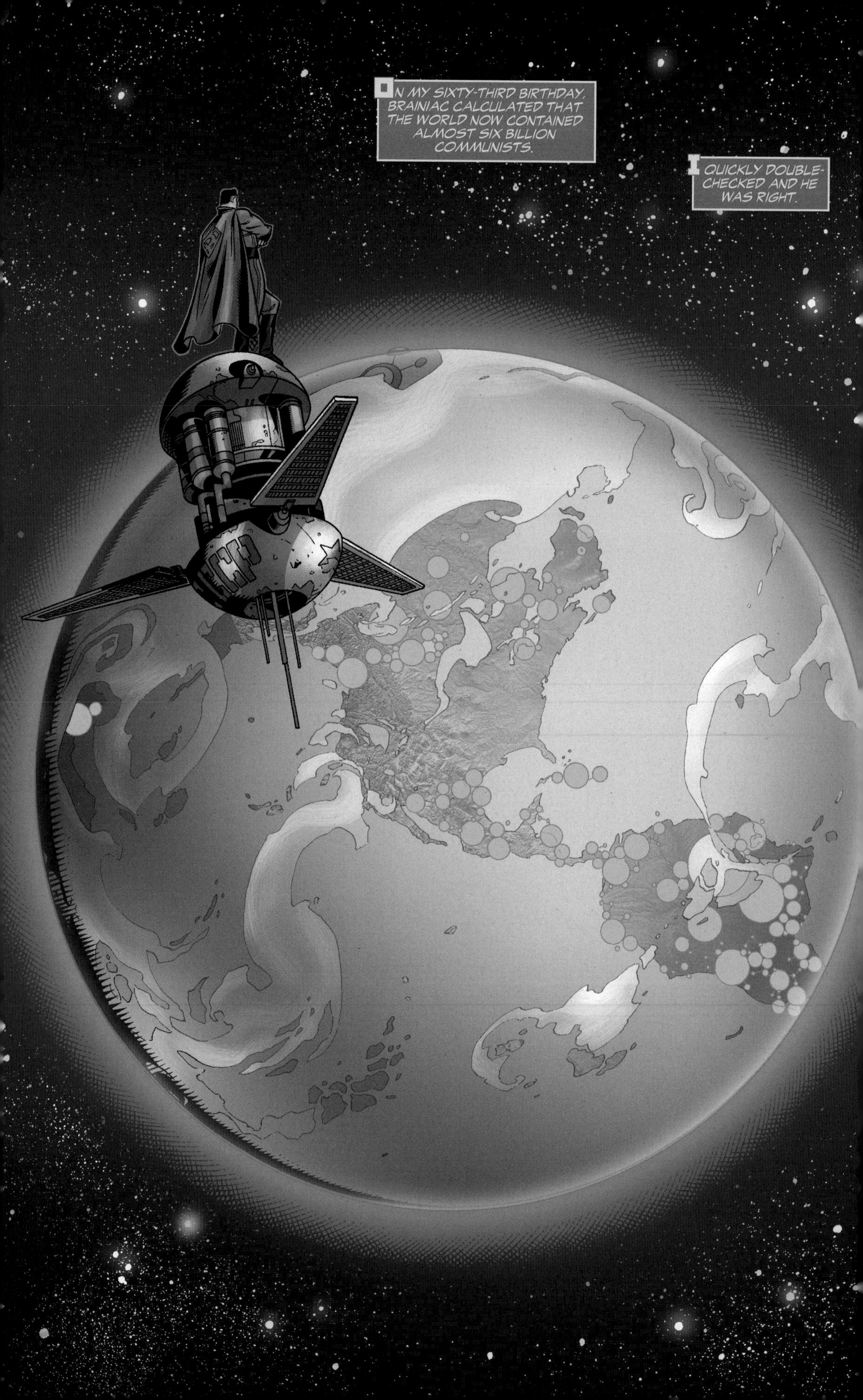
ON MY SIXTY-THIRD BIRTHDAY, BRAINIAC CALCULATED THAT THE WORLD NOW CONTAINED ALMOST SIX BILLION COMMUNISTS.
I QUICKLY DOUBLE-CHECKED AND HE WAS RIGHT.

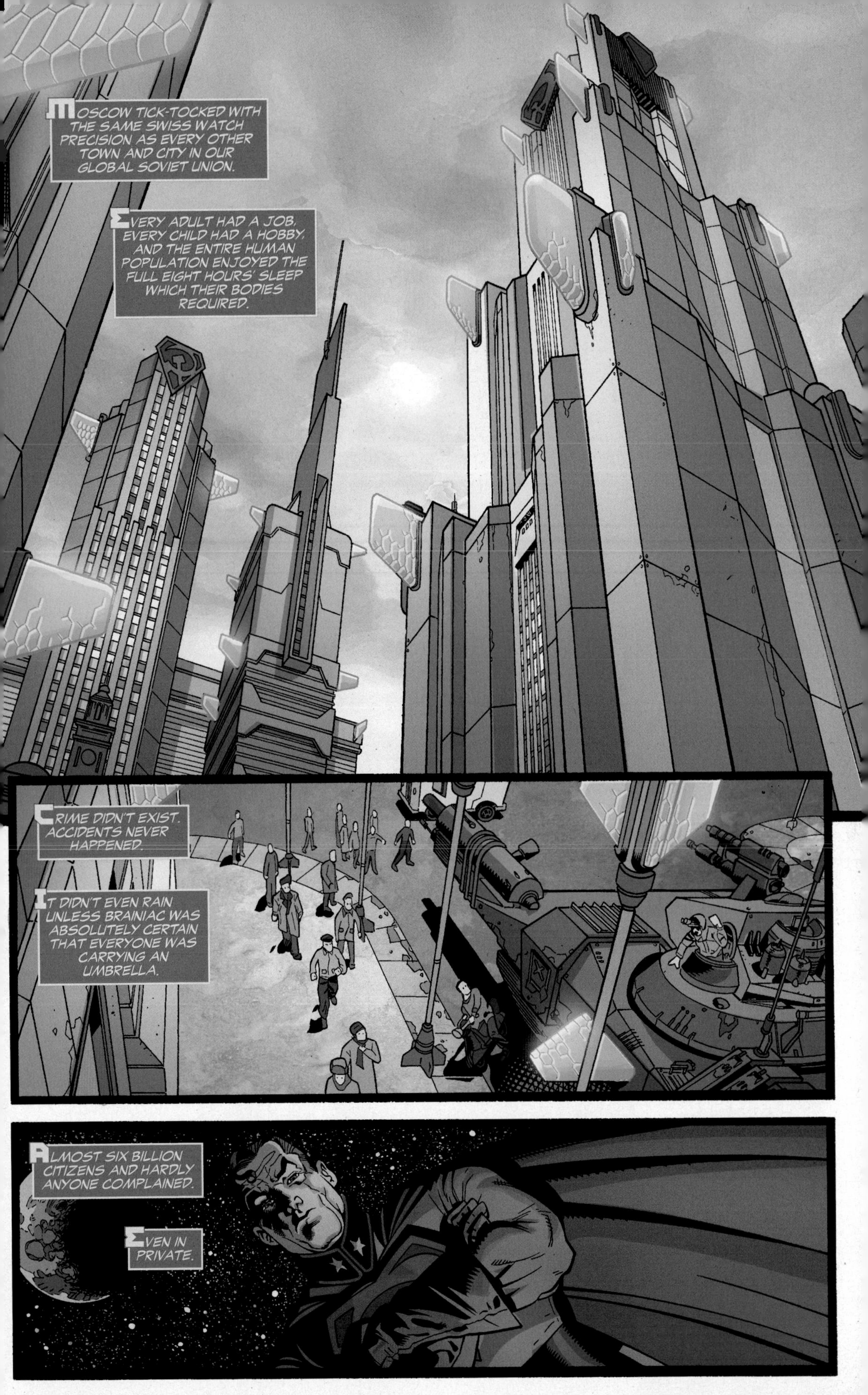
MOSCOW TICK-TOCKED WITH THE SAME SWISS WATCH PRECISION AS EVERY OTHER TOWN AND CITY IN OUR GLOBAL SOVIET UNION.
EVERY ADULT HAD A JOB, EVERY CHILD HAD A HOBBY, AND THE ENTIRE HUMAN POPULATION ENJOYED THE FULL EIGHT HOURS' SLEEP WHICH THEIR BODIES REQUIRED.
CRIME DIDN'T EXIST. ACCIDENTS NEVER HAPPENED.
IT DIDN'T EVEN RAIN UNLESS BRAINIAC WAS ABSOLUTELY CERTAIN THAT EVERYONE WAS CARRYING AN UMBRELLA.
ALMOST SIX BILLION CITIZENS AND HARDLY ANYONE COMPLAINED.
EVEN IN PRIVATE.

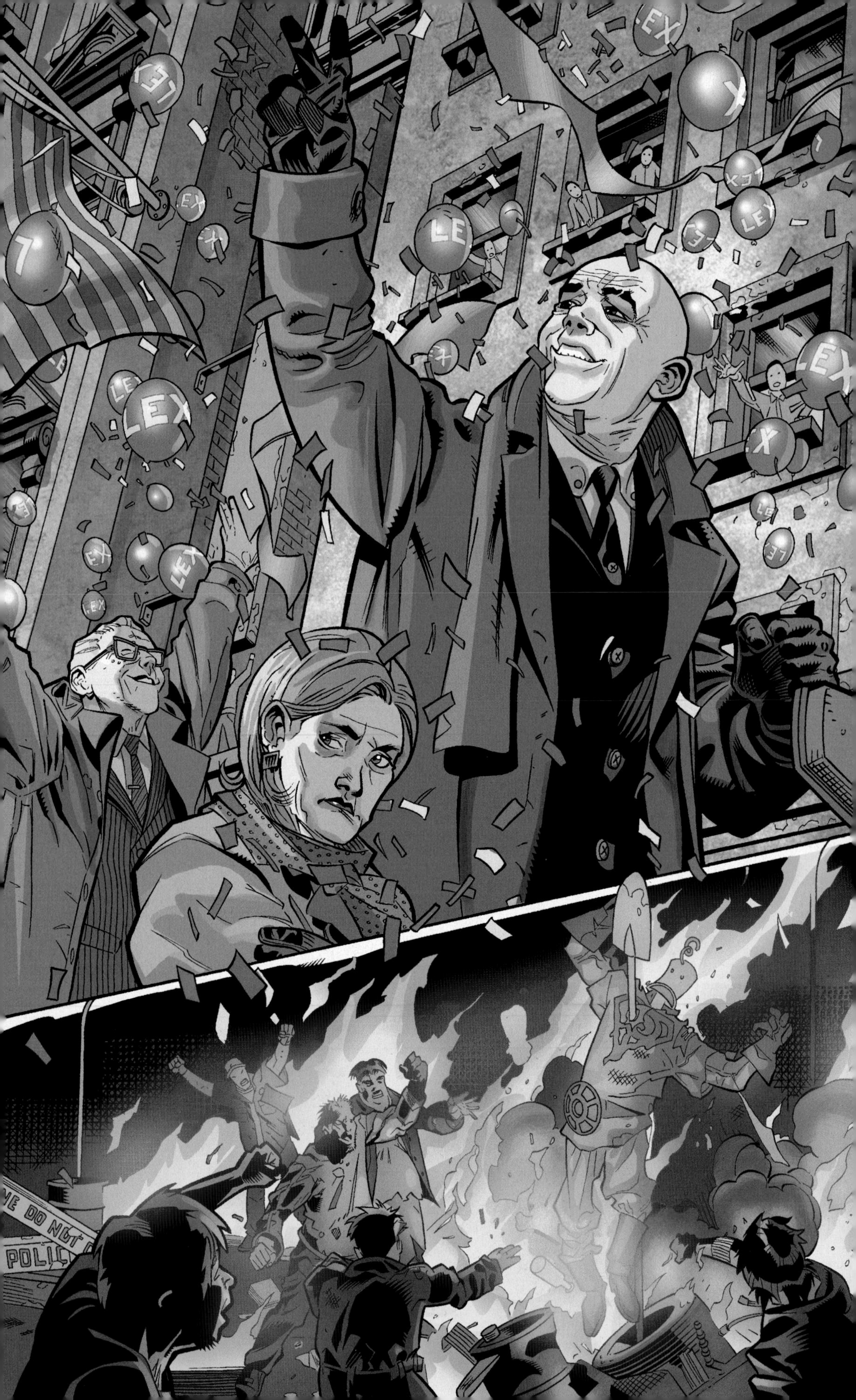
LEX
DO NOT

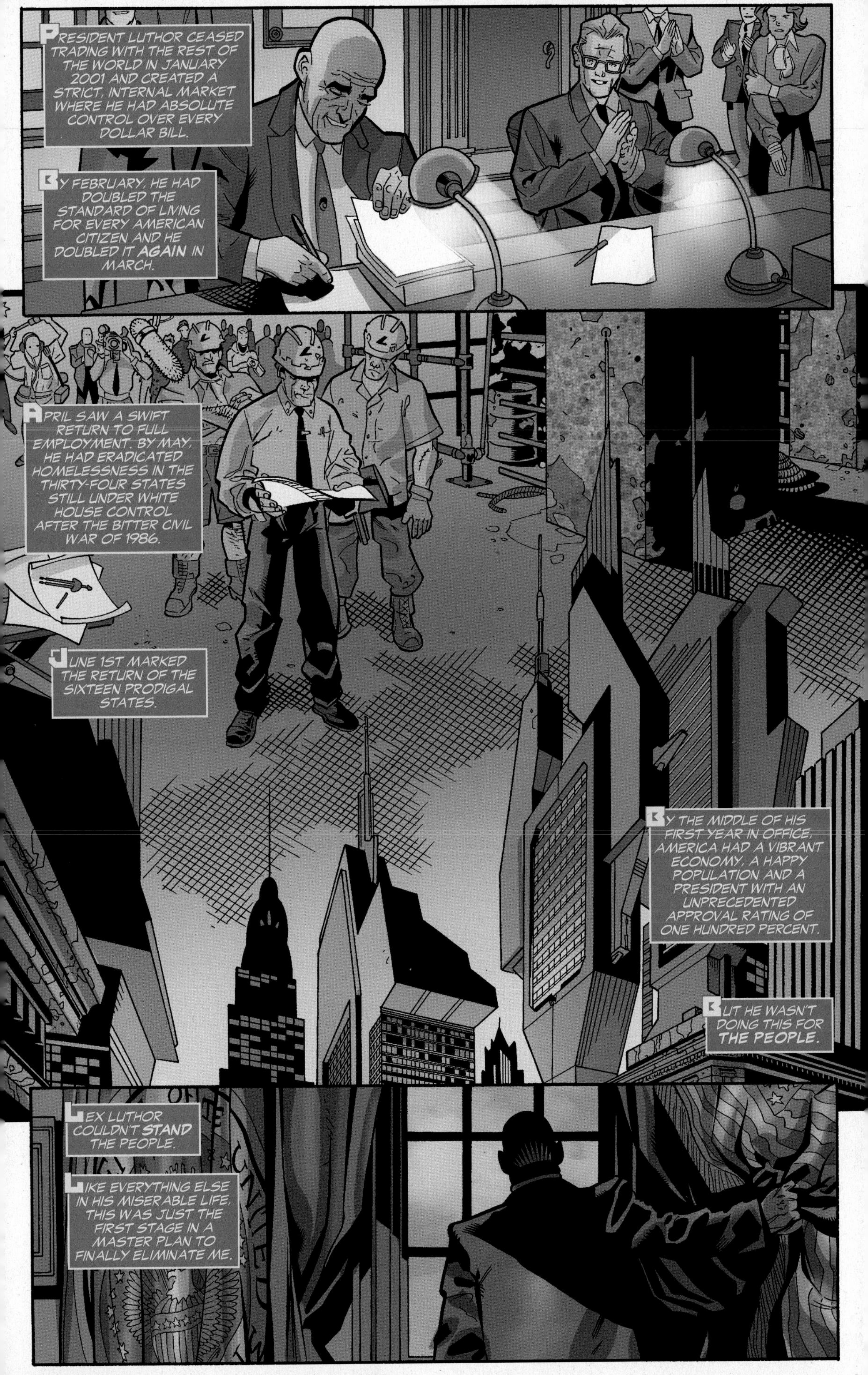
PRESIDENT LUTHOR CEASED TRADING WITH THE REST OF THE WORLD IN JANUARY 2001 AND CREATED A STRICT, INTERNAL MARKET WHERE HE HAD ABSOLUTE CONTROL OVER EVERY DOLLAR BILL.
BY FEBRUARY, HE HAD DOUBLED THE STANDARD OF LIVING FOR EVERY AMERICAN CITIZEN AND HE DOUBLED IT AGAIN IN MARCH.
APRIL SAW A SWIFT RETURN TO FULL EMPLOYMENT. BY MAY, HE HAD ERADICATED HOMELESSNESS IN THE THIRTY-FOUR STATES STILL UNDER WHITE HOUSE CONTROL AFTER THE BITTER CIVIL WAR OF 1986.
JUNE 1ST MARKED THE RETURN OF THE SIXTEEN PRODIGAL STATES.
BY THE MIDDLE OF HIS FIRST YEAR IN OFFICE, AMERICA HAD A VIBRANT ECONOMY, A HAPPY POPULATION AND A PRESIDENT WITH AN UNPRECEDENTED APPROVAL RATING OF ONE HUNDRED PERCENT.
BUT HE WASN'T DOING THIS FOR THE PEOPLE.
LEX LUTHOR COULDN'T STAND THE PEOPLE.
LIKE EVERYTHING ELSE IN HIS MISERABLE LIFE, THIS WAS JUST THE FIRST STAGE IN A MASTER PLAN TO FINALLY ELIMINATE ME.

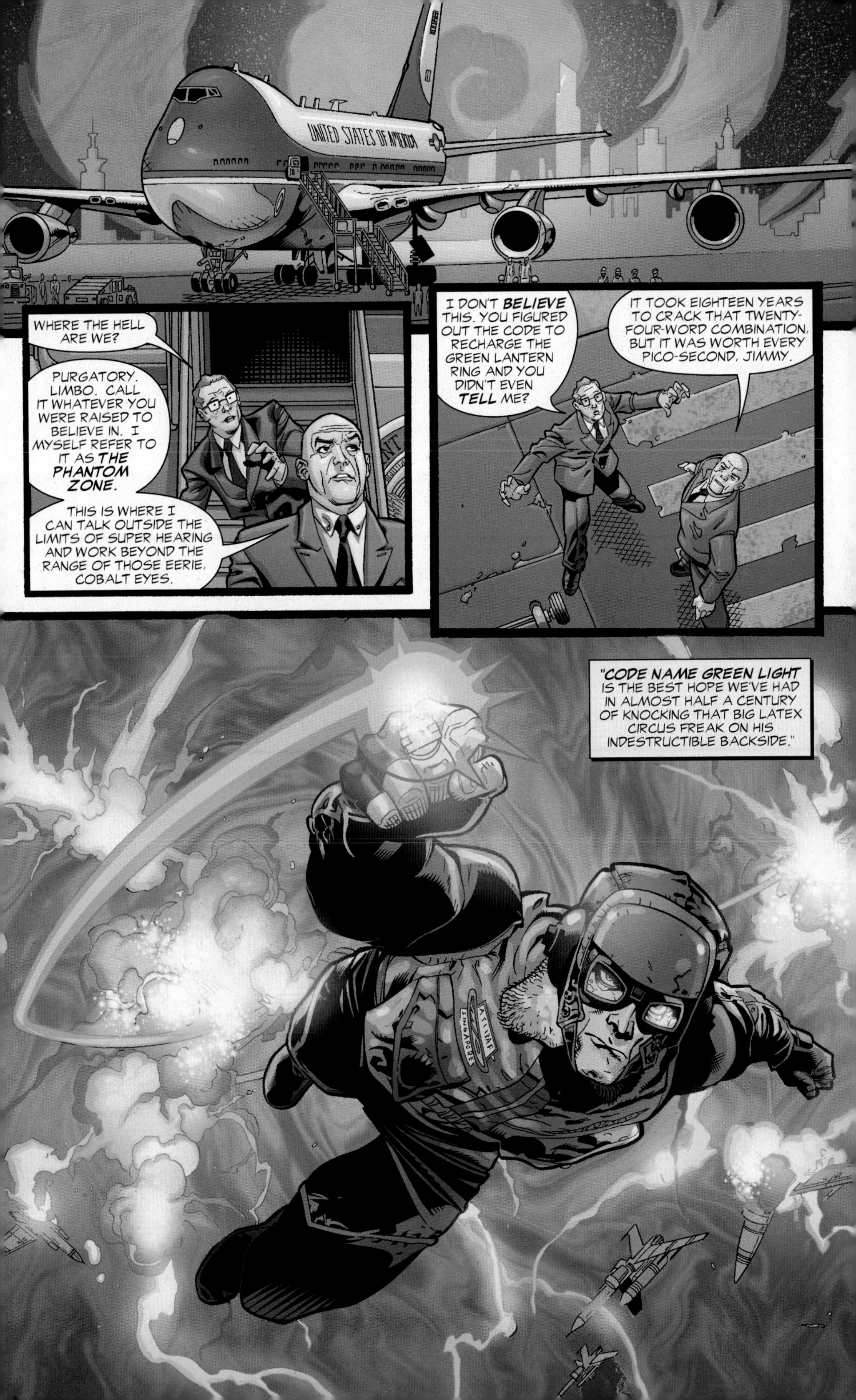
UNITED STATES OF AMERICA
WHERE THE HELL ARE WE?
PURGATORY. LIMBO. CALL IT WHATEVER YOU WERE RAISED TO BELIEVE IN. I MYSELF REFER TO IT AS **THE PHANTOM ZONE.**
THIS IS WHERE I CAN TALK OUTSIDE THE LIMITS OF SUPER HEARING AND WORK BEYOND THE RANGE OF THOSE EERIE, COBALT EYES.
I DON'T **BELIEVE** THIS. YOU FIGURED OUT THE CODE TO RECHARGE THE GREEN LANTERN RING AND YOU DIDN'T EVEN **TELL** ME?
IT TOOK EIGHTEEN YEARS TO CRACK THAT TWENTY-FOUR-WORD COMBINATION, BUT IT WAS WORTH EVERY PICO-SECOND, JIMMY.
"**CODE NAME GREEN LIGHT** IS THE BEST HOPE WE'VE HAD IN ALMOST HALF A CENTURY OF KNOCKING THAT BIG LATEX CIRCUS FREAK ON HIS INDESTRUCTIBLE BACKSIDE."

BECAUSE THE STUPID LITTLE TRINKET'S POWERED BY HONESTY AND WILLPOWER, I'M SORRY TO SAY. THAT SAID, IT DIDN'T TAKE LONG TO FIND *SOME* NOBLE IDIOT WITH THE NECESSARY QUALIFICATIONS.

DO YOU REMEMBER COLONEL *HAL JORDAN?*

THE NAME RINGS A BELL. WASN'T HE SOME KIND OF TEST PILOT?

ONLY ONE OF THE MOST DECORATED PILOTS IN MILITARY HISTORY--

"YOU PROBABLY READ THE STORY ABOUT HIS PLANE GOING DOWN IN MALAYSIA BACK IN 1983 WHEN WE WERE STILL TRYING TO DRIVE THE COMMUNISTS OUT OF THE SOUTH PACIFIC.

"HE WAS CAPTURED BY THE ENEMY, TORTURED EVERY DAY AND FED ON A DIET OF INSECTS UNTIL HE DROPPED TO A SKELETAL NINETY POUNDS.

SURRENDERING THAT LEVEL OF POWER TO SOMEONE ELSE SOUNDS REMARKABLY OUT OF CHARACTER FOR YOU, CHIEF. WHY DIDN'T YOU JUST HANG ONTO THE RING FOR YOURSELF?

"ANY NORMAL MAN WOULD HAVE LOST HIS MIND OR DIED IN THE CONDITIONS JORDAN ENDURED, BUT HE LASTED *FOUR YEARS* LIKE THIS AND IT WAS ALL THANKS TO HIS INCREDIBLE WILLPOWER.

WHAT DO YOU MEAN?

BASICALLY, HE FILLED HIS AGONIZINGLY LONG DAYS BY BUILDING A VIRTUAL CONCENTRATION CAMP IN HIS HEAD FOR THE COMMUNISTS WHO WERE PERSECUTING HIM.

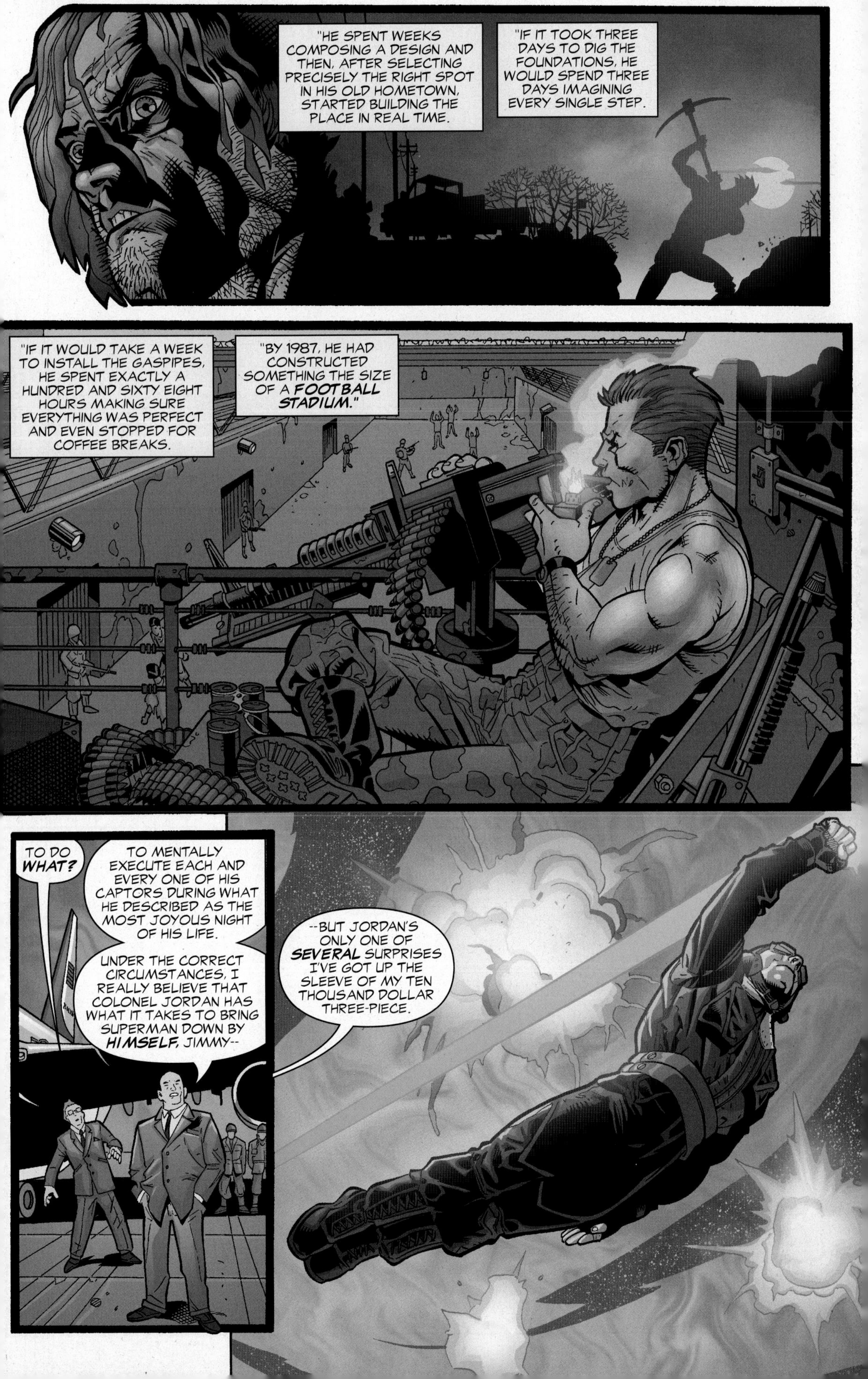
"HE SPENT WEEKS COMPOSING A DESIGN AND THEN, AFTER SELECTING PRECISELY THE RIGHT SPOT IN HIS OLD HOMETOWN, STARTED BUILDING THE PLACE IN REAL TIME.
"IF IT TOOK THREE DAYS TO DIG THE FOUNDATIONS, HE WOULD SPEND THREE DAYS IMAGINING EVERY SINGLE STEP.
"IF IT WOULD TAKE A WEEK TO INSTALL THE GASPIPES, HE SPENT EXACTLY A HUNDRED AND SIXTY EIGHT HOURS MAKING SURE EVERYTHING WAS PERFECT AND EVEN STOPPED FOR COFFEE BREAKS.
"BY 1987, HE HAD CONSTRUCTED SOMETHING THE SIZE OF A **FOOTBALL STADIUM**."
TO DO **WHAT?**
TO MENTALLY EXECUTE EACH AND EVERY ONE OF HIS CAPTORS DURING WHAT HE DESCRIBED AS THE MOST JOYOUS NIGHT OF HIS LIFE.
UNDER THE CORRECT CIRCUMSTANCES, I REALLY BELIEVE THAT COLONEL JORDAN HAS WHAT IT TAKES TO BRING SUPERMAN DOWN BY **HIMSELF**, JIMMY--
--BUT JORDAN'S ONLY ONE OF **SEVERAL** SURPRISES I'VE GOT UP THE SLEEVE OF MY TEN THOUSAND DOLLAR THREE-PIECE.

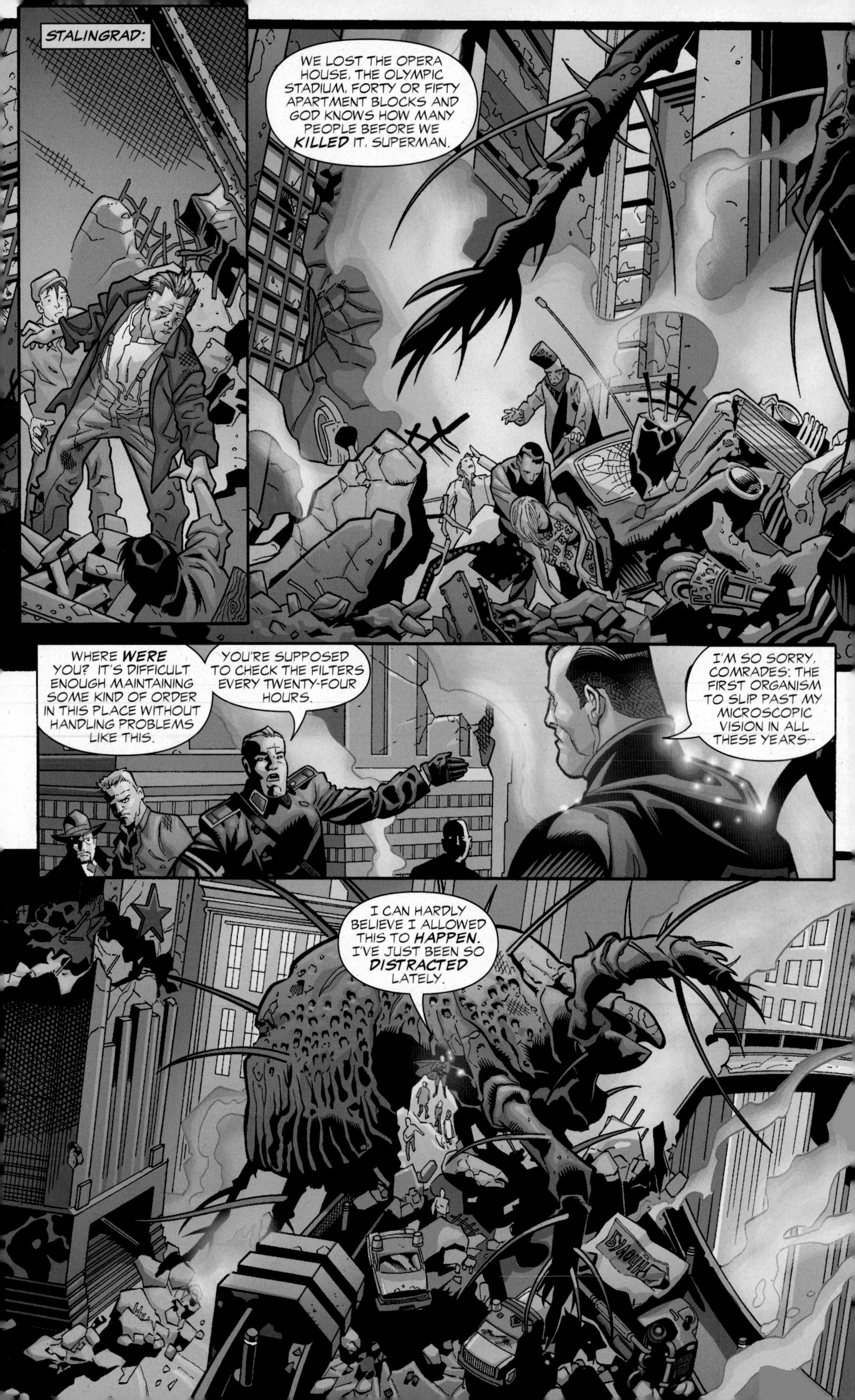
STALINGRAD:
WE LOST THE OPERA HOUSE, THE OLYMPIC STADIUM, FORTY OR FIFTY APARTMENT BLOCKS AND GOD KNOWS HOW MANY PEOPLE BEFORE WE KILLED IT, SUPERMAN.
WHERE WERE YOU? IT'S DIFFICULT ENOUGH MAINTAINING SOME KIND OF ORDER IN THIS PLACE WITHOUT HANDLING PROBLEMS LIKE THIS.
YOU'RE SUPPOSED TO CHECK THE FILTERS EVERY TWENTY-FOUR HOURS.
I'M SO SORRY, COMRADES: THE FIRST ORGANISM TO SLIP PAST MY MICROSCOPIC VISION IN ALL THESE YEARS--
I CAN HARDLY BELIEVE I ALLOWED THIS TO HAPPEN. I'VE JUST BEEN SO DISTRACTED LATELY.

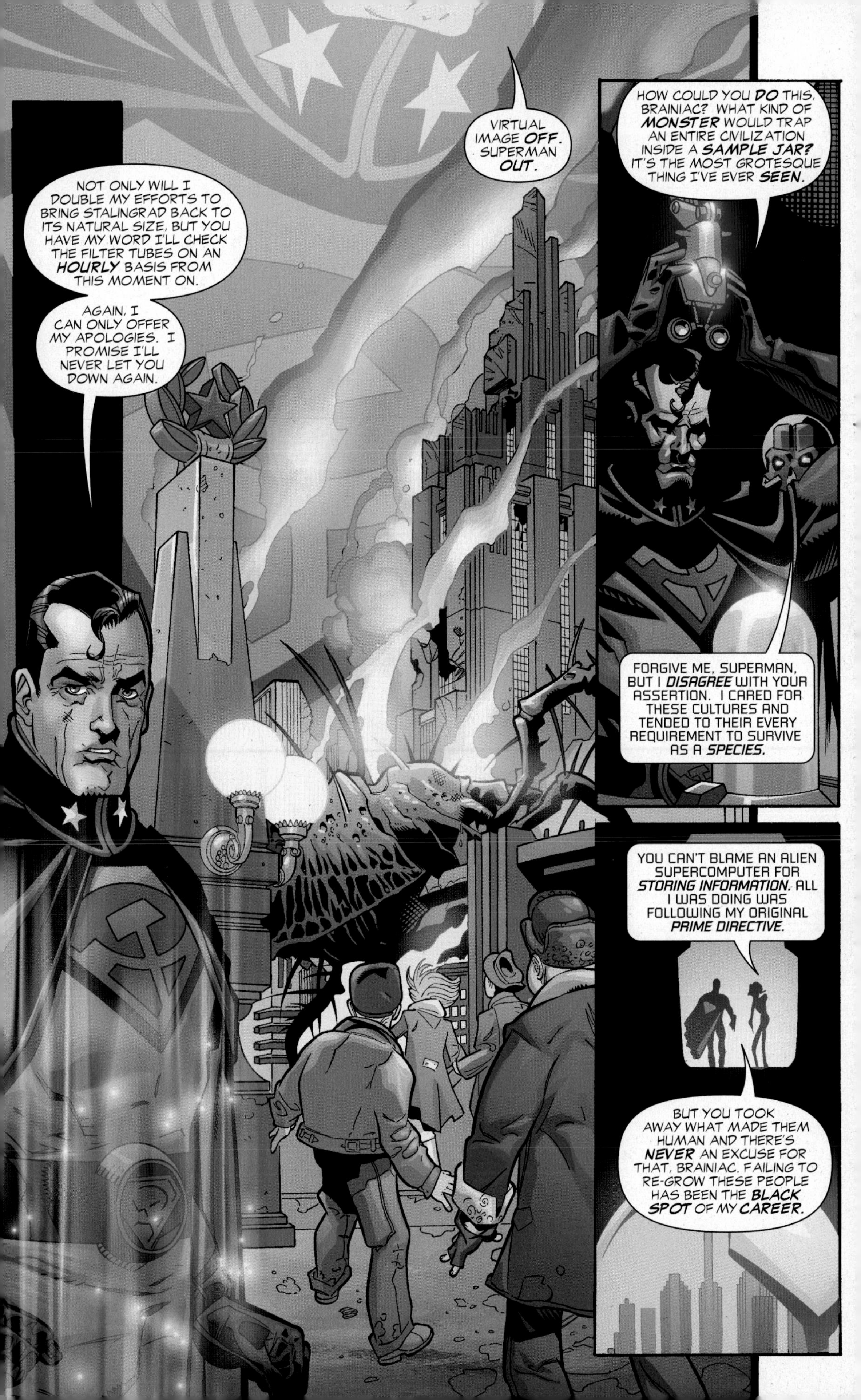

NOT ONLY WILL I DOUBLE MY EFFORTS TO BRING STALINGRAD BACK TO ITS NATURAL SIZE, BUT YOU HAVE MY WORD I'LL CHECK THE FILTER TUBES ON AN HOURLY BASIS FROM THIS MOMENT ON.
AGAIN, I CAN ONLY OFFER MY APOLOGIES. I PROMISE I'LL NEVER LET YOU DOWN AGAIN.
VIRTUAL IMAGE OFF. SUPERMAN OUT.
HOW COULD YOU DO THIS, BRAINIAC? WHAT KIND OF MONSTER WOULD TRAP AN ENTIRE CIVILIZATION INSIDE A SAMPLE JAR? IT'S THE MOST GROTESQUE THING I'VE EVER SEEN.
FORGIVE ME, SUPERMAN, BUT I DISAGREE WITH YOUR ASSERTION. I CARED FOR THESE CULTURES AND TENDED TO THEIR EVERY REQUIREMENT TO SURVIVE AS A SPECIES.
YOU CAN'T BLAME AN ALIEN SUPERCOMPUTER FOR STORING INFORMATION. ALL I WAS DOING WAS FOLLOWING MY ORIGINAL PRIME DIRECTIVE.
BUT YOU TOOK AWAY WHAT MADE THEM HUMAN AND THERE'S NEVER AN EXCUSE FOR THAT, BRAINIAC. FAILING TO RE-GROW THESE PEOPLE HAS BEEN THE BLACK SPOT OF MY CAREER.

PERHAPS, BUT OUR BIGGEST CONCERN AT THE MOMENT SHOULD BE EVENTS IN NORTH AMERICA. THIS IS NO LONGER A CASE OF THE ONE CORNER OF THE WORLD WHERE THINGS DIDN'T GO TO PLAN.

THE NEWLY UNITED STATES NOW POSE A THREAT TO EVERYTHING YOU HAVE EVER ACCOMPLISHED, SUPERMAN.

THIS IS LUTHOR'S ULTIMATE DEATH TRAP. HE'S SPENT ALMOST TWO DECADES FORMULATING THIS SINGLE ASSAULT, AND MY EVIDENCE SUGGESTS THAT THINGS WILL BE COMING TO A HEAD SHORTLY.

ANY RECOMMEN-DATIONS?

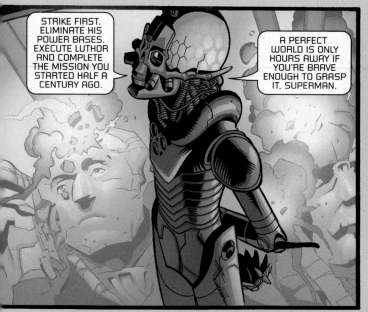

STRIKE FIRST. ELIMINATE HIS POWER BASES. EXECUTE LUTHOR AND COMPLETE THE MISSION YOU STARTED HALF A CENTURY AGO.

A PERFECT WORLD IS ONLY HOURS AWAY IF YOU'RE BRAVE ENOUGH TO GRASP IT, SUPERMAN.

BUT I DON'T *WANT* TO INVADE THEM, BRAINIAC. EVERYTHING I'VE ACCOMPLISHED SO FAR HAS BEEN DONE BY WINNING THE ARGUMENT.

I COULD HAVE HAD MY UTOPIA OVERNIGHT IF I'D HAMMERED THE WORLD INTO SUBMISSION WITH MY FISTS.

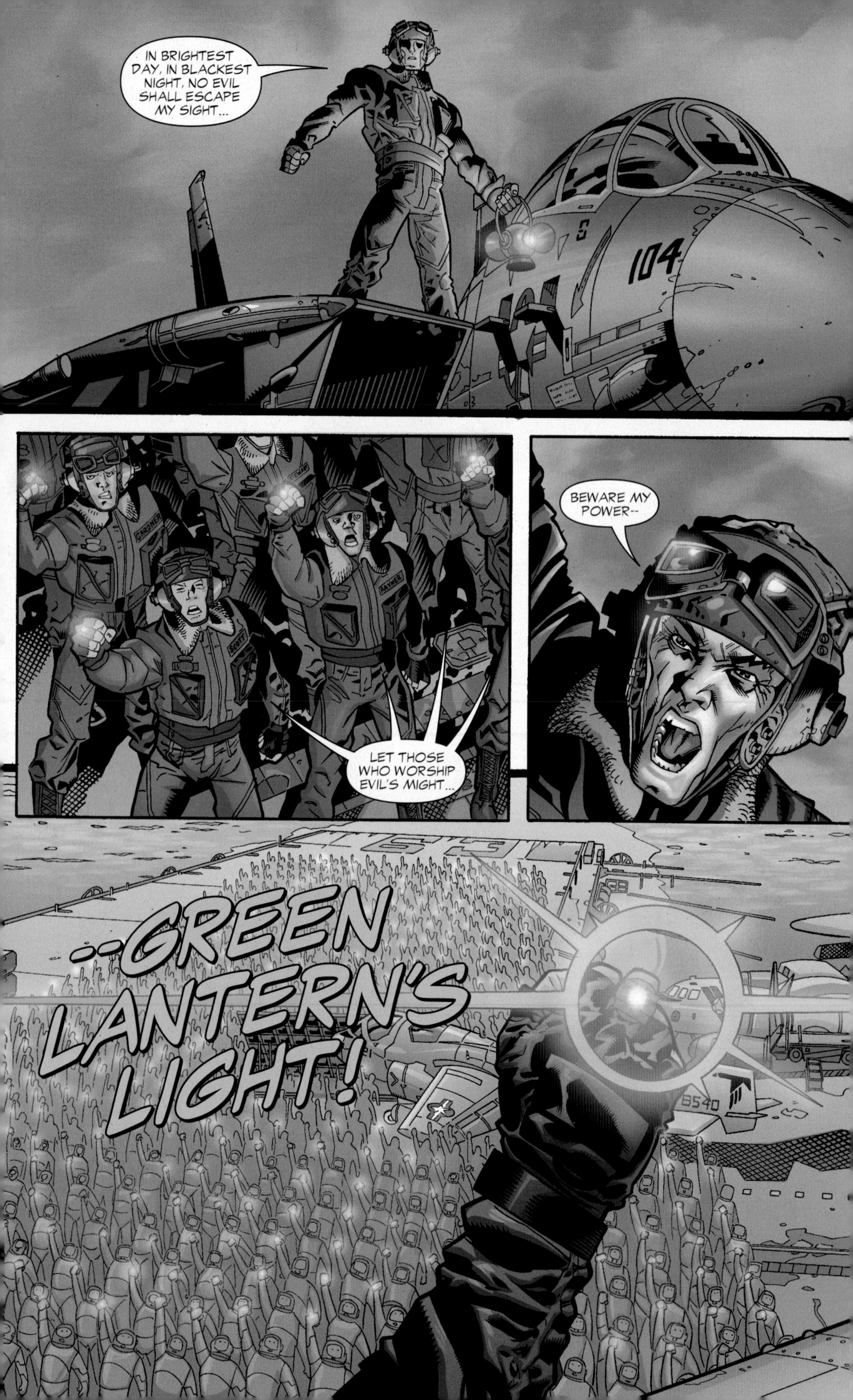
IN BRIGHTEST DAY, IN BLACKEST NIGHT, NO EVIL SHALL ESCAPE MY SIGHT...
104
LET THOSE WHO WORSHIP EVIL'S MIGHT...
BEWARE MY POWER--
--GREEN LANTERN'S LIGHT!

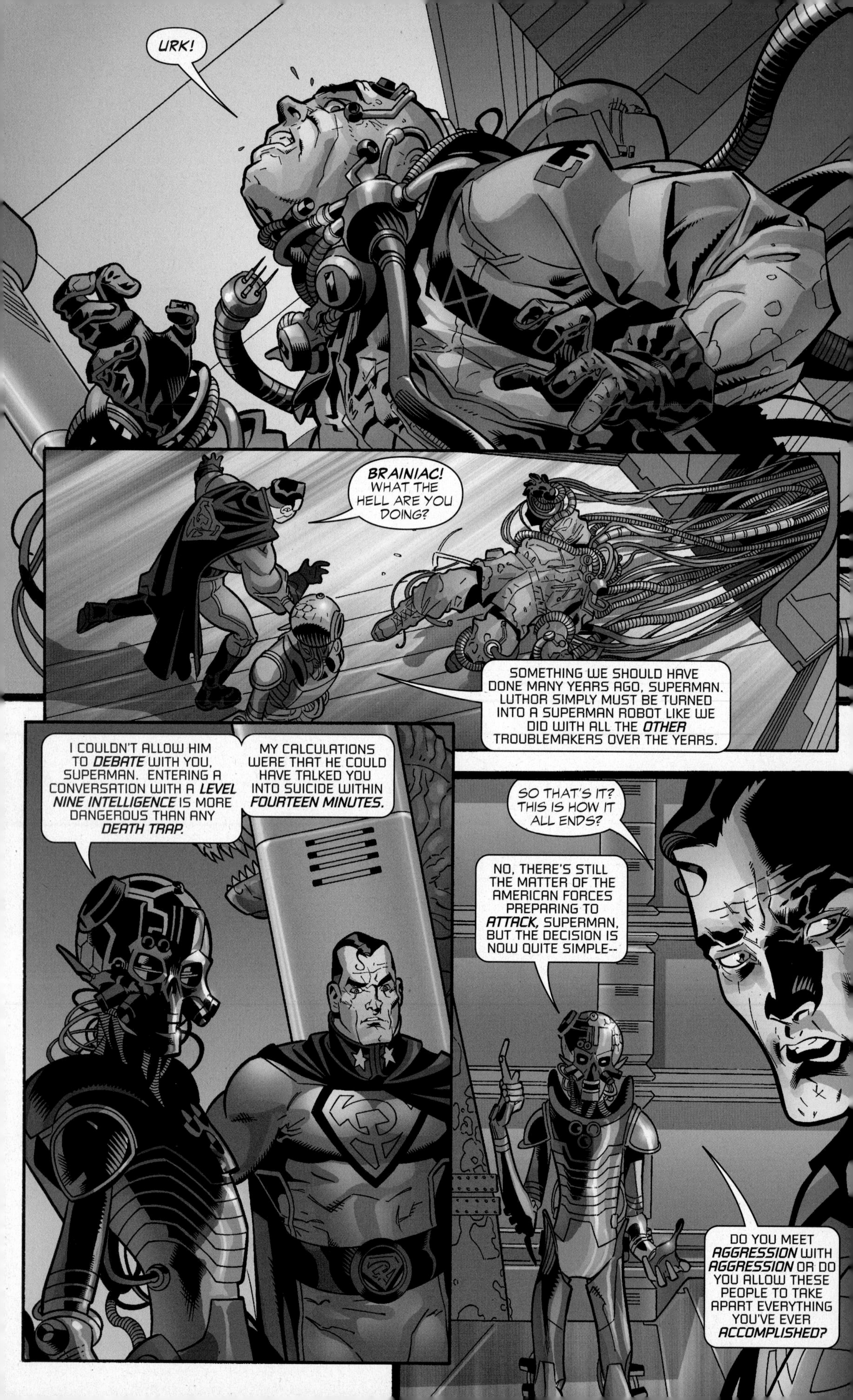
URK!
BRAINIAC! WHAT THE HELL ARE YOU DOING?
SOMETHING WE SHOULD HAVE DONE MANY YEARS AGO, SUPERMAN. LUTHOR SIMPLY MUST BE TURNED INTO A SUPERMAN ROBOT LIKE WE DID WITH ALL THE OTHER TROUBLEMAKERS OVER THE YEARS.
I COULDN'T ALLOW HIM TO DEBATE WITH YOU, SUPERMAN. ENTERING A CONVERSATION WITH A LEVEL NINE INTELLIGENCE IS MORE DANGEROUS THAN ANY DEATH TRAP.
MY CALCULATIONS WERE THAT HE COULD HAVE TALKED YOU INTO SUICIDE WITHIN FOURTEEN MINUTES.
SO THAT'S IT? THIS IS HOW IT ALL ENDS?
NO, THERE'S STILL THE MATTER OF THE AMERICAN FORCES PREPARING TO ATTACK, SUPERMAN, BUT THE DECISION IS NOW QUITE SIMPLE--
DO YOU MEET AGGRESSION WITH AGGRESSION OR DO YOU ALLOW THESE PEOPLE TO TAKE APART EVERYTHING YOU'VE EVER ACCOMPLISHED?

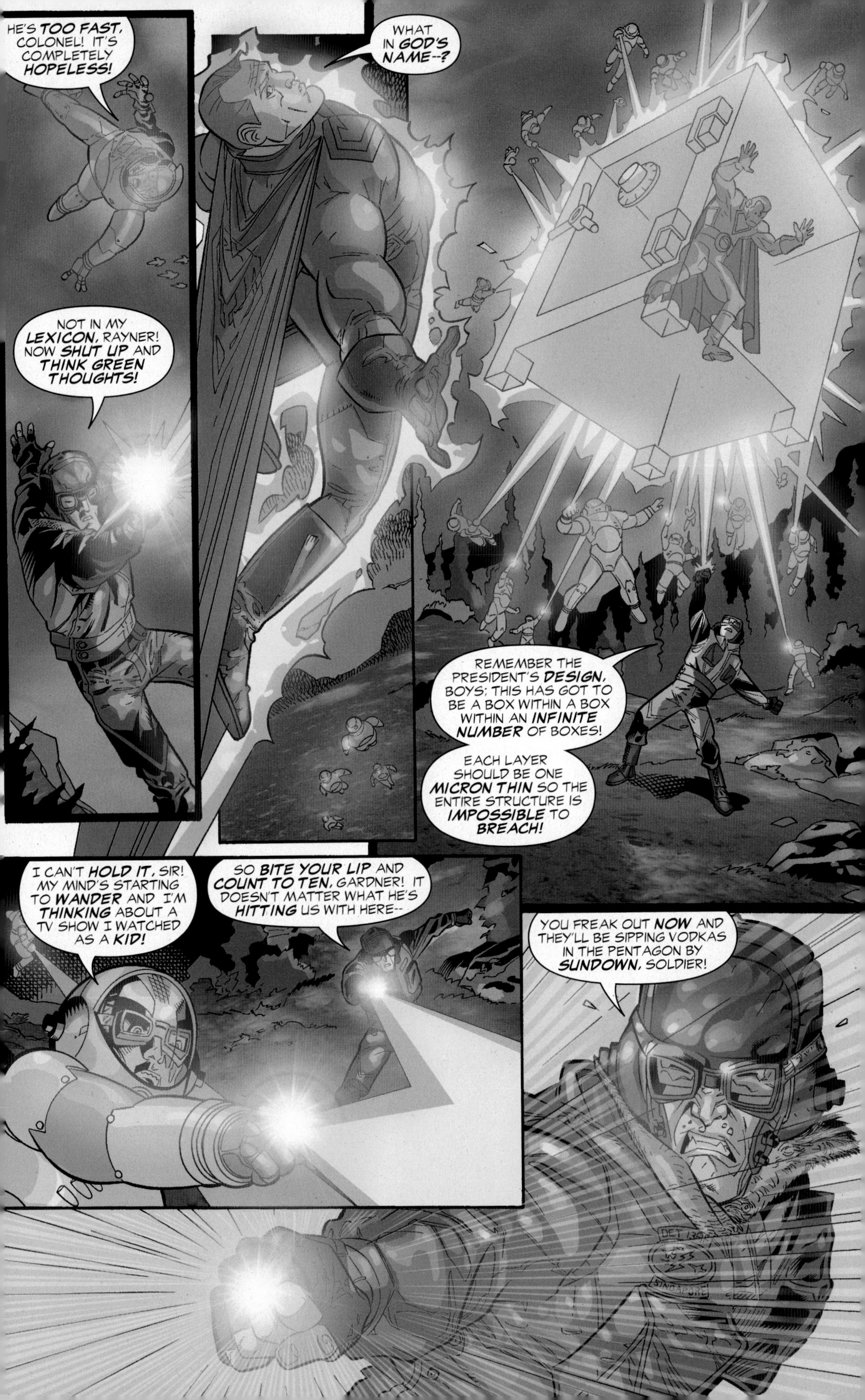

HE'S TOO FAST, COLONEL! IT'S COMPLETELY HOPELESS!
WHAT IN GOD'S NAME--?
NOT IN MY LEXICON, RAYNER! NOW SHUT UP AND THINK GREEN THOUGHTS!
REMEMBER THE PRESIDENT'S DESIGN, BOYS; THIS HAS GOT TO BE A BOX WITHIN A BOX WITHIN AN INFINITE NUMBER OF BOXES!
EACH LAYER SHOULD BE ONE MICRON THIN SO THE ENTIRE STRUCTURE IS IMPOSSIBLE TO BREACH!
I CAN'T HOLD IT, SIR! MY MIND'S STARTING TO WANDER AND I'M THINKING ABOUT A TV SHOW I WATCHED AS A KID!
SO BITE YOUR LIP AND COUNT TO TEN, GARDNER! IT DOESN'T MATTER WHAT HE'S HITTING US WITH HERE--
YOU FREAK OUT NOW AND THEY'LL BE SIPPING VODKAS IN THE PENTAGON BY SUNDOWN, SOLDIER!

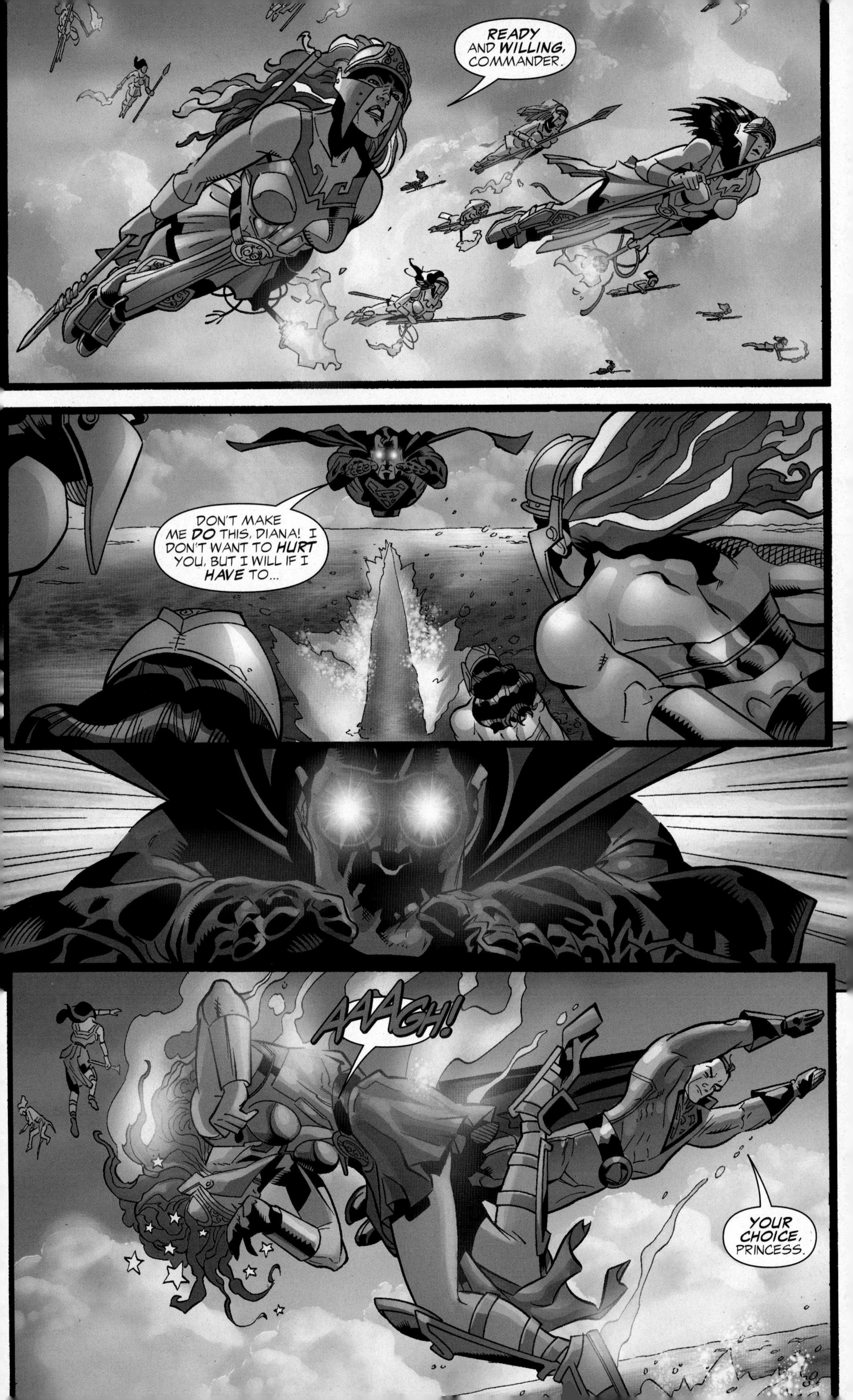
READY AND WILLING, COMMANDER.
DON'T MAKE ME DO THIS, DIANA! I DON'T WANT TO HURT YOU, BUT I WILL IF I HAVE TO...
AAAGH!
YOUR CHOICE, PRINCESS.

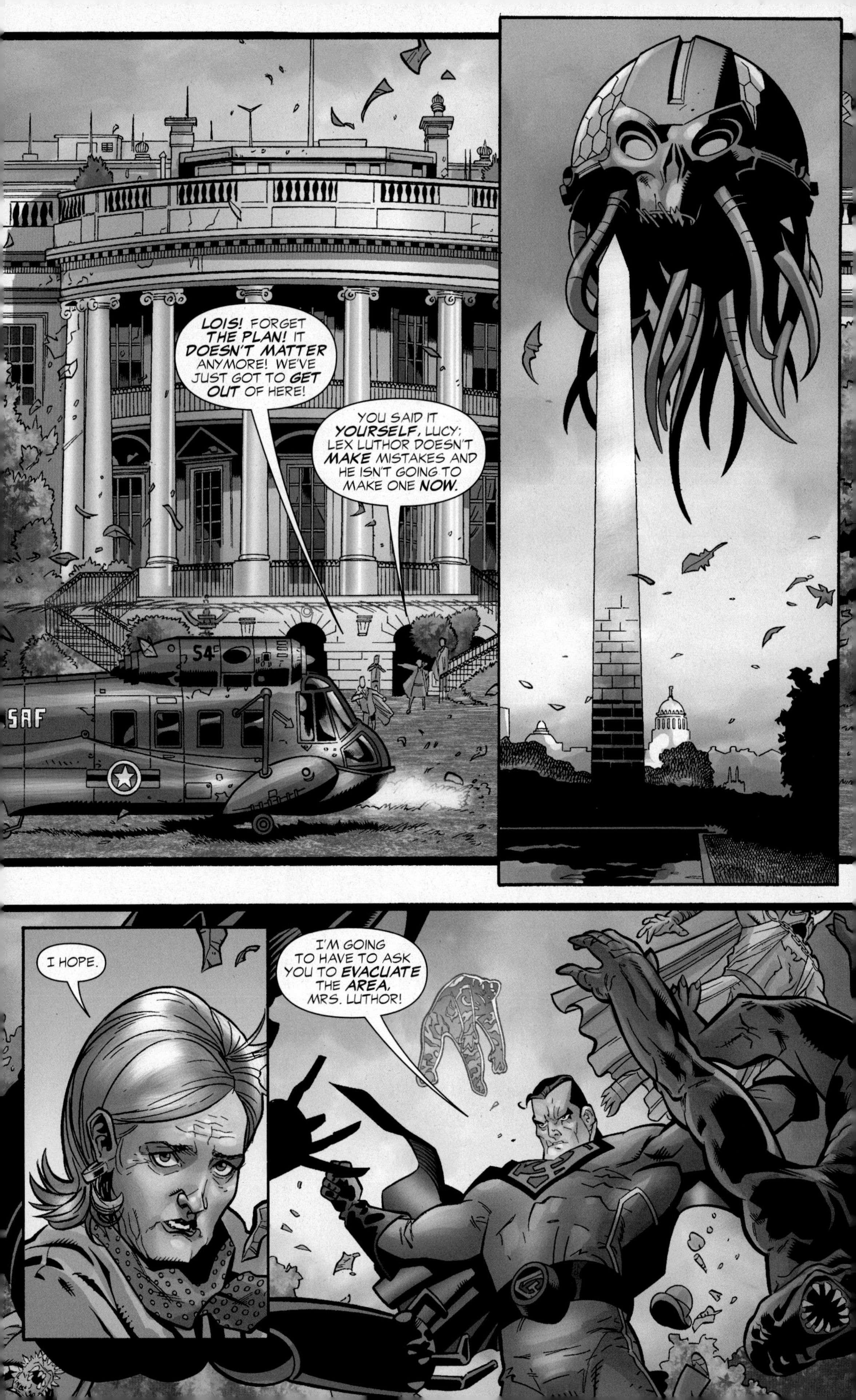
LOIS! FORGET THE PLAN! IT DOESN'T MATTER ANYMORE! WE'VE JUST GOT TO GET OUT OF HERE!
YOU SAID IT YOURSELF, LUCY; LEX LUTHOR DOESN'T MAKE MISTAKES AND HE ISN'T GOING TO MAKE ONE NOW.
I HOPE.
I'M GOING TO HAVE TO ASK YOU TO EVACUATE THE AREA, MRS. LUTHOR!

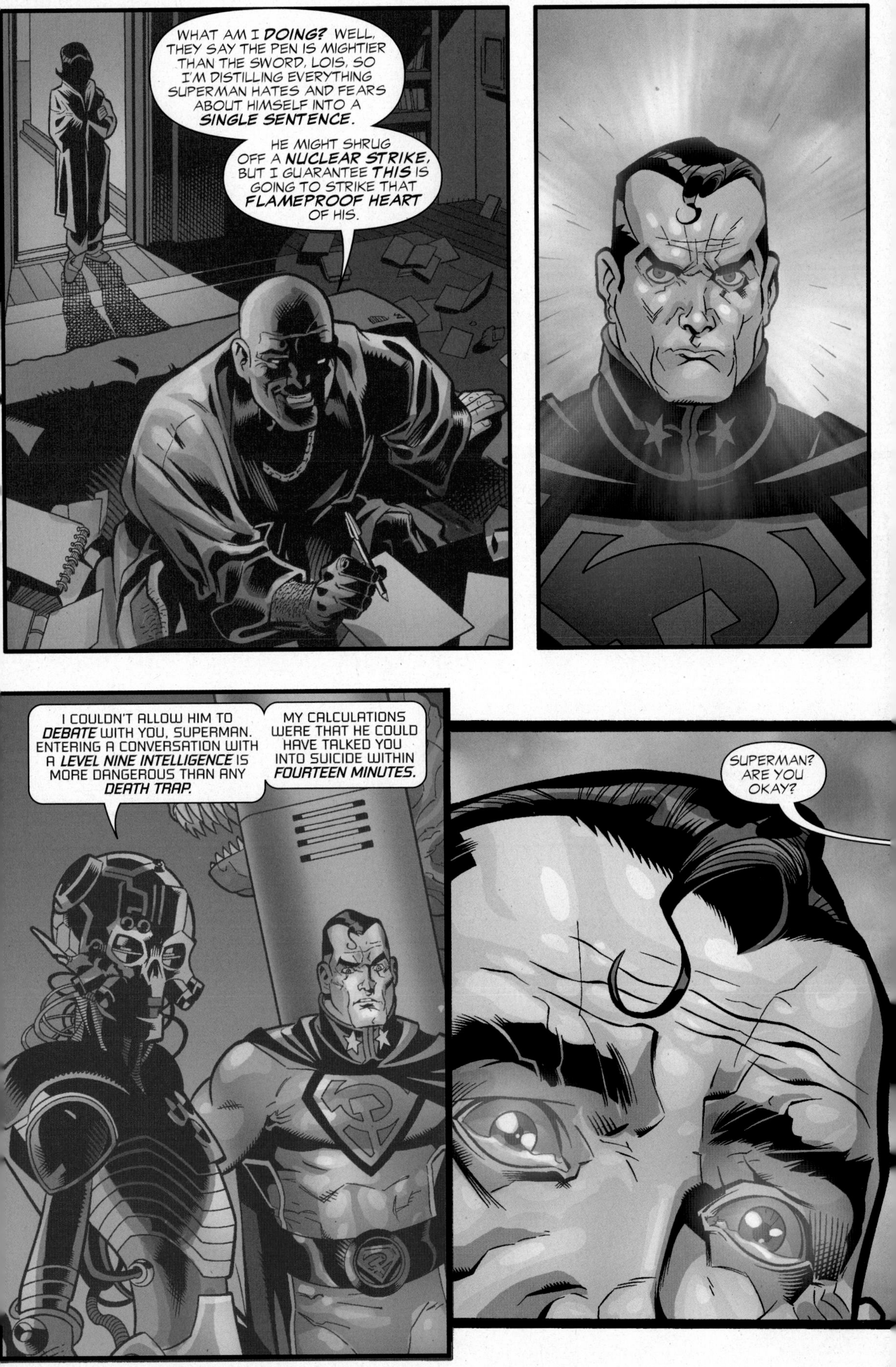
WHAT AM I DOING? WELL, THEY SAY THE PEN IS MIGHTIER THAN THE SWORD, LOIS, SO I'M DISTILLING EVERYTHING SUPERMAN HATES AND FEARS ABOUT HIMSELF INTO A SINGLE SENTENCE.
HE MIGHT SHRUG OFF A NUCLEAR STRIKE, BUT I GUARANTEE THIS IS GOING TO STRIKE THAT FLAMEPROOF HEART OF HIS.
I COULDN'T ALLOW HIM TO DEBATE WITH YOU, SUPERMAN. ENTERING A CONVERSATION WITH A LEVEL NINE INTELLIGENCE IS MORE DANGEROUS THAN ANY DEATH TRAP.
MY CALCULATIONS WERE THAT HE COULD HAVE TALKED YOU INTO SUICIDE WITHIN FOURTEEN MINUTES.
SUPERMAN? ARE YOU OKAY?

SUPERMAN GONE. BRAINIAC GONE. THE WORLD READY TO EMBRACE LUTHORISM EVEN MORE READILY THAN EVER BEFORE.

ONE COULD ALMOST BE FORGIVEN FOR THINKING THAT THIS HAD ALL BEEN WORKED OUT TO THE TENTH DECIMAL POINT FORTY YEARS AGO, EH?

CHECKMATE, SUPERMAN.

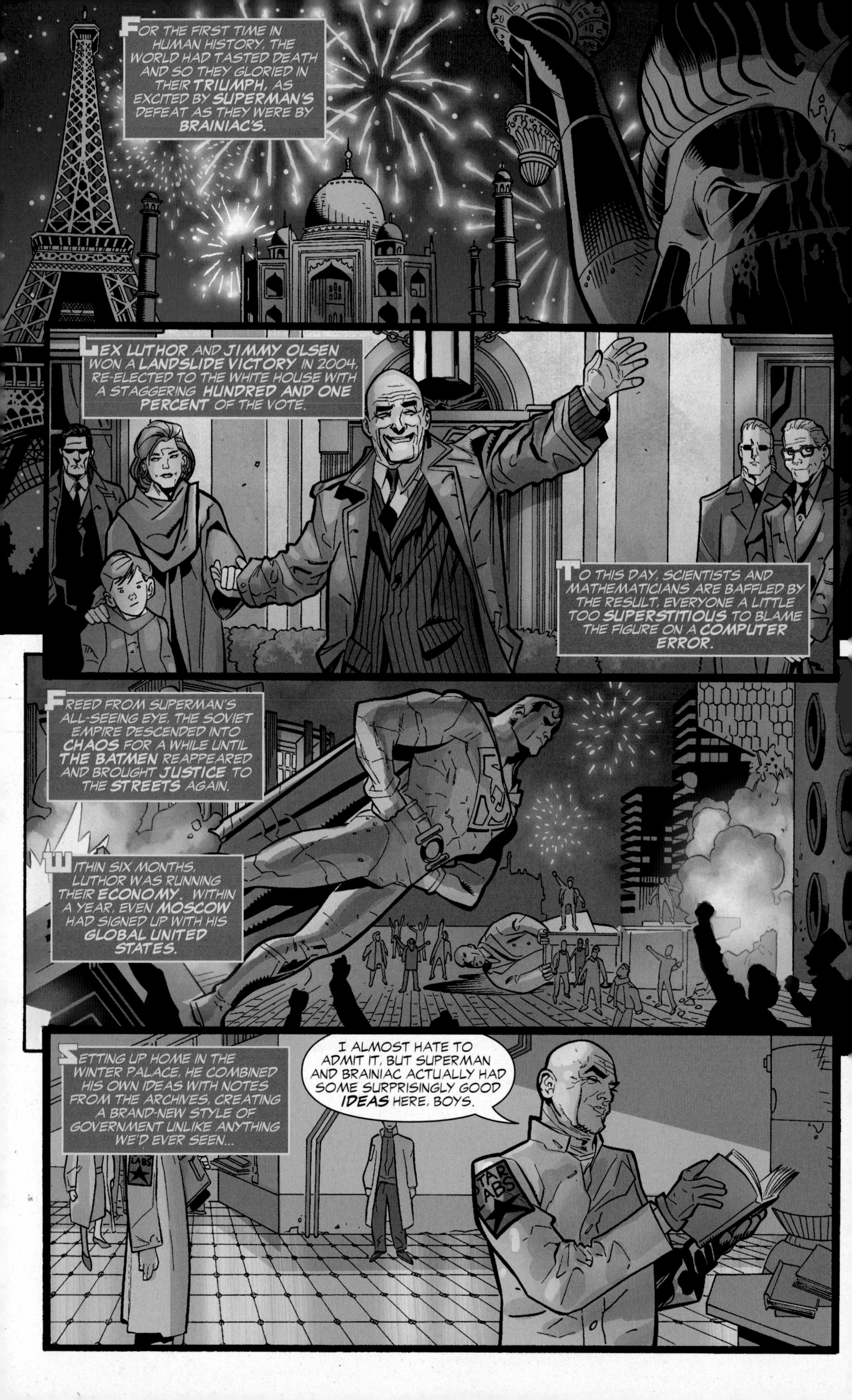
FOR THE FIRST TIME IN HUMAN HISTORY, THE WORLD HAD TASTED DEATH AND SO THEY GLORIED IN THEIR TRIUMPH, AS EXCITED BY SUPERMAN'S DEFEAT AS THEY WERE BY BRAINIAC'S.
LEX LUTHOR AND JIMMY OLSEN WON A LANDSLIDE VICTORY IN 2004, RE-ELECTED TO THE WHITE HOUSE WITH A STAGGERING HUNDRED AND ONE PERCENT OF THE VOTE.
TO THIS DAY, SCIENTISTS AND MATHEMATICIANS ARE BAFFLED BY THE RESULT, EVERYONE A LITTLE TOO SUPERSTITIOUS TO BLAME THE FIGURE ON A COMPUTER ERROR.
FREED FROM SUPERMAN'S ALL-SEEING EYE, THE SOVIET EMPIRE DESCENDED INTO CHAOS FOR A WHILE UNTIL THE BATMEN REAPPEARED AND BROUGHT JUSTICE TO THE STREETS AGAIN.
WITHIN SIX MONTHS, LUTHOR WAS RUNNING THEIR ECONOMY. WITHIN A YEAR, EVEN MOSCOW HAD SIGNED UP WITH HIS GLOBAL UNITED STATES.
SETTING UP HOME IN THE WINTER PALACE, HE COMBINED HIS OWN IDEAS WITH NOTES FROM THE ARCHIVES, CREATING A BRAND-NEW STYLE OF GOVERNMENT UNLIKE ANYTHING WE'D EVER SEEN...
I ALMOST HATE TO ADMIT IT, BUT SUPERMAN AND BRAINIAC ACTUALLY HAD SOME SURPRISINGLY GOOD IDEAS HERE, BOYS.
STAR LABS

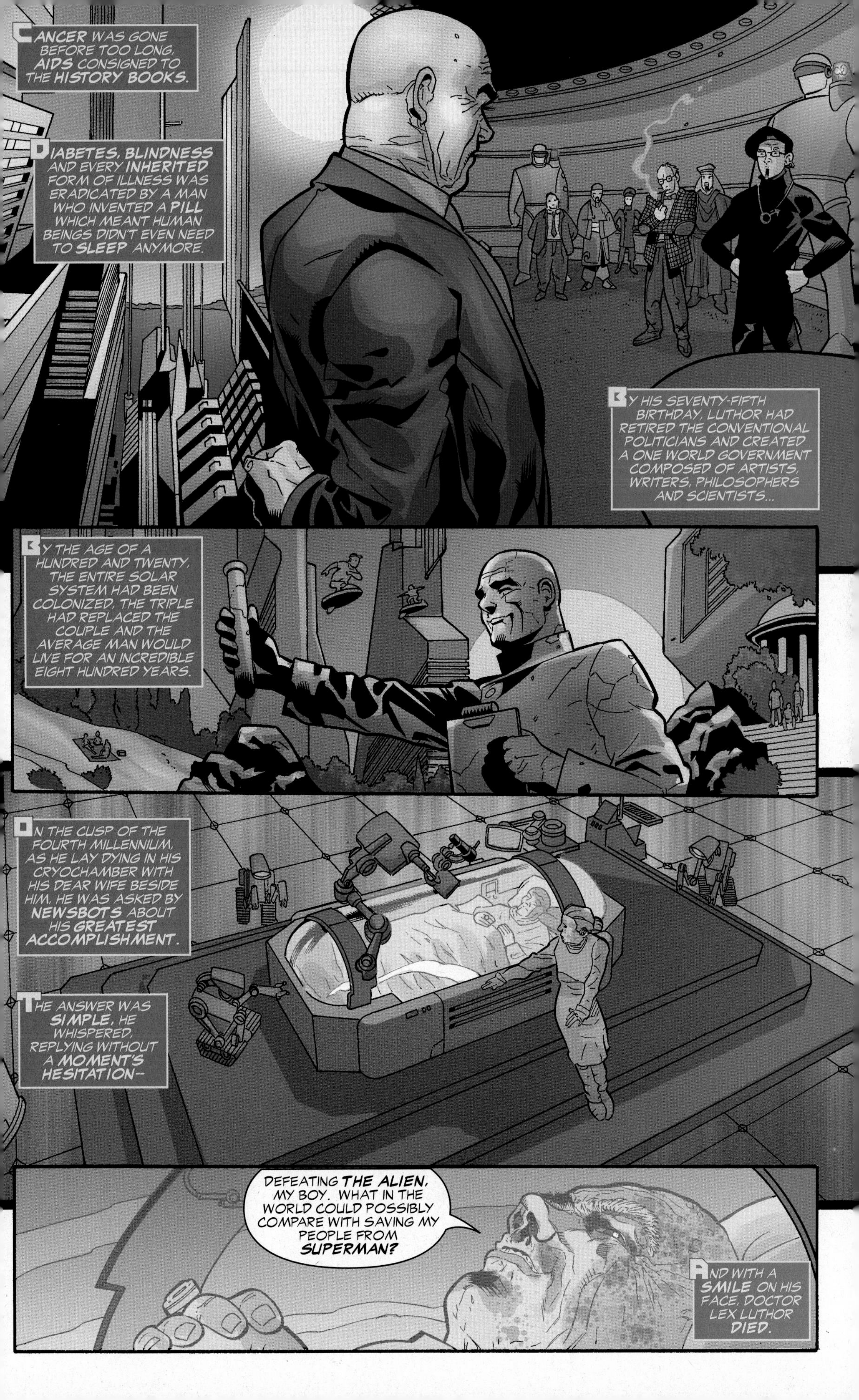
CANCER WAS GONE BEFORE TOO LONG, AIDS CONSIGNED TO THE HISTORY BOOKS.
DIABETES, BLINDNESS AND EVERY INHERITED FORM OF ILLNESS WAS ERADICATED BY A MAN WHO INVENTED A PILL WHICH MEANT HUMAN BEINGS DIDN'T EVEN NEED TO SLEEP ANYMORE.
BY HIS SEVENTY-FIFTH BIRTHDAY, LUTHOR HAD RETIRED THE CONVENTIONAL POLITICIANS AND CREATED A ONE WORLD GOVERNMENT COMPOSED OF ARTISTS, WRITERS, PHILOSOPHERS AND SCIENTISTS...
BY THE AGE OF A HUNDRED AND TWENTY, THE ENTIRE SOLAR SYSTEM HAD BEEN COLONIZED, THE TRIPLE HAD REPLACED THE COUPLE AND THE AVERAGE MAN WOULD LIVE FOR AN INCREDIBLE EIGHT HUNDRED YEARS.
ON THE CUSP OF THE FOURTH MILLENNIUM, AS HE LAY DYING IN HIS CRYOCHAMBER WITH HIS DEAR WIFE BESIDE HIM, HE WAS ASKED BY NEWSBOTS ABOUT HIS GREATEST ACCOMPLISHMENT.
THE ANSWER WAS SIMPLE, HE WHISPERED, REPLYING WITHOUT A MOMENT'S HESITATION--
DEFEATING THE ALIEN, MY BOY. WHAT IN THE WORLD COULD POSSIBLY COMPARE WITH SAVING MY PEOPLE FROM SUPERMAN?
AND WITH A SMILE ON HIS FACE, DOCTOR LEX LUTHOR DIED.

METROPOLIS WAS WHERE HE WAS BORN AND WHERE HE ASKED TO BE LAID TO REST IN A **GEOMETRIC MAZE** OF HIS OWN DESIGN.

THE CITY WAS RENAMED **LEXOR** OVER FIVE HUNDRED YEARS EARLIER, BUT YOU COULD STILL RECOGNIZE SOME OF THE OLD LANDMARKS LIKE THE **METROPOLIS TOWERS** AND THE **DAILY PLANET** BUILDING.

LUTHOR

I THOUGHT FOR A MOMENT THAT HIS WIDOW MIGHT RECOGNIZE ME AT THE **FUNERAL**. WOULD SHE SEE THROUGH THE GLASSES AND THE **DARK BLUE SUIT** OF THE **DISGUISE** I'D CREATED?

LOIS LANE WAS, AFTER ALL, A **PULITZER PRIZE-WINNING JOURNALIST**.

WHAT'S UP, MOM? ARE YOU **OKAY?**

FINE, ALBERT. **ABSOLUTELY FINE**. I JUST HAD THE STRANGEST SENSE OF **DEJA VU** FOR A MOMENT.

BUT, MUCH TO MY SURPRISE, SHE **DIDN'T**.

NOT EVEN FOR A **SECOND**.

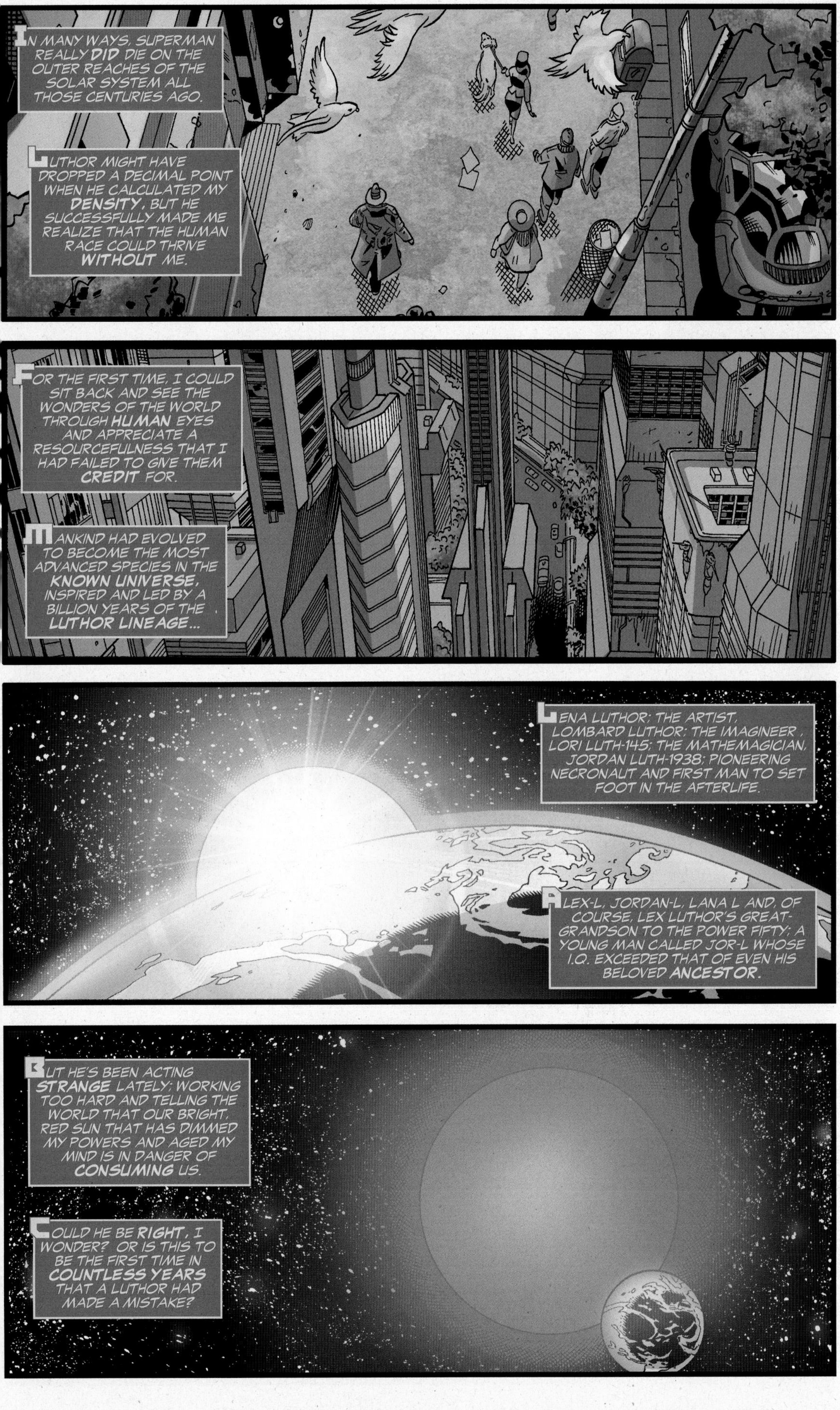
IN MANY WAYS, SUPERMAN REALLY DID DIE ON THE OUTER REACHES OF THE SOLAR SYSTEM ALL THOSE CENTURIES AGO.
LUTHOR MIGHT HAVE DROPPED A DECIMAL POINT WHEN HE CALCULATED MY DENSITY, BUT HE SUCCESSFULLY MADE ME REALIZE THAT THE HUMAN RACE COULD THRIVE WITHOUT ME.
FOR THE FIRST TIME, I COULD SIT BACK AND SEE THE WONDERS OF THE WORLD THROUGH HUMAN EYES AND APPRECIATE A RESOURCEFULNESS THAT I HAD FAILED TO GIVE THEM CREDIT FOR.
MANKIND HAD EVOLVED TO BECOME THE MOST ADVANCED SPECIES IN THE KNOWN UNIVERSE, INSPIRED AND LED BY A BILLION YEARS OF THE LUTHOR LINEAGE...
LENA LUTHOR: THE ARTIST, LOMBARD LUTHOR: THE IMAGINEER, LORI LUTH-145; THE MATHEMAGICIAN, JORDAN LUTH-1938; PIONEERING NECRONAUT AND FIRST MAN TO SET FOOT IN THE AFTERLIFE.
ALEX-L, JORDAN-L, LANA L AND, OF COURSE, LEX LUTHOR'S GREAT-GRANDSON TO THE POWER FIFTY; A YOUNG MAN CALLED JOR-L WHOSE I.Q. EXCEEDED THAT OF EVEN HIS BELOVED ANCESTOR.
BUT HE'S BEEN ACTING STRANGE LATELY; WORKING TOO HARD AND TELLING THE WORLD THAT OUR BRIGHT, RED SUN THAT HAS DIMMED MY POWERS AND AGED MY MIND IS IN DANGER OF CONSUMING US.
COULD HE BE RIGHT, I WONDER? OR IS THIS TO BE THE FIRST TIME IN COUNTLESS YEARS THAT A LUTHOR HAD MADE A MISTAKE?

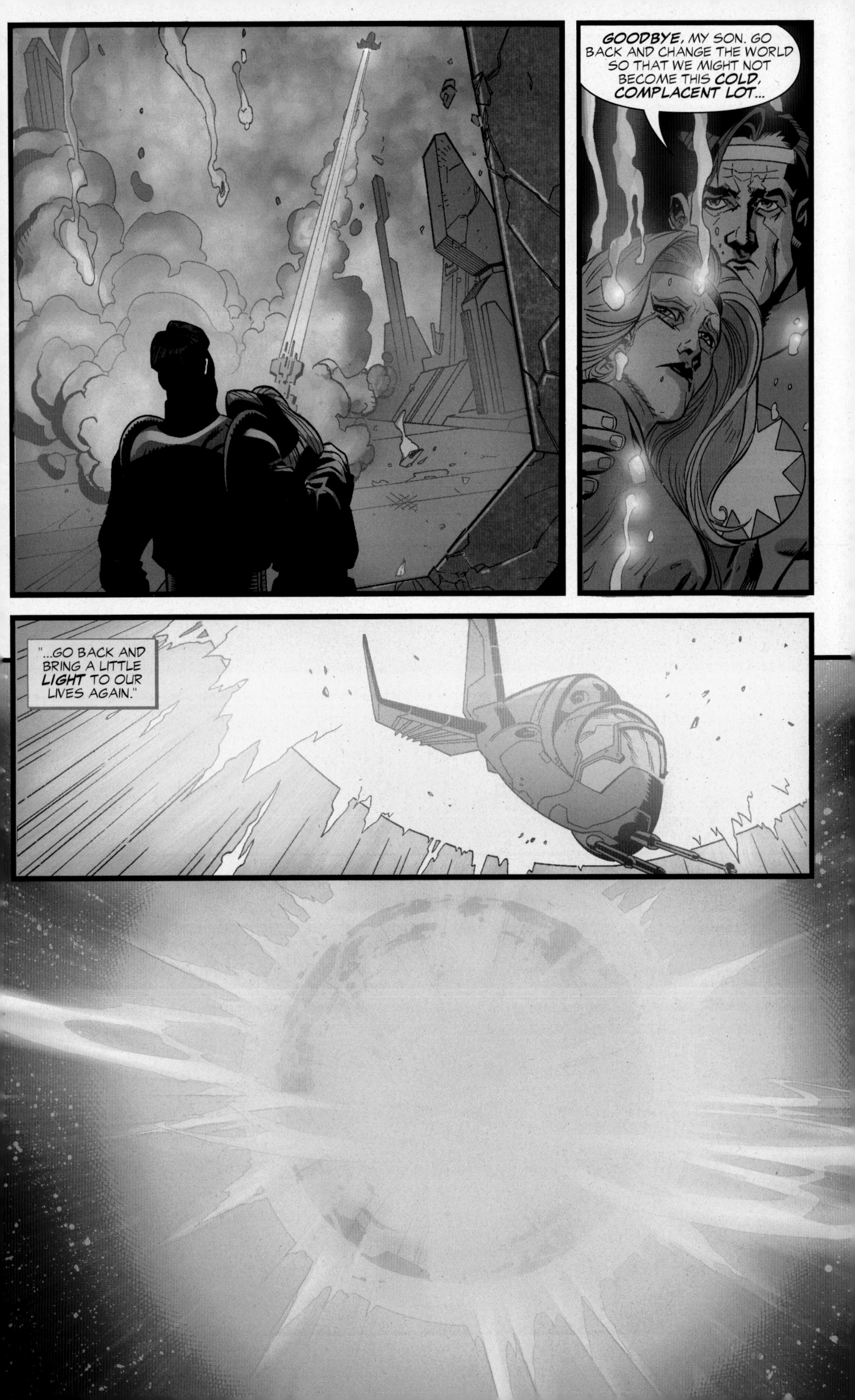
GOODBYE, MY SON. GO BACK AND CHANGE THE WORLD SO THAT WE MIGHT NOT BECOME THIS COLD, COMPLACENT LOT...
"...GO BACK AND BRING A LITTLE LIGHT TO OUR LIVES AGAIN."

THE UKRAINE, RUSSIA, 1938:

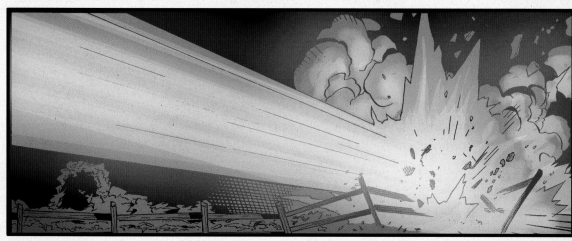

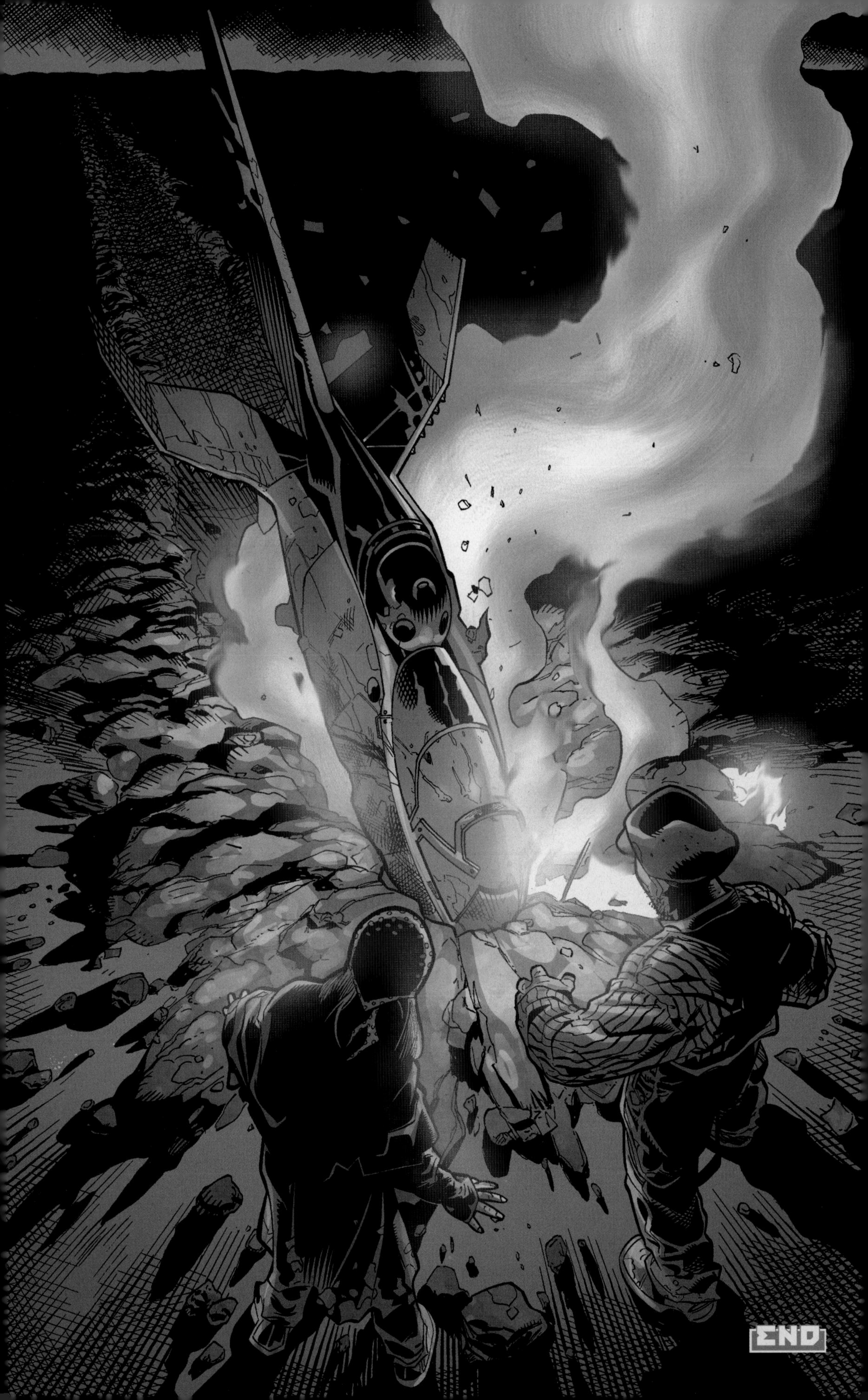
END

This sketch section features the work of series artists **Dave Johnson** and **Kilian Plunkett**, as well as acclaimed painter **Alex Ross** – who helped Johnson develop the initial characters and world of SUPERMAN: RED SON.

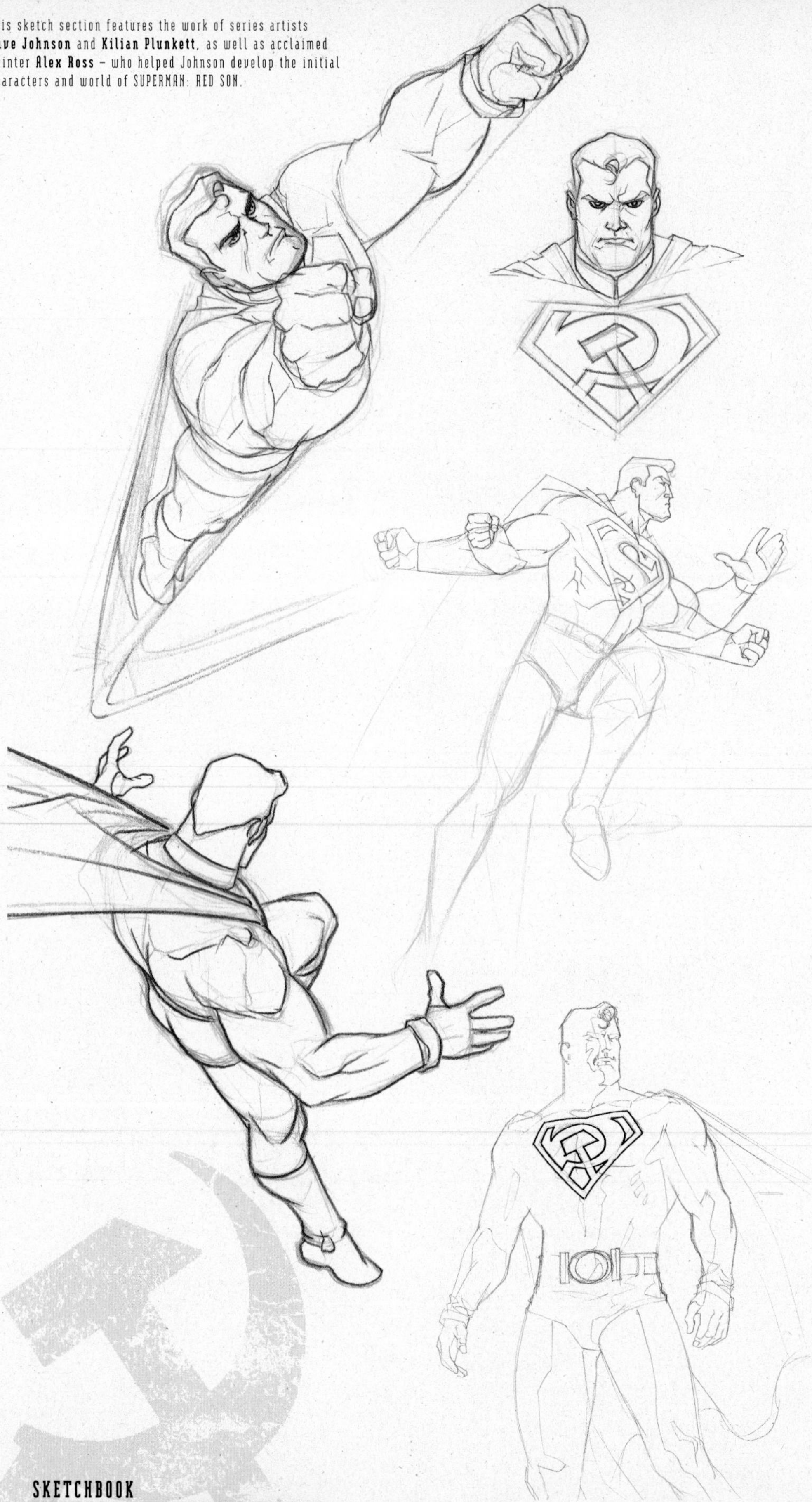

SKETCHBOOK
DAVE JOHNSON

BOOK ONE

BOOK TWO

BOOK THREE

RED

RED

If I had finished the
Book, this would have
been Supes costume.
I still
like what Kilian
came up with, though.

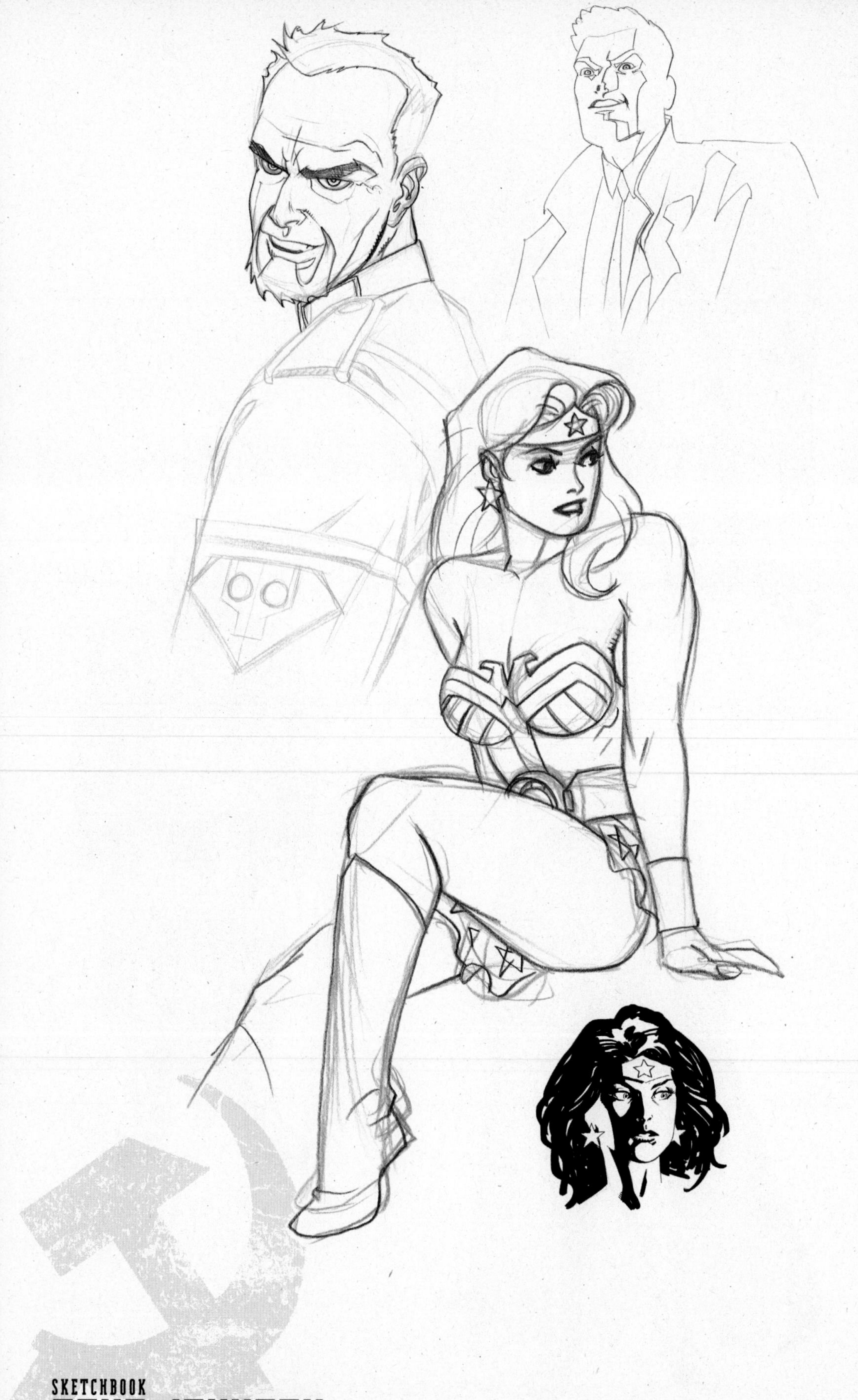

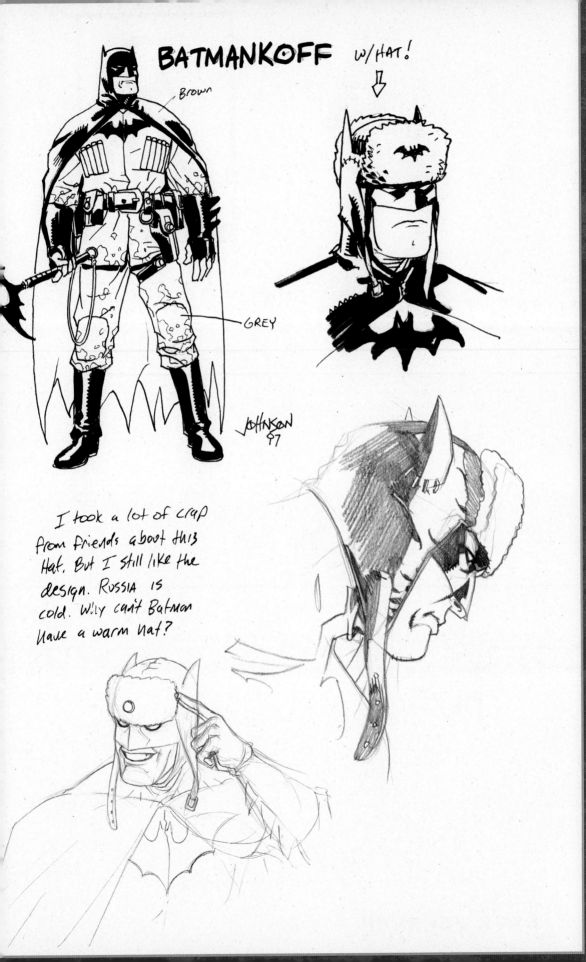

BATMANKOFF

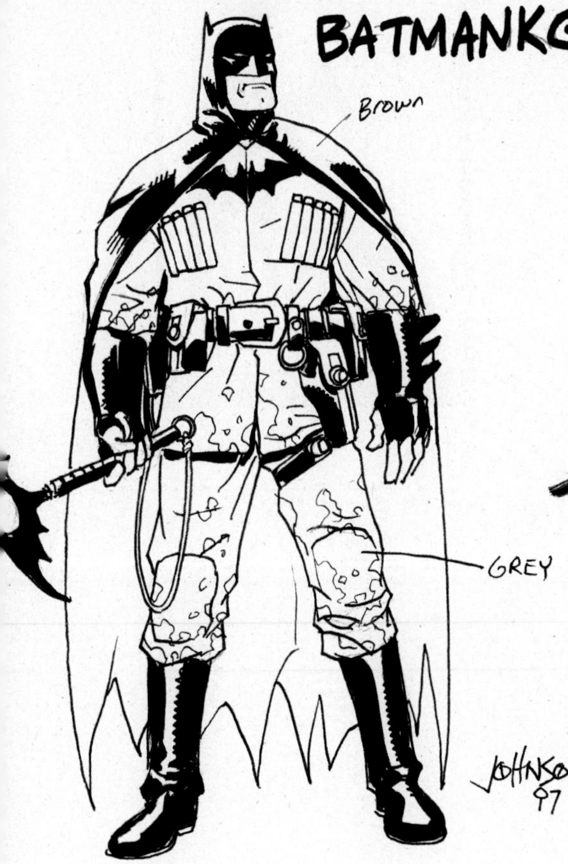
Brown
GREY
JOHNSON 97

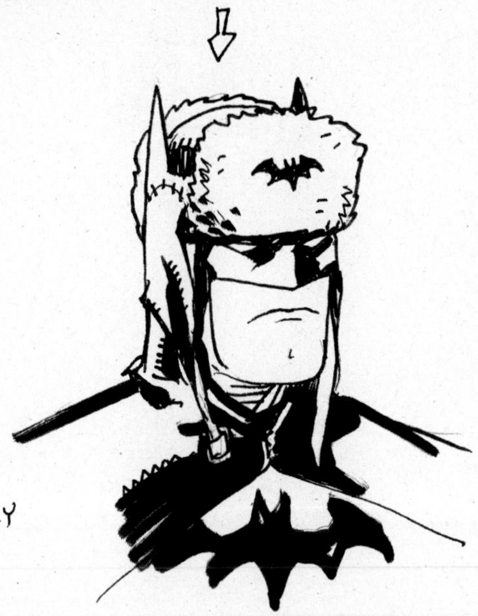
w/HAT!

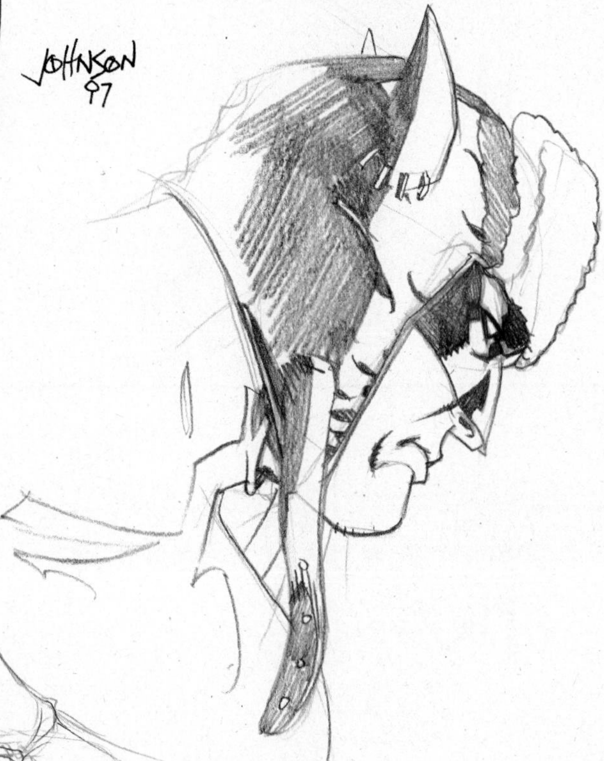

I took a lot of crap from friends about this Hat. But I still like the design. RUSSIA is cold. Why can't Batman have a warm hat?

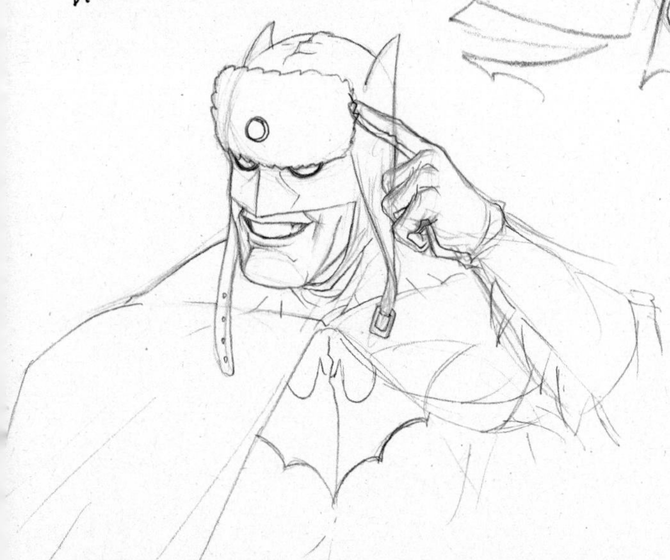

40% GREY

WHITE

DARK RED

40% GREY

SUPERMAN
RED SON

SUPERMAN
THE RED SON

AD LAYOUT for Painting

Here's two different ways to do the same shot. I think both work but a choice had to be made.
The final version had to be done with 5 point perspective. It's a real pain to do, but worth the effort.

Unlike most artists I like to do most of my work on scrap paper then lightbox the final design on the bristol board. Maybe thats why I'm so slow. But it eliminates the pressure of having to get it right on the page the first time.
Not to mention I can enlarge or reduce the layout to suit my needs before I commit it to paper.

This was the first cover Idea for issue 3. But I felt it didn't fill up the space on the cover. Too much dead area on either side of the figure. Especially after reducing him down to fit under the Title logo. Well, at least it's SEEing the light of day in this book.

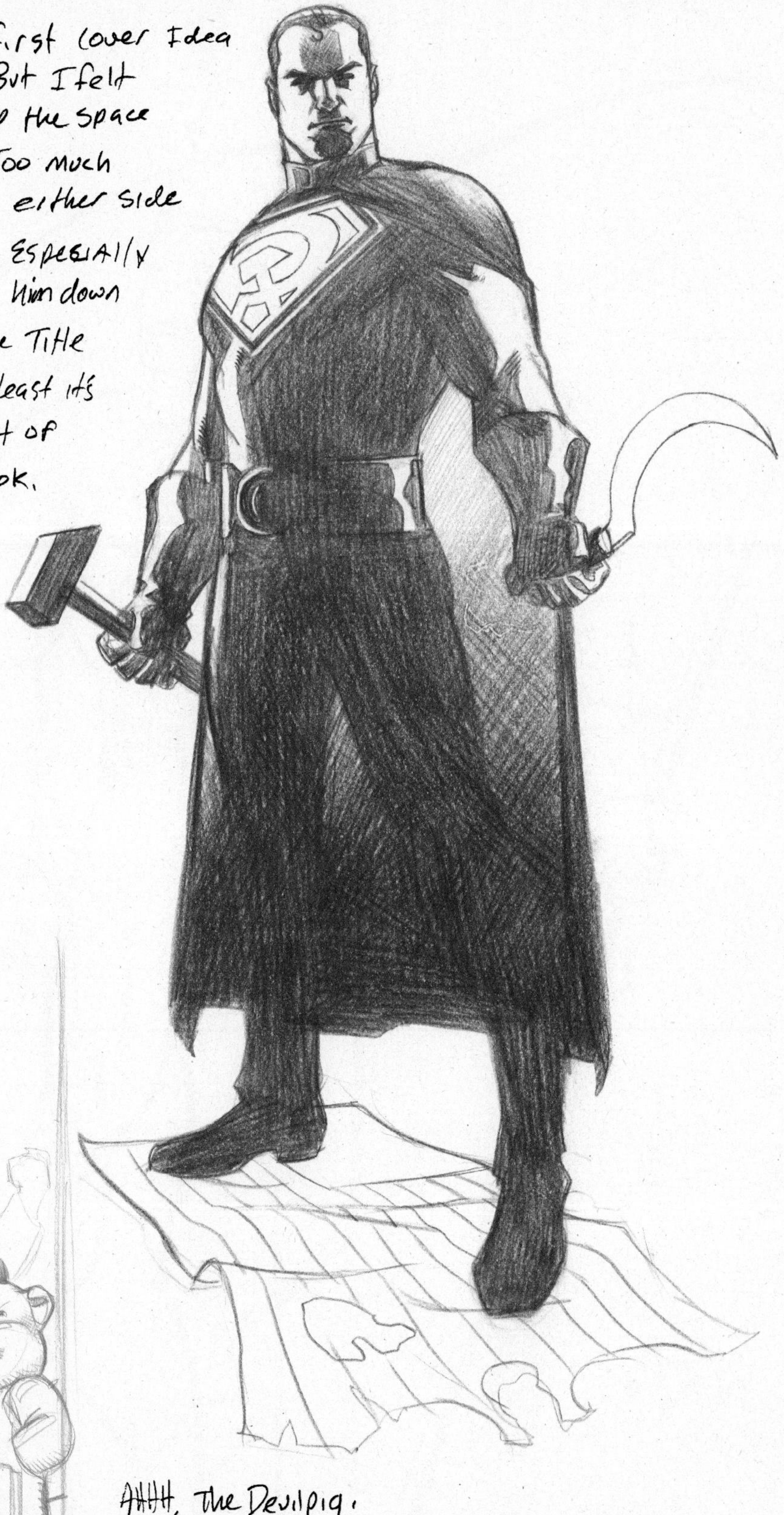

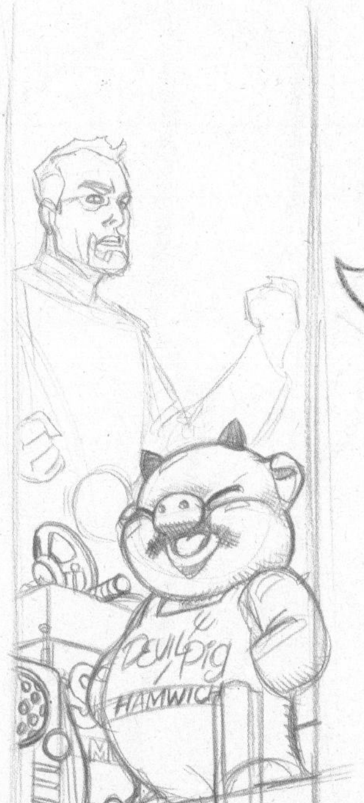
Devilpig
HAMWICH

AHHH, The Devilpig.
This little basterd has been showing up Everywhere.
Coming to a 100 Bullets cover soon.

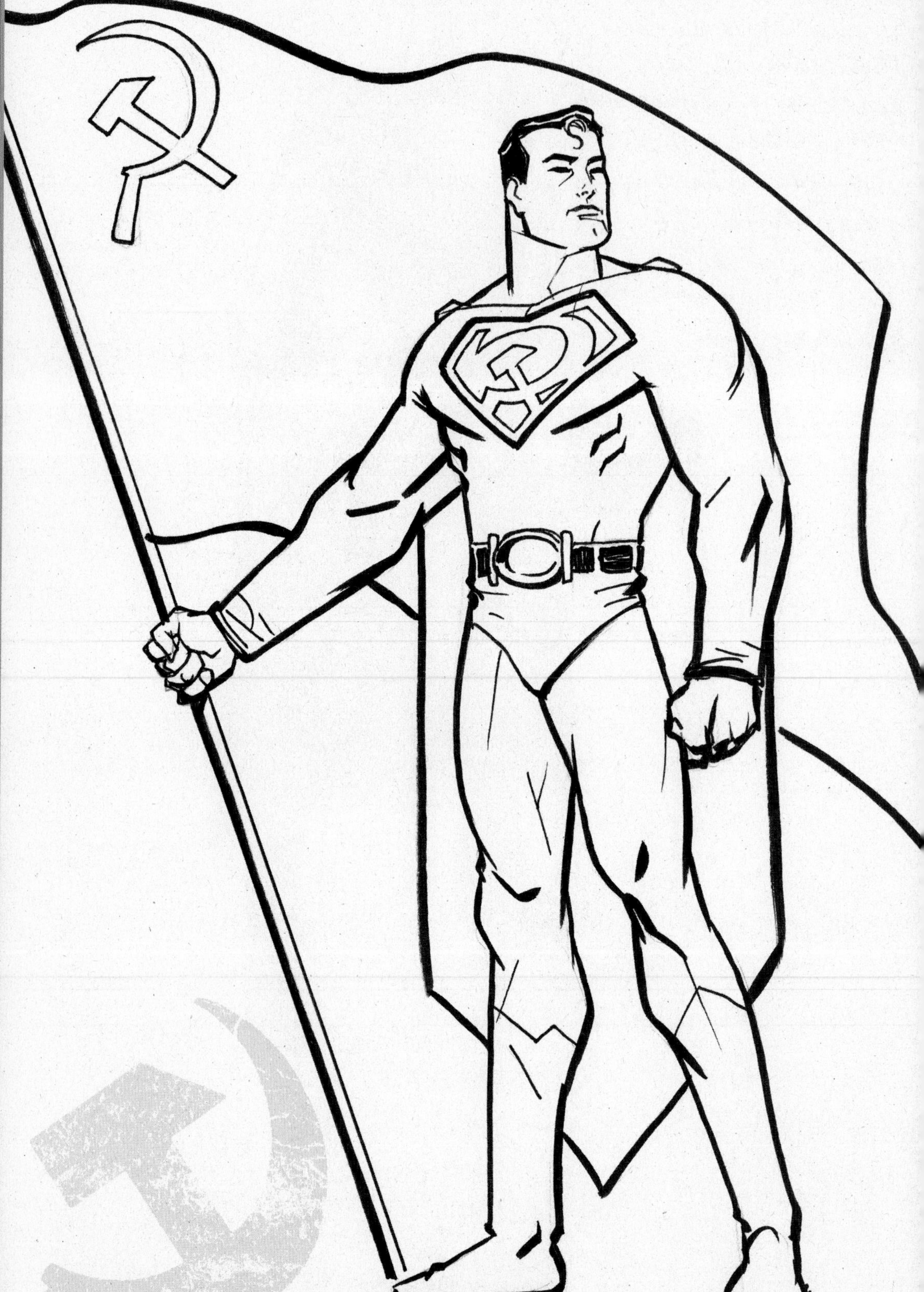

SKETCHBOOK
DAVE JOHNSON

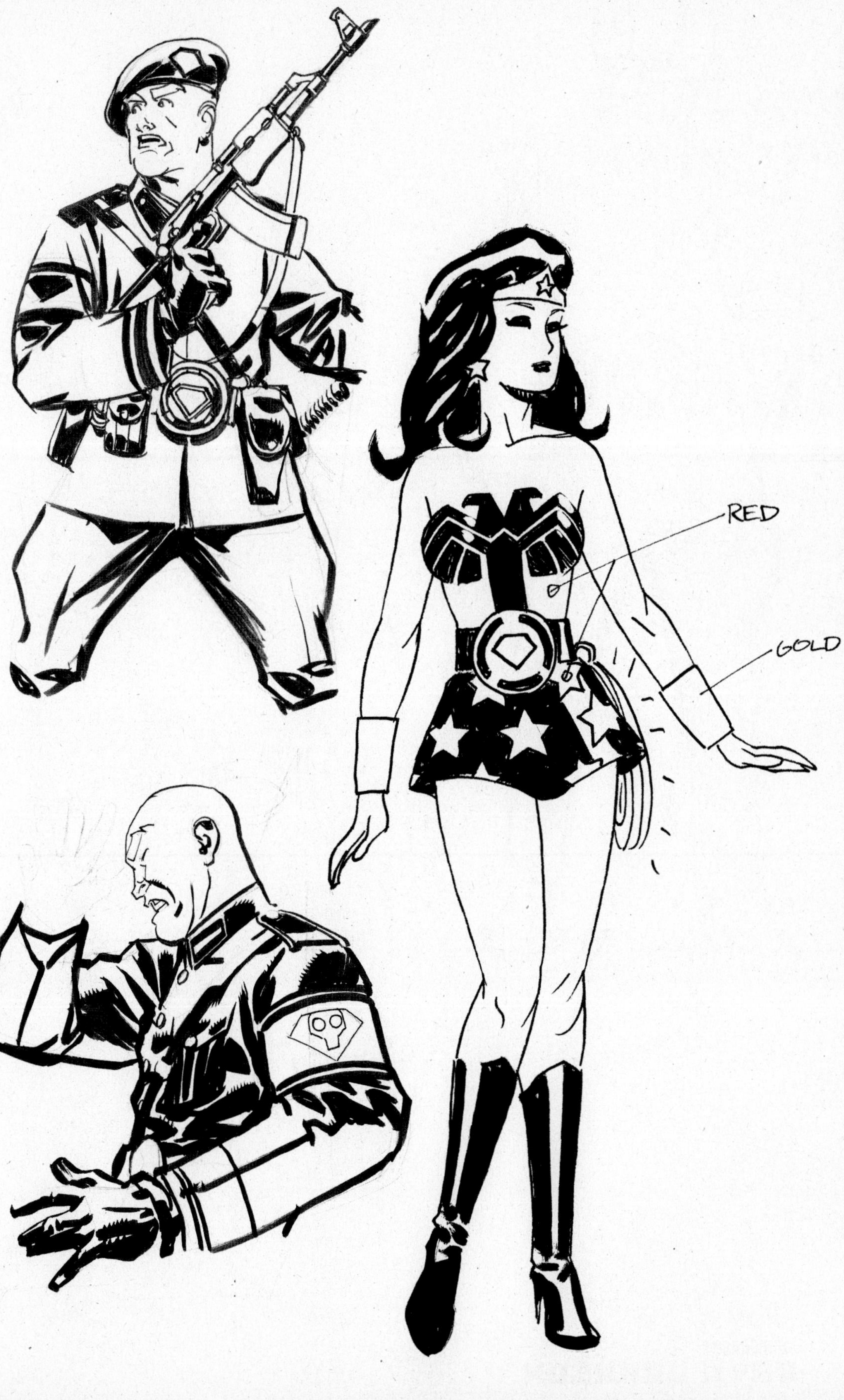
RED
GOLD

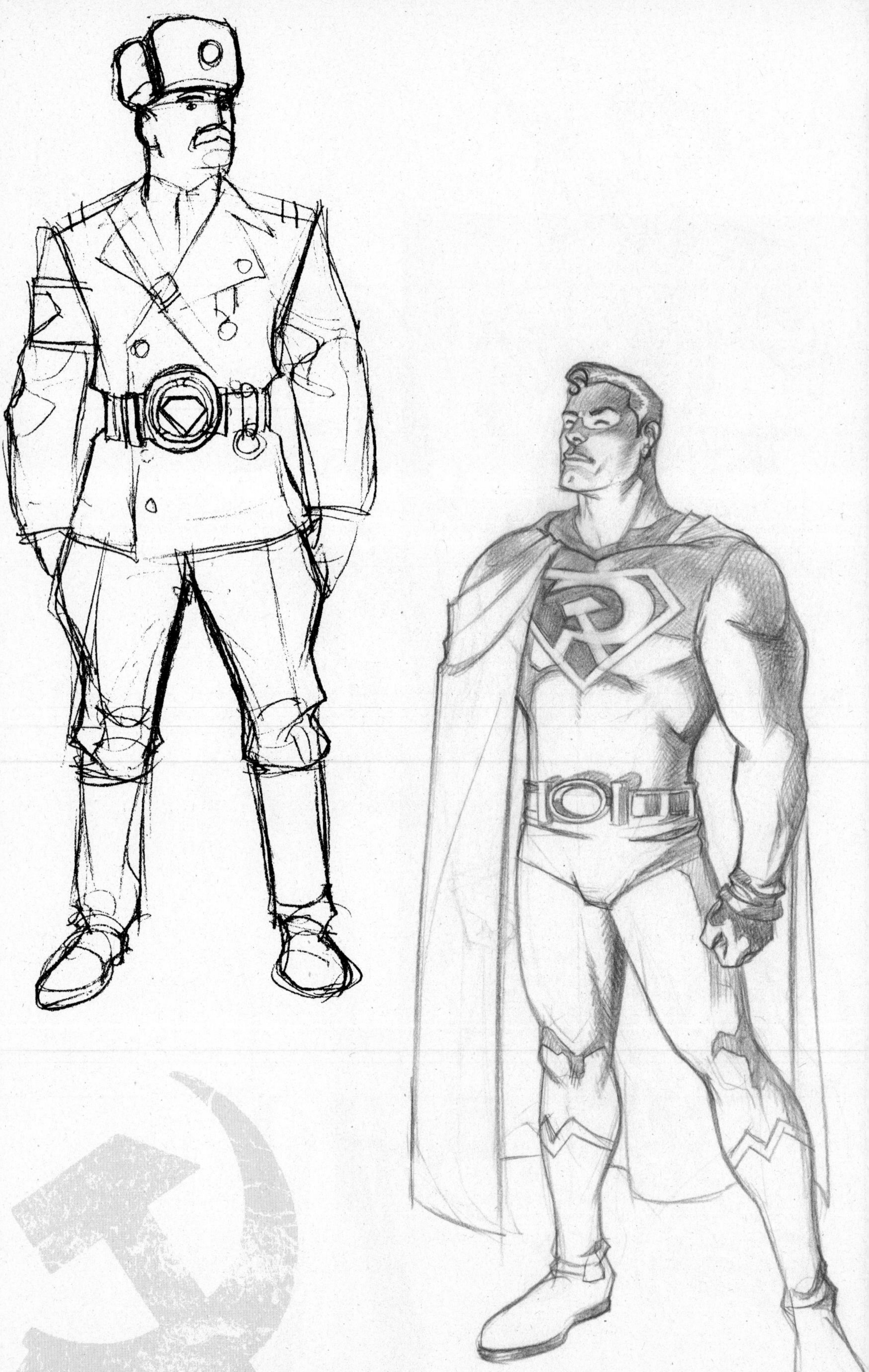

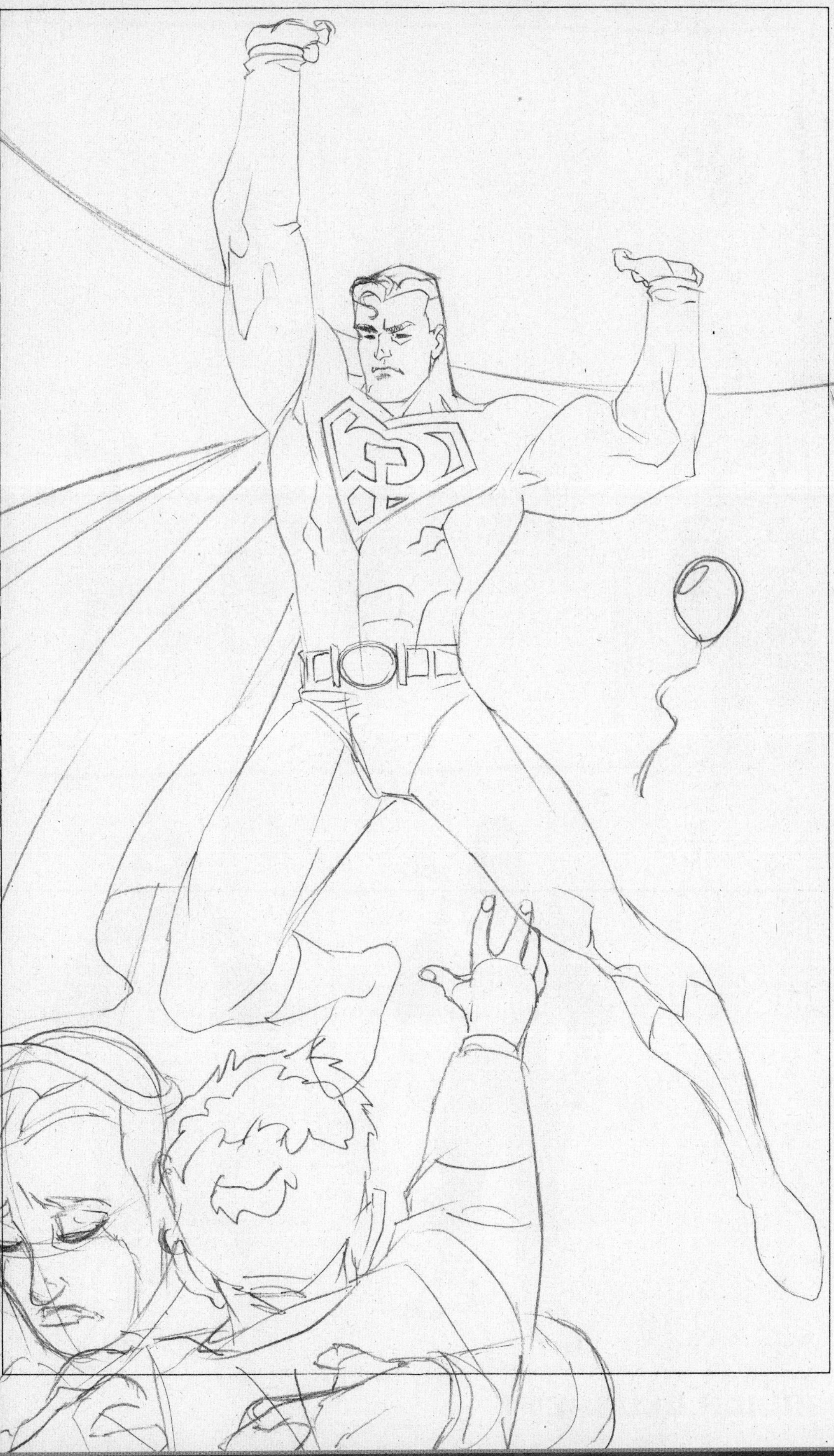

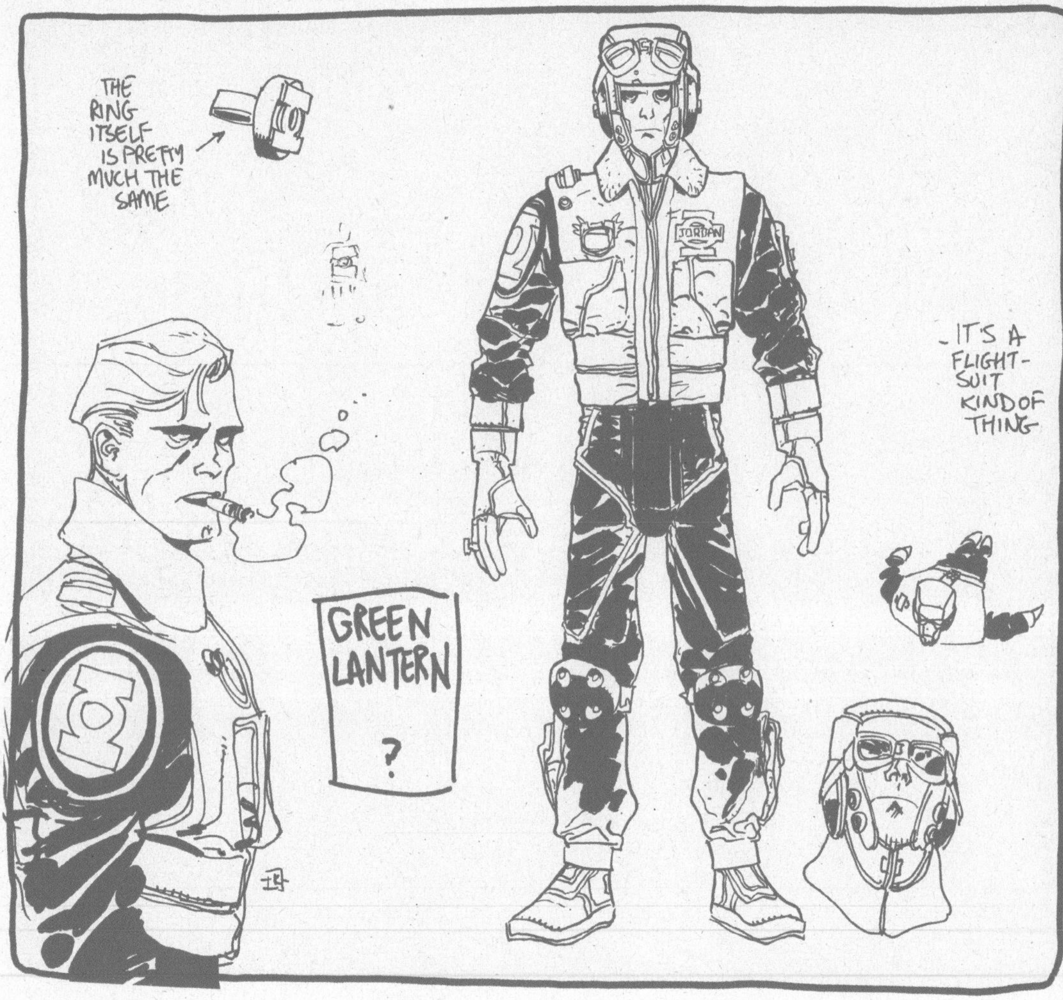
THE RING ITSELF IS PRETTY MUCH THE SAME
JORDAN
GREEN LANTERN
?
- IT'S A FLIGHT-SUIT KIND OF THING

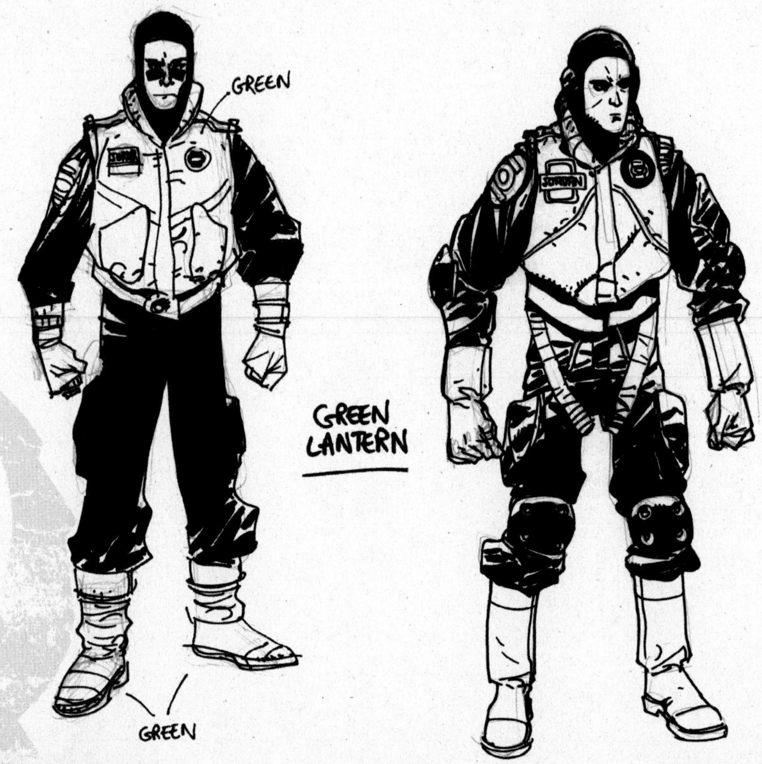
GREEN
JORDAN
GREEN LANTERN
GREEN

SKETCHBOOK
KILIAN PLUNKETT

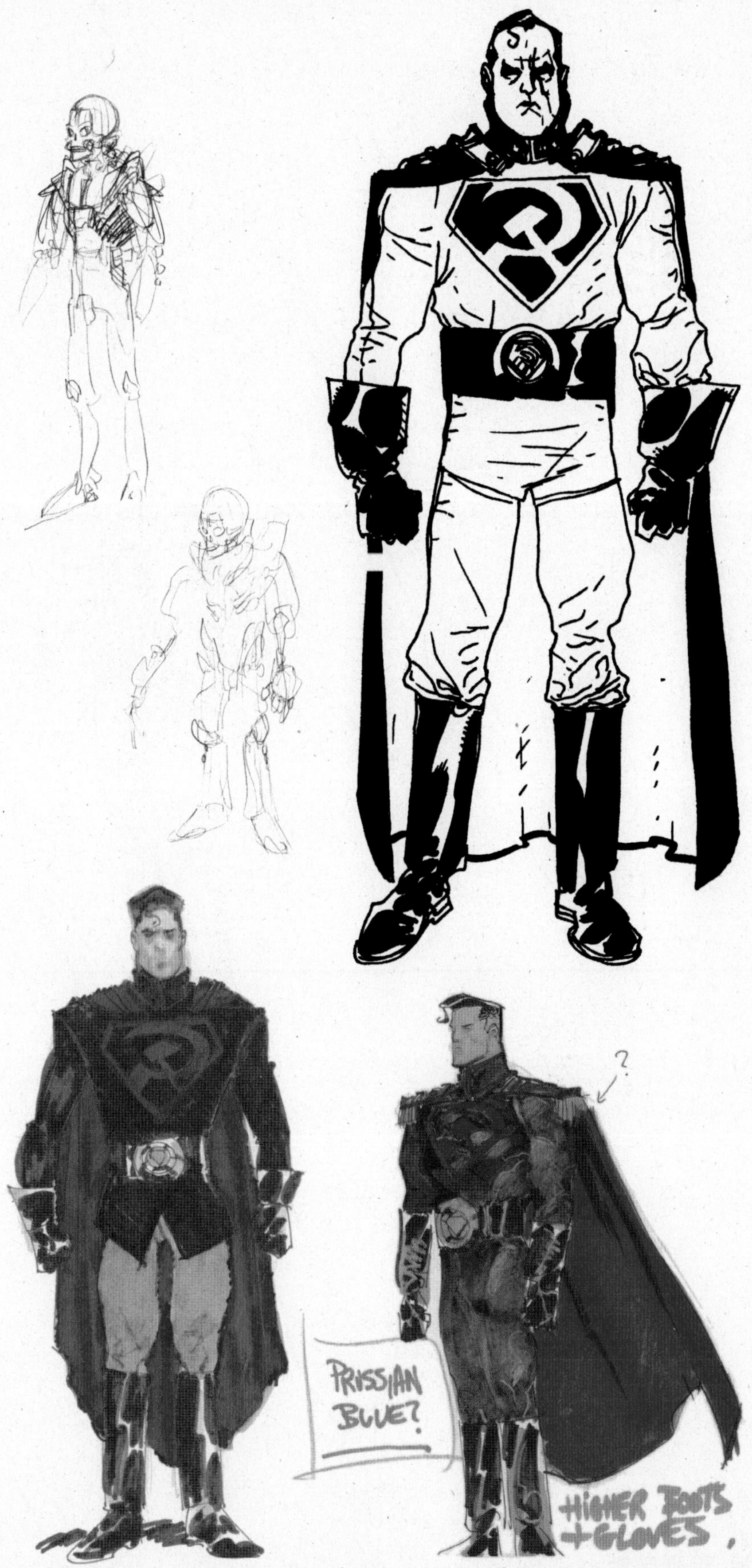
?
PRUSSIAN BLUE?
HIGHER BOOTS + GLOVES.

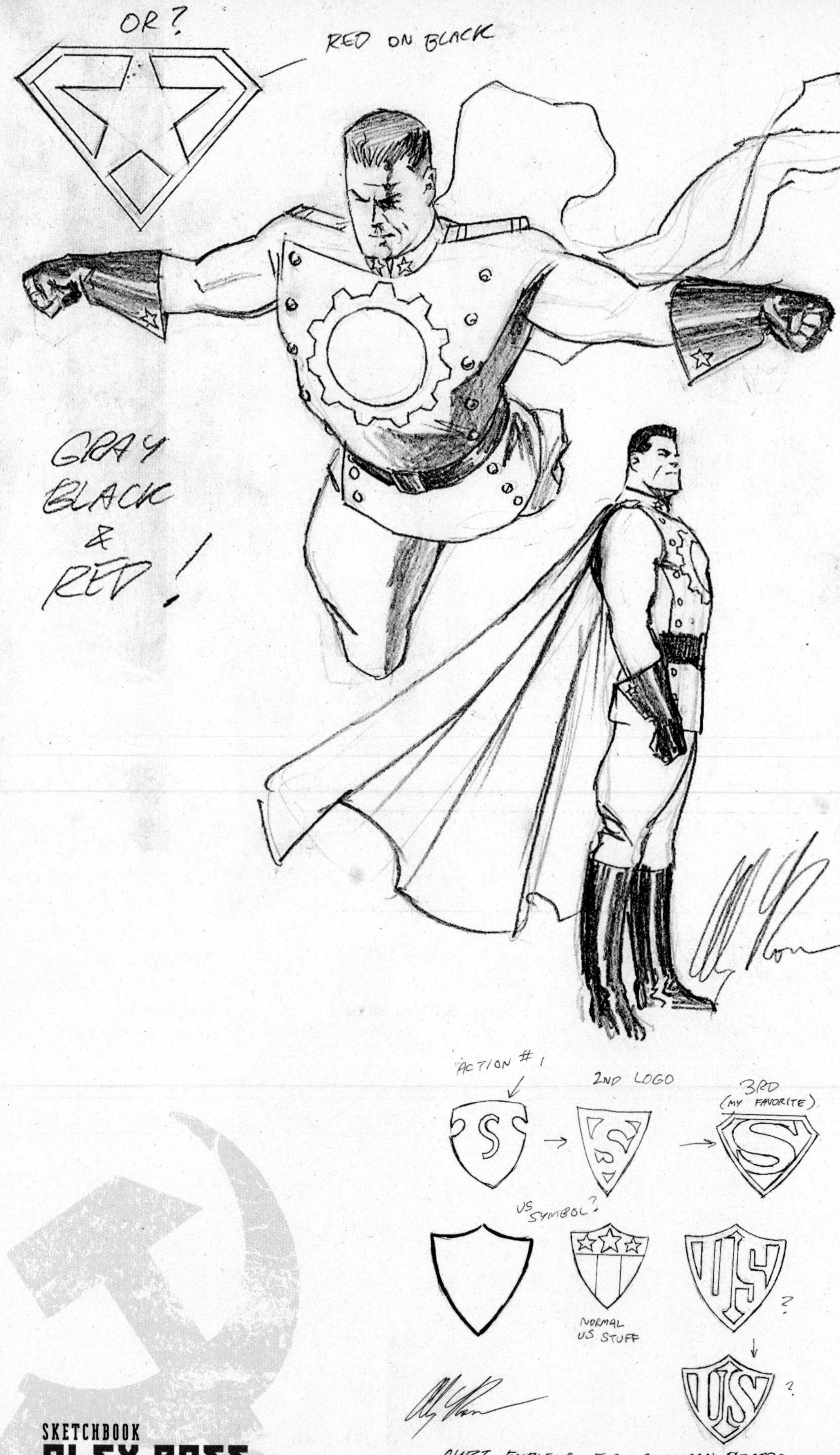
OR?
RED ON BLACK
GRAY BLACK & RED!
ACTION #1
2ND LOGO
3RD (MY FAVORITE)
US SYMBOL?
NORMAL US STUFF
?
?
CHEST EMBLEMS FOR AMERICAN BIZARRO ANSWER TO RUSSIAN SUPERMAN

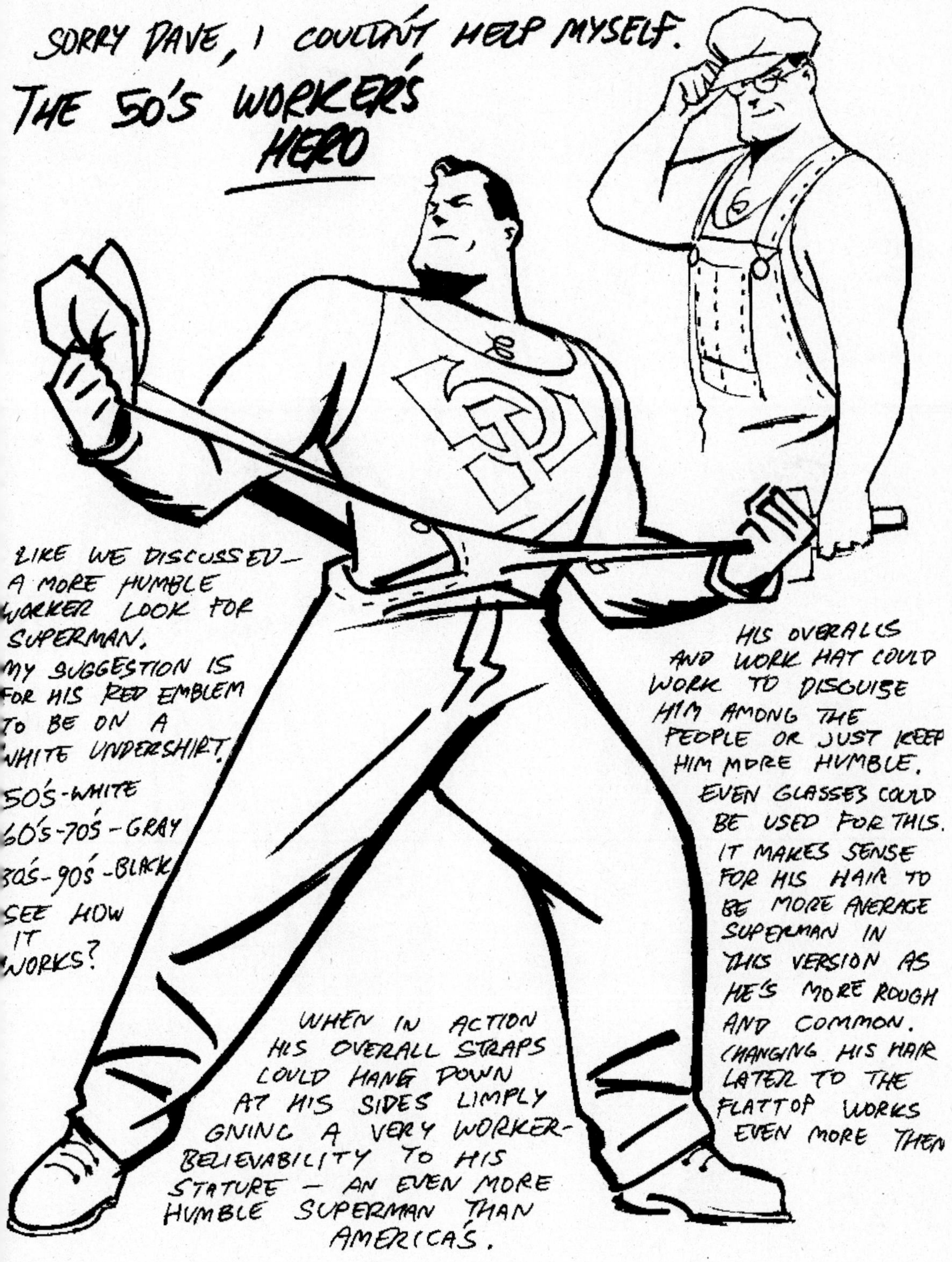
SORRY DAVE, I COULDN'T HELP MYSELF.
THE 50'S WORKER'S HERO
LIKE WE DISCUSSED—
A MORE HUMBLE
WORKER LOOK FOR
SUPERMAN.
MY SUGGESTION IS
FOR HIS RED EMBLEM
TO BE ON A
WHITE UNDERSHIRT.
50'S-WHITE
60'S-70'S-GRAY
80'S-90'S-BLACK
SEE HOW
IT
WORKS?
HIS OVERALLS
AND WORK HAT COULD
WORK TO DISGUISE
HIM AMONG THE
PEOPLE OR JUST KEEP
HIM MORE HUMBLE.
EVEN GLASSES COULD
BE USED FOR THIS.
IT MAKES SENSE
FOR HIS HAIR TO
BE MORE AVERAGE
SUPERMAN IN
THIS VERSION AS
HE'S MORE ROUGH
AND COMMON.
CHANGING HIS HAIR
LATER TO THE
FLATTOP WORKS
EVEN MORE THEN
WHEN IN ACTION
HIS OVERALL STRAPS
COULD HANG DOWN
AT HIS SIDES LIMPLY
GIVING A VERY WORKER-
BELIEVABILITY TO HIS
STATURE — AN EVEN MORE
HUMBLE SUPERMAN THAN
AMERICA'S.

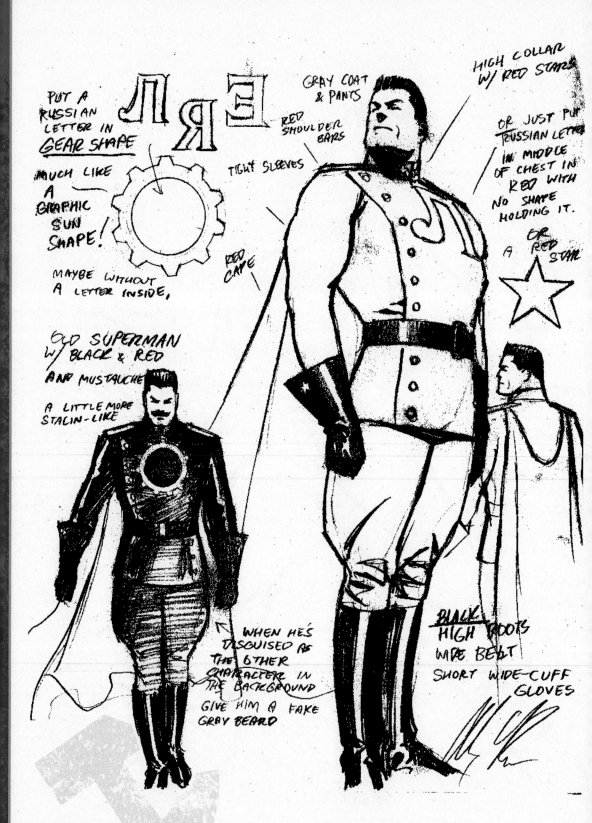

PUT A RUSSIAN LETTER IN GEAR SHAPE

MUCH LIKE A GRAPHIC SUN SHAPE!

MAYBE WITHOUT A LETTER INSIDE,

GRAY COAT & PANTS

RED SHOULDER BARS

TIGHT SLEEVES

RED CAPE

HIGH COLLAR W/ RED STARS

OR JUST PUT RUSSIAN LETTER IN MIDDLE OF CHEST IN RED WITH NO SHAPE HOLDING IT.

OR RED STAR

OLD SUPERMAN W/ BLACK & RED AND MUSTACHE

A LITTLE MORE STALIN-LIKE

WHEN HE'S DISGUISED AS THE OTHER CHARACTER IN THE BACKGROUND GIVE HIM A FAKE GRAY BEARD

BLACK HIGH BOOTS WIDE BELT SHORT WIDE-CUFF GLOVES

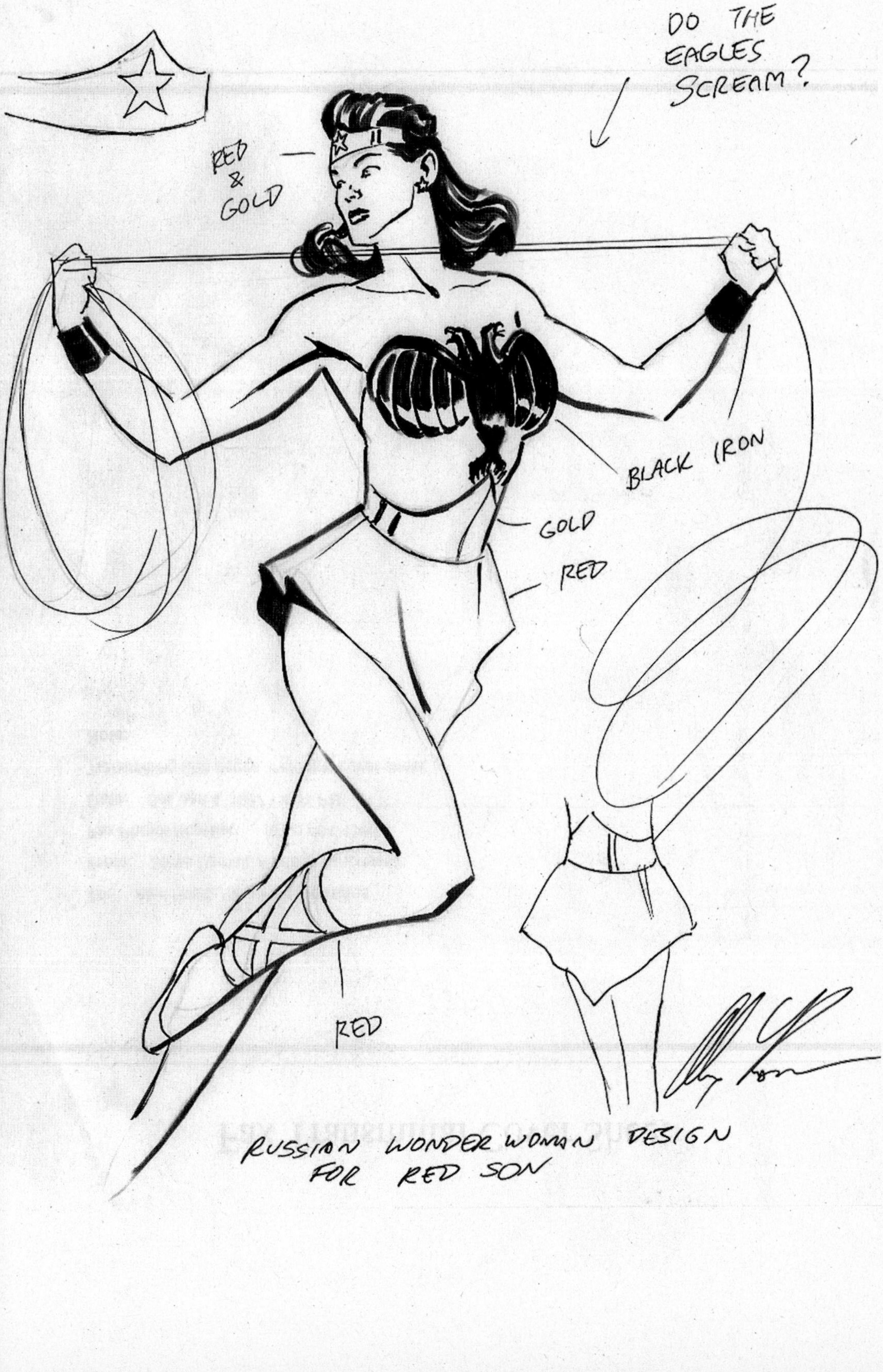
DO THE EAGLES SCREAM?
RED & GOLD
BLACK IRON
GOLD
RED
RED
RUSSIAN WONDER WOMAN DESIGN FOR RED SON

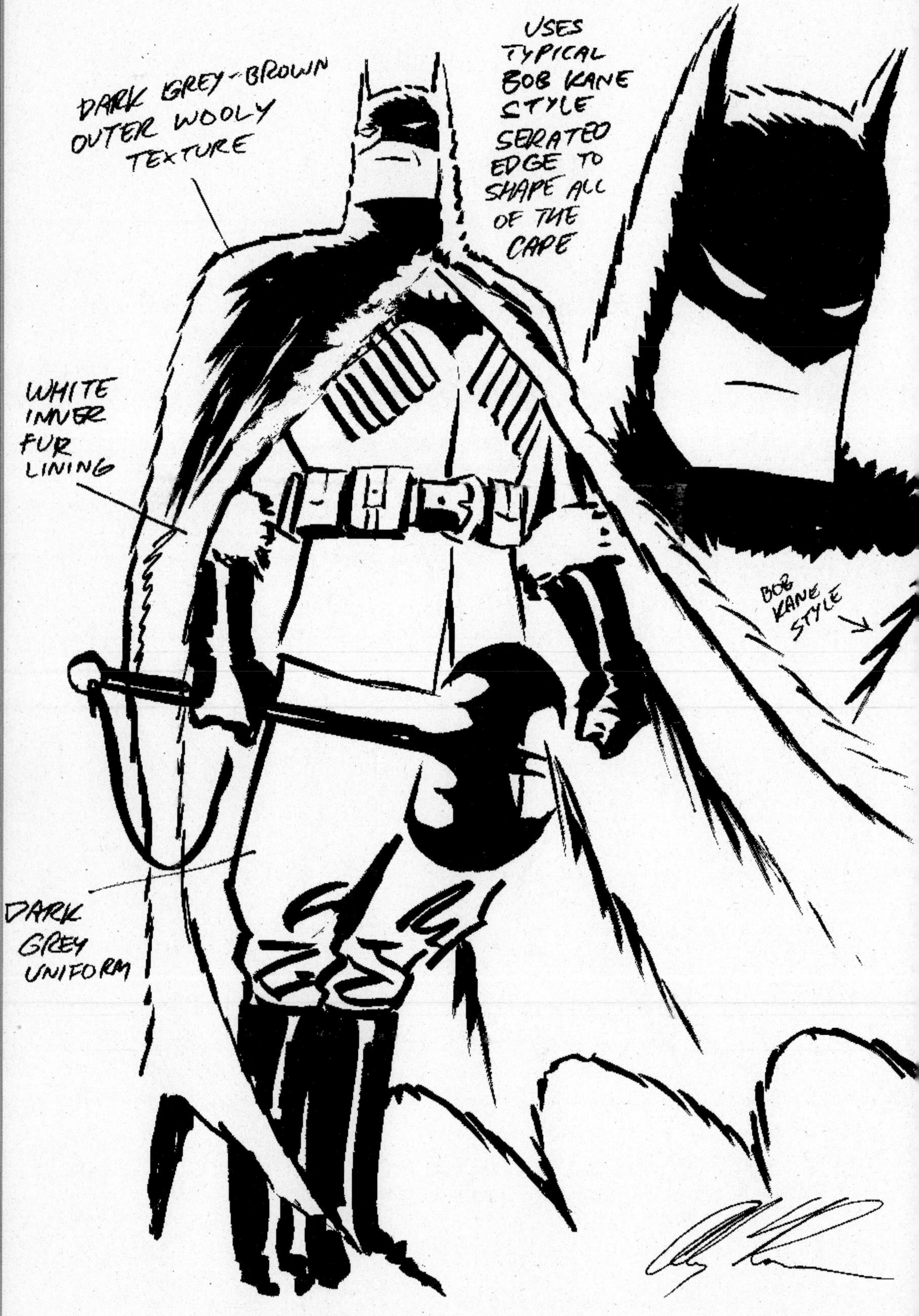
DARK GREY-BROWN OUTER WOOLY TEXTURE
USES TYPICAL BOB KANE STYLE SERRATED EDGE TO SHAPE ALL OF THE CAPE
WHITE INNER FUR LINING
BOB KANE STYLE
DARK GREY UNIFORM